The Critica

on

Music

Edited by

Brigitte Bogar and Christopher Innes

RosettaBooks®

Contents

General Editor's Preface 7

Introduction. 9

Bernard Shaw and His Times: A Chronology 21

A Note on the Text. 27

Part I: Critical Approaches 31

   1. How To Become a Musical Critic. 32

   2. Some Instruments and How to Play Them 38

   3. Fine Strokes of Comedy 43

Part II: Musical Theory 49

   1. Mozart's Finality 50

   2. The Religion of the Pianoforte 56

Part III: Vocalists. 75

   1. Men and Women of the Day. 76

   2. Vocalists of the Season (13 June) 79

   3. Vocalists of the Season (20 June) 80

   4. Vocalists of the Season (27 June) 82

   5. Madame Nilsson 84

   6. Goodbye, Patti. 87

   7. The Passing of Trebelli 89

Part IV: Opera and Operetta. 95

   1. Pauline. 96

   2. English Opera 100

   3. Bach and Don Pasquale 103

   4. Opera and Empty Bravado 106

   5. On Opera in Translation. 107

   6. Opera in Italian. 110

   7. Palmy Days at the Opera 113

   8. The Don Giovanni Centenary. 118

   9. Jean De Reszke's Romeo 120

10. Trovatore and the Huguenots 123
11. Signor Lago's Opera Season 129
12. Jack-Acting 135
13. A Non-Mozartian Don 141
14. Incognita 147
15. The Third Act of Ernani 154
16. Verdi's Falstaff 160
17. Utopian Gilbert and Sullivan 166
18. Half a Century Behind 171
19. Born-Again Italian Opera 178
20. La Navarraise 185
21. German Opera at Drury Lane 192
Part V: Richard Wagner 201
    1. The Wagner Festival 202
    2. Wagner at Covent Garden Theatre 203
    3. A Butchered Lohengrin 205
    4. Bassetto at Bayreuth 207
    5. Siegfried at Covent Garden 210
    6. Wagner's Theories 216
Part VI: Oratorios and Religious Music 225
    1. The Redemption at the Crystal Palace 226
    2. Parry's Judith 229
    3. Miss Smyth's Decorative Instinct 234
    4. The Most Utter Failure Ever Achieved 240
Part VII: Family 249
    1. Amateur Opera at Londonderry House 250
    2. The 789th Performance of Dorothy 252
Part VIII: Instrumental Concerts 257
    1. Mozart and Haydn with Strings 258
    2. Herr Richter and His Blue Ribbon 259
    3. Crystal Palace Variety 264
    4. The Grieg Concert 266
    5. Circenses 268
Part IX: The Voice 275
    1. A Pamphlet on the Voice 276

2. A Typical "Popular" Vocalist 277

3. A Volume on Voice Training 279

4. Specialists in Singing........................... 281

THE VOICE 288

Singing in Tune................................. 288

Pronunciation 292

The Common Dread of Classical Music 296

Qualifications of a Singer 300

Physiology of the Vocal Organs................... 306

Classifications of Voices 312

Effort 315

Sources and Further Reading...................... 317

General Editor's Preface

Bernard Shaw is not the household name he once was, but in the 1920s and 1930s he was certainly the world's most famous English-language playwright, and arguably one of the most famous people in the world. His plays were internationally performed and acclaimed, his views on matters great and small were relentlessly solicited by the media, he was pursued by paparazzi long before the word was even invented, the biggest names in politics, the arts, entertainment, even sports—Gandhi, Nehru, Churchill, Rodin, Twain, Wells, Lawrence of Arabia, Elgar, Einstein, Garbo, Chaplin, Stalin, Tunney and many more—welcomed his company, and his correspondents in the tens of thousands of letters he wrote during his long lifetime constitute a veritable who's who of world culture and politics. And Shaw remains the only person ever to have been awarded both a Nobel Prize and an Oscar.

Shaw's reputation rests securely not just on his plays, a dozen or so of which have come to be recognized as classics—*Man and Superman, Major Barbara, Pygmalion,* and *Saint Joan* perhaps now the most familiar of them—but also on his early work as a music, art, literary, and theater critic, and on his lifelong political activism. After he moved to London from his native Dublin in 1876, and after completing five novels, he established himself as one of London's most controversial, feared, and admired critics, and while he eventually retired from earning his living as a critic in order to focus on playwriting, he continued to lecture and write about cultural and other issues—religion, for example—with scorching intelligence. As for politics, his early commitment to Socialism, and his later expressed admiration for Communism and contempt for Capitalism, meant that while his views were relentlessly refuted by the establishment press they could rarely be ignored—hardly surprising given the logic and passion that underpinned them.

Winston Churchill once declared Shaw to be "the greatest living master of letters in the English-speaking world," and the selections from Shaw's reviews, essays, speeches, and correspondence contained in the five volumes of this Critical Shaw series provide abundant evidence to validate Churchill's high regard. Shaw wrote—and spoke—voluminously, and his complete works on the topics covered by this series—Literature, Music, Religion, Theater, and Politics—would fill many more than five volumes. The topics reflect Shaw's deepest interests and they inspired some of his most brilliant nondramatic writing. The selections in each volume give a comprehensive and representative survey of his thinking, and show him to be not just the great rhetorician that Churchill and others acknowledged, but also one of the great public intellectuals of the twentieth century.

Leonard Conolly
Robinson College, Cambridge
December 2015

Introduction

by Brigitte Bogar

The published edition of Bernard Shaw's complete music criticism adds up to three volumes totaling 2,289 pages [originally edited by Dan H. Laurence, London: Bodley Head, 1981]. Volume III also includes occasional pieces he wrote up into the 1940s. This edition focuses solely on Shaw's reviews between 1876 and 1898—the era he focuses specifically on writing criticism for music columns in newspapers and journals—as well as publishing for the first time notes he wrote on the vocal training in 1882. We are designing the selection here to mirror Shaw's various focuses, to highlight his musical ideas, but also to include his wider range of general artistic commentary and show his political attitudes, which are a recurrent aspect of his reviews.

The sheer volume of Shaw's critical articles reviewing musical events in London and elsewhere in England, in conjunction with journeys he made to cover performances of Wagner's work in Bayreuth, indicates his active influence in the world of music. He was one of the most comprehensive reviewers of music during the late nineteenth century, dealing with the music scene in both newspaper pieces and journal articles, weekly or frequently more often, over a remarkable length of twenty-two years. Indeed his work covered every aspect of the musical world, from composition to performance; and he commented on every musical genre from operas, operettas and musical comedies, through oratorios as well as religious masses, to instrumental concerts and even band music. In addition, he wrote on music criticism, with significant effect, and reviewed books published on music, as well as musical conferences. He also wrote explicitly on economic and political aspects of the art, and even on the social nature of audiences as well as promoting socialist ideals. This extensive range, together with a frequently critical tone, demonstrates that Shaw counts as one of the major music critics writing in English.

Shaw first became a music critic at the urging of his surrogate father, Vandeleur Lee, when in 1876 Shaw followed his mother and sisters to London. (They had left with Vandeleur Lee some years earlier and lived together.) On arriving in London, Shaw, who had left his position as a clerk in Dublin wishing to pursue a literary career, focused on research and writing novels in the Reading Room at the British Museum. In November that year, Lee was hired as a critic for *The Hornet* and he engaged Shaw to ghostwrite the reviews for him. Perhaps unsurprisingly—given Shaw's background, and since Lee was a vocal coach and opera conductor—Shaw's primary focus in his early music criticism is on opera, vocal music and vocal technique. He wrote unsigned pieces for *The Hornet* from 29th of November 1876 until 26th of September 1877. In 1882, he also agreed to ghostwrite an updated version for a proposed new edition of Vandeleur Lee's book on vocal training: *The Voice, Its Artistic Production, Development and Preservation* (1870). Lee's original work had been highly influential through focusing on a new medical approach and on the physiological theory of sound production, thus promoting a noticeably altered form of vocal training. The technique that Lee developed featured a newly discovered scientific instrument, the "Laryngoscope." Shaw was so familiar with this book that his updated notes are revisions to the original that in fact clearly express his own views. Indeed he added whole chapters to the original manuscript, such as sections on "Singing in Tune" and on "Pronunciation." The new text (held in the New York Public Library), which got abandoned by Shaw when Lee separated from Shaw's mother, was never completed, due to Lee's unexpectedly early death in 1886. Shaw's writings on "The Voice," so far unpublished, form an appendix to this edition, since they illuminate his knowledge of vocal technique.

Shaw was well qualified to serve as a critic of music—even to the degree that in a couple of his reviews he feels capable of presenting his critical approach satirically. Unlike several of his contemporary late nineteenth-century music critic-colleagues, such as John Fuller Maitland and Francis Hueffer, Shaw had an extensive knowledge of music from his family background. He had actually grown up in a musical family, and he played several instruments himself. His mother was an opera singer in Dublin, coached by Vandeleur Lee; and indeed, she herself composed songs. In addition, his younger sister Lucy became a professional singer on the London stage. As a young teenager, Shaw taught himself operatic scores—claiming that he had the ability to sing Mendelssohn's *Athalie*, Handel's *Messiah*, Verdi's *Trovatore*, Donizetti's *Lucrezia*, Gounod's *Faust* and (above all) Mozart's *Don Giovanni* from cover to cover. After his mother's departure for London, Shaw taught himself to play various instruments, in particular the piano. While he was a music critic, Shaw also composed music: both for women he was interested in, such as a singer and member of the Fabian Society Grace Gilhurst, the actress Florence Farr, or his socialist political companion Dollie Radford—although unfortunately very few of these compositions seem to have survived—and for use with his plays. However, in his plays, with the signal exception of *Saint Joan*, there is no mention of Shaw's music or songs in the scripts, which probably means that these compositions only ever appeared in the first productions, supervised by Shaw himself. (These and other pieces Shaw used have been recorded for the first time ever by Brigitte Bogar and are available on a new CD: for copies contact brigitte.bogar@gmail.com.)

In addition, Shaw's musical knowledge underpins his plays. For example the "Dream Scene" of *Man and Superman*, where Mozart's music is featured, as well as the figure of Donna Anna from *Don Giovanni*, deliberately echoes his mother's favorite opera role from Dublin. An even more specific example is Professor Higgins' methods of speech training in *Pygmalion* (1912), which directly repeat Shaw's notes for "The Voice," with the equipment of Henry Higgins' laboratory exactly paralleling Vandeleur Lee's studio. One prominent feature is a grand piano—but what connects Higgins explicitly with Lee's book is two very specific objects described in Shaw's stage directions: "a laryngoscope" and "a life-size image of half a human head, showing in section the vocal organs," which Lee had published as illustrations. Looking without preconceptions at *Pygmalion*, there is a real surprise. This is a play that centers on the vocal training of a young working class flower-girl to change her cockney diphthong-vowels and elided consonants into the nose-in-the air linguistic precision of a high-born aristocrat. Yet in the original text, there is not one mention of how Higgins achieves this radical voice makeover. The 1913 script of *Pygmalion* avoids any scene or even description of the way Higgins trains Eliza's voice and speech-habits, but the omission is not because Shaw lacks such knowledge: the missing link is in his career as a music critic, connecting this with his career as a dramatist. There is clear evidence of the kind of instructional methods Shaw would have had in mind in several articles dealing with vocal training; and these show a basic—but generally ignored—link between Shaw's early career as a music critic, and his drama.

When *The Hornet* went out of business, Shaw continued to write music reviews for *The Dramatic Review*, *Our Corner* and for *The Magazine of Music*, starting on 8th of February 1885. In the first four months, he wrote six pieces on opera. For three years from 13th of June 1885 until 4th of July 1888, after the separation of Vandeleur Lee and Shaw's mother, Shaw only wrote four reviews devoted solely to opera. During this period the main part of his writings were on an exhibition of old instruments, discussions of pitch, reviews of lectures and books relating to music, and twenty-two concert reviews, although these sometimes included vocal pieces. During this period, he collaborated with the founding of the Fabian Society—the origin of Socialism in England—and subsequently the political aspects of his reviews become more pronounced, expressed in a number of lengthy articles for *Our Corner* (an art magazine that included summaries of opera and concerts, as well as political commentary). From 15th of January 1886, until 13th of February 1888, he wrote for the *The Pall Mall Gazette* (continuing with occasional pieces until March 25, 1889); and this journal is where most of his book reviews were printed. During this period, he generally signed himself as "Corno di Bassetto," ironically choosing what he thought of as an outdated musical instrument for his pseudonym. Almost immediately, after he started writing for *The Star* from 14th of May 1888, opera and vocal technique took his focus again. From there, while his focus remained the same, his career branched out significantly. He started writing for *The World* in May 1890, with sporadic reviews or comments for *The Fortnightly Review*, *The Musical Courier*, the *Daily Chronicle* and other journals—showing his widespread reputation as a critic. August 8, 1894, marks the point where Shaw effectively ended his work as a music critic, although he continued to write occasional pieces, particularly for his previous employer, *The Star*, until 1898.

Throughout his career as a music critic, intermittently Shaw continued to include politics in his writing, as with reviews on the use of children on stage, musicians' unions and women's rights. In his writings, there are hints that Shaw came to see music as such as potentially revolutionary. This political focus is clear in Shaw's early plays, collected under the title "Plays Unpleasant" and written while he was still primarily active as a music critic, completing *Widowers' Houses* in 1892, and *Mrs Warren's Profession* in 1894. Far more explicitly than Shaw's music reviews, these plays attacked the aristocracy (suggesting they gained their elevated position through prostitution) as well as businessmen, who are presented as amassing wealth from exploiting the poor. At the same time, these plays strongly support feminism and women's independence, while also highlighting the plight of the socially disadvantaged. One can see these themes as deriving from the subtexts and from the frequently explicit commentary in his music reviews. Indeed the first of these early plays has a strongly musical reference, being initially titled "Das Rhinegold" by Shaw, in a reference to his favorite composer, Wagner, whose major work *Der Ring des Nibelungen* Shaw interpreted in an anarchistic socialist light.

Opera and vocal reviews may remain the major focus in Shaw's writing for *The World*. Yet at this point, his more academic criticism as well as travel descriptions, politics, music history and theory now take up over 20% of his writings. However, adding everything up, over his whole career as a music critic, opera and vocal criticism account for about 37% of Shaw's reviews; his reviews of instrumental concerts add up to just under 20%; and the "other" topics make up 22.5%. With almost all his instrumental reviews covering a number of concerts in each piece, and frequently including vocal sections, as well as reviews of oratorio and choral works accounting for just over 5% of Shaw's total music reviews, it would be safe to state that opera and vocal performances total well over half of all Shaw's musical writings. It is indeed mainly in the case of opera, operetta and oratorios that his reviews focus on just a single performance.

Possibly this bias towards vocal performance reflects the musical situation in London during the last part of the Victorian era, since in London during Shaw's time as a music critic the most important musical events were the great Choir Festivals at which one could hear works by Bach, Handel, and particularly Mendelssohn. It also clearly echoes Shaw's own predilections. While his reviews certainly deal with oratorios, usually sharply criticized for the way they were performed, Shaw generally focuses throughout on opera and musical theater. Possibly partly reflecting his socialist and so anti-religious views, Shaw was generally dismissive of oratorios, in his reviews criticizing the vocalization and pronunciation of the singers. Indeed, he was very dismissive of the conservatory in general, and specifically the Guildhall School of Music: in particular criticizing the English teaching of pronunciation where "*e che sospire*" from "*Lascia ch'io pianga*"[aria in Handel's opera *Rinaldo*] becomes "Ayee Kayee Soaspearayee."

Nevertheless, in his reviews of opera, operetta and musical theater (including Bayreuth productions of Wagner), Shaw is equally ruthless in his criticism of any singer's diction, vibrato and pitch, as well as referring frequently to faulty pronunciation. Reflecting his notes for the second edition of *The Voice*, in his writings on vocal performances and in his opera reviews Shaw highlights technical aspects such as pure vowels, *coup de glotte*, the laryngoscope, the voice division into three registers, and rounding the back of the throat (the pharynx). He also repeatedly suggests that singers should foster instincts of self-preservation for the voice, taking steps to stop forcing the volume and high pitches that might destroy their voices. At the same time, reflecting perhaps his growing interest in theater, Shaw increasingly criticizes the singers' lack of acting ability on stage.

Shaw's focus is to some extent determined by his background, so that in his reviews Shaw hardly ever mentions major English composers of the eighteenth and nineteenth centuries: John Gay and John Barnett are both only mentioned once; Thomas Arne is mentioned only three times. Purcell gets mentioned less than twenty times. By comparison, Irish composers—Balfe and Wallace—are referred to by name more than ten times each. He discusses Balfe, *The Bohemian Girl* and arias associated with his operas, almost thirty times. It is tempting to question whether Shaw's attention to the two Irish composers is the reason they made it into music history. The only two English composers that get more references are Handel with over one hundred—thirty-plus on *Messiah* alone—and Sullivan with over eighty references—forty of those with Gilbert, although Gilbert and Sullivan's operettas are generally sharply criticized. For instance, in a review of *The Gondoliers*, Shaw judges:

> We know the exact limit of Mr Gilbert's and Sir Arthur Sullivan's talent by this time, as well as we know the width of the Thames at Waterloo Bridge; and I am just as likely to find Somerset House under water next Easter or autumn, as to find The Gondoliers one hair's-breadth better than The Mikado." (The Star, 13 December 1899: a review not included in this selection.)

In distinct contrast are the German composers, such as Beethoven, Liszt, Brahms, Mozart and Wagner, all of whom are very favorably featured throughout Shaw's writings, with Wagner being the most prominent, having over two hundred entries in Shaw's reviews—not including the entire discussion in Shaw's book, *The Perfect Wagnerite* (first published in 1898).

As his reviews depict, in London during this period, Italian opera was the fashion; and many English composers actually had their operas first performed in Italian translations. Even the first performance of Wagner's *Der Fliegende Holländer* in England (Drury Lane 1870) had the libretto translated into

Italian. In 1890 Shaw complained that Wagner was seldom performed in England, commenting that more people had explored the Congo than had seen *Die Walküre* (*The Star*, 14 February 1890: a review not included here). Shaw did his best to promote Wagner, whose work he interpreted from a socialist perspective, and also Mozart. However, his preferred composer during his time as a music critic is definitely Wagner, whom he identifies with politically as well as musically; and his study of Wagner's operas, *The Perfect Wagnerite*, gives a socialist/Shavian reading and overview of *The Ring*, exposing a general theme of love and humanity versus money and capitalist exploitation. Shaw also, both in his study and his earlier reviews, singles out Wagner's use of *leitmotifs* to express the nature of a character or a specific emotion, demonstrating how these give a symphonic wholeness to an entire performance, unifying it musically and evoking the poetic qualities of a story. As Shaw argues, Wagner is not only responsible for a completely new development in opera, which he labels as "music-drama," but he also forms the culmination of nineteenth-century music, just as Mozart forms the apex of eighteenth-century music. Following this approach, while supportive and positive about Wagner's operas in his music reviews, after Wagner's death Shaw begins to criticize the productions in Bayreuth, and in the Preface to his fourth and final edition of *The Perfect Wagnerite* (1922) Shaw comments that in the aftermath of the First World War Wagner had become toothless and old-fashioned.

Since the basis for Shaw's approach to music was his vocal knowledge, he focused significantly more on opera and vocal music than any other music critic in England did at the time. The extensive coverage of opera in his music criticism certainly emphasized that, to Shaw, this musical genre dominated all other forms of music; and the way his reviews were distributed in newspapers and journals—particularly with so many of them being anonymous or signed by a pseudonym—would have spread his views widely though society. In his critique of the actual stage productions of the operas in London that he reviews, as well as of the management in these theaters, he suggests that comic and popular modes of staging are not appropriate, even for the theater itself. In other words, opera needs expert and artistic presentation as well as a significant theme and a properly developed story. The weighting of Shaw's musical criticism on opera, together with his aesthetic principles, in effect underlines the elite essence of music as high art. On the surface, this seems to conflict with Shaw's socialist views. As a leading member of the Fabian Society, he helped to found both the London School of Economics (with the perception of the LSE as being an educational institution focusing on left-wing economics) and the British Labour Party. Still, while the aesthetic principles that informed his music criticism might seem exclusive, it is certainly arguable that Shaw was intending to educate ordinary citizens, inducing them into adopting high art as their own.

Supporting this, he completely rejected all operetta or musical versions of his plays, trying (unsuccessfully) to deny the performance rights to a Viennese version of his *Arms and the Man: The Chocolate Soldier [operetta by Oscar Strauss, 1908]*, which turned out to be extremely popular both in Europe and in the United States. He also completely refused a suggestion—from Gabriel Pascal, the director who had made the film of the play, and whom Shaw referred to as "a genius"—that *Pygmalion* be turned into a musical, which meant that *My Fair Lady* could only be adapted from the play after Shaw's death. Reflecting this, in his reviews "popular" musical forms seem hardly approvable, with even his commentary on his sister Lucy's success, *Dorothy*, being extremely critical (see page 252). Yet in writing so much about opera Shaw was clearly intending to improve the artistic appreciation of the general public: by no means simply to change opera into high art for a social elite, even if this might be the actual result of his music criticism. Therefore, while Balfe's operas seldom received performances on the London stage during Shaw's time as a music critic, in Shaw's extensive references to him and to his operas (motivated by their shared Irish background) it can be seen that he is attempting to promote the popular quality of opera, as well as underlining their unrecognized artistic quality. This is reinforced again by the significance of Shaw being one of the leading people in establishing and defending Wagner's reputation in England. By promulgating the idea of *Gesamtkunstwerk* in contrast to operetta and comic opera, including Gilbert and Sullivan, Shaw is promoting opera as the alternative to standard popular musical theater.

As shown above, Shaw's family background clearly influenced his critical writings, as well as later his work as a playwright. Being a musician and singer himself gave him a particular understanding of the voice as an instrument, and helps explain why the opera and vocal reviews took up the main part of Shaw's focus, especially in his earlier years. In addition, from his work for Vandeleur Lee on *The Voice*, Shaw gained extensive knowledge of pronunciation, which would later create a link between his career as a music critic, and his later dramas. While music criticism may seem a specialized vocation, across the whole of Shaw's multifarious career an overall consistency is seen.

Yet even beyond his fame as a dramatist, Bernard Shaw has been counted as one of the most significant music critics of the nineteenth and twentieth centuries, as shown in the evaluation by an eminent music critic of the mid-twentieth century. Harold Schonberg, who wrote for *The New York Times*, singled out Shaw, claiming his reviews as a measure for all music criticism (6 July 1980 — reprinted in *The New York Times Guide to the Arts of the Twentieth Century*, 2002). This in itself makes his reviews worth reading, in addition to the added insight his musical statements give to scholars interested in Shaw, who should take note that they contribute a significantly different aspect to the general interpretation of his plays.

Bernard Shaw and His Times: A Chronology

[This chronology is common to all five volumes in the Critical Shaw series, and reflects the topics of the series: Politics, Theater, Literature, Music, and Religion. For a comprehensive and detailed chronology of Shaw's life and works, see A. M. Gibbs, A Bernard Shaw Chronology (Basingstoke: Palgrave, 2001).]

1856   Shaw born in Dublin (26 July).

1859   Charles Darwin publishes On the Origin of Species by Means of Natural Selection.

1864   Herbert Spencer publishes Principles of Biology (and coins the phrase "survival of the fittest").

1865   The Salvation Army is founded by Methodist preacher William Booth.

1870   The doctrine of papal infallibility is defined as dogma at the First Vatican Council.

1876   Shaw moves from Dublin to London. He begins ghostwriting music reviews for Vandeleur Lee for The Hornet.

1879   Shaw begins writing music reviews for The Saturday Musical Review, The Court Journal, and other publications. He writes his first novel, Immaturity, quickly followed by four others: The Irrational Knot (1880), Love Among the Artists (1881), Cashel Byron's Profession (1882), and An Unsocial Socialist (1883).

1883 Shaw reads Karl Marx's *Das Kapital* (in a French trans-lation) in the British Museum Reading Room.

1884 The Fabian Society is founded; Shaw joins in the same year. He publishes his first book review in *The Christ-ian Scientist*.

1885 Shaw begins publishing book reviews regularly in *The Pall Mall Gazette*.

1886 Eleanor Marx, daughter of Karl Marx, organizes a reading of Ibsen's *A Doll's House*; Shaw reads the part of Krogstad.

1889 Having written music reviews for over a decade, Shaw becomes a full-time critic for *The Star*, and then (in 1890) *The World*.

1891 Shaw publishes *The Quintessence of Ibsenism* (revised and updated in 1922).

1892 Shaw's first play, *Widowers' Houses*, is performed.

1893 Founding of the Independent Labour Party, a socialist advocacy group.

1894 Shaw resigns from *The World* and henceforth writes only occasional music reviews. *Arms and the Man* is first performed. Shaw becomes acquainted with aspir-ing theatre critic Reginald Golding Bright.

1895 Shaw becomes full-time drama critic for *The Saturday Review*. He publishes a lengthy review column almost every week for the next two and a half years.

1897 Shaw is elected a member of the Vestry of the Parish of St Pancras (until 1903).

1898 Shaw marries Charlotte Payne-Townshend and resigns as *The Saturday Review* drama critic. He publishes *The Perfect Wagnerite* and *Plays: Pleasant and Unpleasant*. One of the "unpleasant" plays, *Mrs Warren's Profession*, is refused a performance licence by the Lord Chamberlain; the ban will stay in effect until 1924.

1901 *Caesar and Cleopatra* is first performed, with music written by Shaw. Queen Victoria dies.

1904 J. E. Vedrenne and Harley Granville Barker begin their management of the Court Theatre (until 1907), with Shaw as a principal playwright. Eleven Shaw plays are performed in three seasons.

1905 *Man and Superman* is first performed. Albert Einstein publishes his theory of relativity.

1906 Founding of the Labour Party. *Major Barbara* and *The Doctor's Dilemma* are first performed.

1908 *Der tapfere Soldat*, an unauthorized operetta loosely based on *Arms and the Man*, with music by Oscar Straus and libretto by Rudolf Bernauer and Leopold Jacobson, is first performed in Vienna. It is later staged (1910) in translation as *The Chocolate Soldier*.

1909 *The Shewing-up of Blanco Posnet* is refused a licence by the Lord Chamberlain. W. B. Yeats and Lady Gregory stage it at the Abbey Theatre in Dublin. Shaw appears as a witness before the Joint Select Committee of the House of Lords and the House of Commons on Stage Plays (Censorship).

1911 Shaw joins the managing council of the Royal Academy of Dramatic Art. His strong support of RADA's programs will include bequeathing RADA a third of his royalties. Shaw writes an introduction for the Waverley edition of Dickens's *Hard Times*.

1913 *Pygmalion* is first performed.

1914 Beginning of the First World War. Shaw publishes *Common Sense About the War*.

1916 Easter Rising in Dublin against British rule of Ireland.

1917 The Russian Revolution overthrows the imperialist government and installs a communist government under Vladimir Ilyich Lenin. The United States joins the war against Germany. On 17 July Czar Nicholas II and his family are executed.

1918 Representation of the People Act gives the vote to all men over twenty-one, and to women over thirty if they meet certain qualifications (e.g., property owners, university graduates). End of the First World War.

1920 *Heartbreak House* is first performed. Shaw completes *Back to Methuselah*, a five-play cycle on evolutionary themes. League of Nations formed.

1921 The Irish Free State gains independence from Britain. Shaw writes the preface to *Immaturity*.

1922 Joseph Stalin becomes general secretary of the Communist Party Central Committee. Benito Mussolini becomes Italian prime minister.

1923 *Saint Joan* is first performed, with music written by Shaw.

1924 Ramsay MacDonald becomes the first Labour prime minister, in a Labour-Liberal coalition government.

1925 Adolf Hitler publishes *Mein Kampf* [*My Struggle*].

1926 General strike in Great Britain, 4–13 May. Shaw is awarded the 1925 Nobel Prize for Literature.

1928 Representation of the People (Equal Franchise) Act gives the vote to all women over twenty-one. Shaw publishes *The Intelligent Woman's Guide to Socialism and Capitalism*. *The Apple Cart* is first performed.

1929 The Wall Street Crash, 28–29 October, which signalled the beginning of the Great Depression. Shaw speaks as a delegate to the third International Congress of the World League for Sexual Reform. Sir Barry Jackson establishes the Malvern Festival, dedicated to Shaw's plays.

1931 Shaw visits Russia. He celebrates his seventy-fifth birthday on 26 July in Moscow's Concert Hall of Nobles with two thousand guests. He meets Stalin on 29 July.

1932 Unemployment reaches 3.5 million in Great Britain. South Wales and the industrial north experience mass unemployment and poverty. *Too True to Be Good* receives its English première at the Malvern Festival.

1933 Shaw makes his first visit to the United States. He speaks to an audience of thirty-five hundred at the Metropolitan Opera House (11 April). Hitler becomes German chancellor.

1934 *The Six of Calais* is first performed.

1936 Shaw makes his second (and last) visit to the United States. *The Millionairess* is first performed.

1938 *Geneva* is first performed. Shaw rejects a proposal from producer Gabriel Pascal for a musical version of *Pygmalion*.

1939 Beginning of the Second World War.

1941 The United States enters the Second World War.

1943 Charlotte Shaw dies.

1944 Shaw publishes *Everybody's Political What's What?*

1945 End of the Second World War. United Nations formed. The UK Labour Party wins its first majority government. Clement Atlee becomes prime minister. His government implements an extensive nationalization program of British industry and services.

1947 Discovery of the Dead Sea Scrolls in Qumran Caves, West Bank.

1948 World Council of Churches founded in Amsterdam.

1950 Shaw publishes his last book review in *The Observer* (26 March). He dies in Ayot St Lawrence, Hertfordshire (2 November).

A Note on the Text

This selection made from Bernard Shaw's music reviews is intended to give a comprehensive overview of his work in the field. The reviews and articles have also been divided into separate categories, in order to enable a better and more intelligent understanding of his focus and interests. Each one, with the exception of the first item in the opening section, is listed in chronological order. We have chosen to open with one of Shaw's later pieces that looks back over his career as a music critic, because it provides a coherent account of his approach, which should prove illuminating to readers.

These separate categories have been organized as follows. To introduce the selection and provide focus, the first section is titled Critical Approaches: it comprises Shaw's views on music critics and his own career as one of them. This is followed by Musical Theory: a selection of his more theoretical essays about music and its social impact. While Shaw took a strong political attitude in many of his reviews, promoting a revolutionary aspect in music, as well as frequently including critical comments on social hierarchies and financial issues, there are very few reviews devoted solely to these topics. Politics is a subtext that runs throughout, but there is no example that would justify a separate section on this topic.

As stated in the Introduction, the majority of Shaw's musical reviews are focused on vocal performances. Since particularly in his early writings Shaw focused on the most important singers of the period, covering all vocal ranges, the third section is on Vocalists, reflecting this emphasis; and the next section is on Opera and Operetta, which—though it might seem long—is no less a selection than the other sections. Wagner's operas were a major concern for Shaw, culminating in his book-length study of *The Perfect Wagnerite*, first published in 1898. So because it could be argued that these particular works form the culmination of Shaw's music criticism, a separate section has been appended on Richard Wagner. There is also a separate category devoted to Shaw's reviews of Oratorios and Religious Music: one of the most frequent and important types of musical performance in England at the time. Possibly due to his political stance, Shaw is overall highly critical of both the style of performance, and (except for Handel's works) the way the composers have arranged these religious pieces. This is followed by a section on Family Music: given Shaw's strong family background in music, and frequent references to both his surrogate father, the operatic conductor Vandeleur Lee, and to his operetta-singing sister Lucy (whose most famous success was in a comic opera titled *Dorothy*) in his reviews, two articles focusing on them have been set in a separate section. The penultimate section is on Instrumental Concerts: unlike his opera reviews, in each of these Shaw generally covers several separate instrumental concerts, particularly those that include vocal components in their program, in one review. As a final section, we have included Shaw's unpublished writings (for the proposed second edition of Vandeleur Lee's 1870 book) on The Voice: introduced by a selection of his book reviews relating to the topic of vocal teaching, these pieces offer a scientific basis for Shaw's musical opinions as well as underpinning his predominant focus on vocal performance.

The verbal style and syntax of Shaw's writing at this period have been carefully followed; and as his reviews demonstrate, his style is somewhat different from contemporary verbal customs. For instance, he never uses italics for the title of a play, or opera, or musical theater; nor does he use inverted commas for song titles. Shaw's original spelling and punctuation have been retained. Shaw apparently presumes that his audience has a detailed knowledge of singing and opera, since he frequently refers to songs and arias by their name or first lines, without indicating where they come from. His most frequent references and comparisons are made to Shakespeare (whose name Shaw always spells without the final 'e') and to characters from the novels of Charles Dickens. Since Shaw considered that Dickens was the major author defining the consciousness of his own generation, he very seldom attributes characters to the particular novel they appear in; and in order to make his references comprehensible the titles, as well as other nineteenth-century theatrical references that would have been familiar to his readers of the time, have been inserted in square brackets. Some names, for instance in the "Amateur Opera" review of 1882, are impossible to track down—while what can be found seems irrelevant (one person appears to have been a Seventh Day Adventist, another eventually became a Rear Admiral in the British navy)—so there is no information appended to their names. In other cases birth and death dates, or brief explanatory notes, are included in square brackets. In cases where there are multiple references to the same person or event, added information is given only in the initial reference.

Full bibliographical details for the sources that offer a useful background are provided in Sources and Further Reading, where secondary sources on Shaw's musical writings are also listed.

Part I: Critical Approaches

Bernard Shaw comments frequently on his own critical writings about music during his reviews, and some of his pieces are solely about himself as a music critic, or about his qualifications. Since these offer insights into his approach to the various musical genres and the way he evaluates the performances he writes about, it was felt that a selection of these should precede the other categories into which his reviews have been divided. In all other sections the pieces are listed chronologically. However, here it is clear that the opening of this whole selection should be a piece written towards the middle/ end of his career as a music critic, since it explicitly focuses on both his career and the qualities necessary to become such a figure.

1. How To Become a Musical Critic

The Scottish Musical Monthly, December 1894
Reprinted in The New Music Review, October 1912

My own plan was a simple one. I joined the staff of a new daily paper as a leader writer. My exploits in this department spread such terror and confusion that my proposal to turn my attention to musical criticism was hailed with inexpressible relief, the subject being one in which lunacy is privileged. I was given a column to myself precisely as I might have been given a padded room in an asylum; and from that time up to the other day—a period of nearly seven years—I wrote every week, in that paper or another, an article under the general heading "Music," the first condition of which was, as a matter of good journalism, that it should be as attractive to the general reader, musician or non-musician, as any other section of the paper in which it appeared. Most editors do not believe that this can be done. But then most editors do not know how to edit. The late Edmund Yates, who did, believed in a good musical column as an important reinforcement to a journal. He placed a whole page of The World at the disposal of his musical critic. And the success of this page proved that in the hands of a capable writer music is quite as good a subject from the purely journalistic point of view as either painting or the drama, whilst the interest taken in it is much more general than in party politics, the stock exchange, or even the police intelligence. Let me add that Edmund Yates had no more special interest in music than he had in chemistry; for young musical critics should be warned that of all editors for their purposes, the musical-amateur editor is the very worst. Only, let me in justice add, too, that the critic who is a musical amateur and nothing else is equally objectionable.

It is quite clear that if musical criticism is to win from all papers the space and consideration allowed it in The World, the critics must be persons of considerable accomplishment. There are three main qualifications for a musical critic, besides the general qualification of good sense and knowledge of the world. He must have a cultivated taste for music; he must be a skilled writer; and he must be a practiced critic. Any of these three may be found without the others; but the complete combination is indispensable to good work. Take up any of our musical papers—those which are taken in by the organist as The Lancet is taken in by the doctor—and you will find plenty of articles written by men of unquestionable competence and even eminence as musicians. These gentlemen may write without charm because they have not served their apprenticeship to literature; but they can at all events express themselves at their comparative leisure as well as most journalists do in their feverish haste; and they can depend on the interest which can be commanded by any intelligent man who has ordinary powers of expression, and who is dealing with a subject he understands. Why, then, are they so utterly impossible as musical critics? Because they cannot criticize. They set to work like schoolmasters to prove that this is "right" and that "wrong"; they refer disputed points to school authorities who have no more authority in the republic of art than the head master of Eton has in the House of Commons; they jealously defend their pet compositions and composers against rival claims like ladies at a musical at-home; they shew no sense of the difference between a professor teaching his class how to resolve the chord of the dominant seventh and a critic standing in the presence of the whole world and its art, and submitting his analysis of the work of an artist whose authority is at least equal to his own. A man may have counterpoint at his finger ends; but if, being no more than a second-rate music teacher, he petulantly treats composers of European reputation as intrusive and ignorant pretenders who ought to be suppressed—a very different thing from genuine criticism, however unfavorable, of their works—he obviously puts himself out of the question as a member of the staff of any general newspaper or magazine.

It is not so easy to cite instances of writers who fail because, being critics, they have neither literary skill nor musical culture. A man cannot become an expert in criticism without practicing on art of some kind; and if that art is not music, then he naturally confines himself to the art he is accustomed to handle, writing about it if he has the requisite literary faculty, and if not, teaching it. As to the literary artist who is neither musician nor critic, he has every inducement to devote himself to pure literature, like Mr [Robert Louis] Stevenson or Mr Rudyard Kipling, and no temptation whatever to eke out his income by sham musical criticism. But since, for the purposes of journalism, the literary qualification is the main one—since no editor who is supplied with entertaining "copy" ever asks whether it is criticism or gossip, or cares whether its technology is a bit sounder than the sham sailing directions given in Gulliver's ship, cases are not lacking of journalists taking the post of musical critic merely because it is the only opening that presents itself, and concealing their deficiencies by plenty of descriptive reporting and scraps of news about music and musicians. If such a critic has critical and musical faculty latent in him, he will learn his business after some years; but some writers of this sort have not the faculty, and never learn.

It is worth remarking here—at least I cannot resist mentioning it—that the experienced editor has usually found the mere musician critic so useless on a paper, and the mere journalist critic so sufficient for all purposes, that the critic whose articles are at all readable by people who only read to be amused is usually suspected by his fellow journalists of being a musical impostor, a suspicion which reaches absolute certainty in the mind of his editor. When my own articles on music first began to attract some attention, the cream of the joke was supposed by many persons to be the fact that I knew nothing whatever about music. Several times it happened to me to be introduced to admirers who, on discovering from my reply to the question, "What put it into your head to write about music?" that I did so because it happened to be the art I knew most about, have turned away cruelly disappointed and disillusioned by this prosaic explanation, which seemed to rob my exploits of all their merit. Even when the hypothesis of my total ignorance became untenable, I still used occasionally to encounter people who appealed to me to candidly admit that my knowledge of music did not extend to its technicalities. They missed, I imagine, the Mesopotamianism of the sort of musical writing which parades silly little musical parsing exercises to impress the laity exactly as the performances of the learned pig impress the rustics at a fair.

A critic who does not know his business has two advantages. First, if he writes for a daily paper he can evade the point, and yet make himself useful and interesting, by collecting the latest news about forthcoming events, and the most amusing scandal about past ones. Second, his incompetence can be proved only by comparing his notice of a month ago with his notice of today, which nobody will take the trouble to do. Any man can write an imposing description of Madame Calvé [1858–1942], or of Slivinski [1865–1930], but if you turn back to his description of Miss Eames [1865–1952] or of Sapellnikoff [1868–1941], you will find, if he is no critic, that the same description did duty for them also, just as it did duty, before he was born, for Catalani [1780–1849] and Pasta [1797–1865], Cramer [1771–1858] and Czerny [1791–1857]. When he attempts to particularize the special qualities of the artists he criticizes, you will find him praising Sarasate [1844–1908] and Paderewski [1860–1941] for exactly those feats which their pupils, Miss Nettie Carpenter [1869–1948] and Miss Szumowska [1868–1938], are able to copy to the life. Whether he is praising or blaming, he always dwells on some of the hundred points that all players and executants have in common, and misses the final ones that make all the difference between mediocrity and genius, and between one artist and another.

I know this by my own experience. Nearly twenty years ago a musician [Vandeleur Lee] who wished to help me accepted a post as musical critic to a London paper. I wrote the criticisms; and he handed the emoluments over to me without deduction, contenting himself with the consciousness of doing generously by a young and forlorn literary adventurer, and with the honor and glory accruing from the reputed authorship of my articles. To them I owe all my knowledge of the characteristics of bad criticism. I cannot here convey an adequate impression of their demerits without overstepping the bounds of decorum. They made me miserable at the time; but I did not know even enough to understand that what was torturing me was the guilt and shame which attend ignorance and incompetence. The paper, with my assistance, died, and my sins are buried with it; but I still keep, in a safe hiding place, a set of the critical crimes I contributed to it, much as a murderer keeps the bloodstained knife under which his victim fell. Whenever I feel that I am getting too conceited, or am conscious of crediting myself with a natural superiority to some younger brother of the craft, I take myself down by reading some of that old stuff—though indeed the bare thought of it is generally sufficient. And yet neither in literary ability nor musical knowledge was I unpardonably deficient at that time. I should have been a very decent critic for my age, if only I had known how to criticize. Not knowing that, however, my musical knowledge and power of literary expression made me much more noxious than if I had been a mere newsman in music and a phrasemonger in journalism. When I broke out again, about ten years later, I had graduated as a critic, as a writer, and as a citizen (a most important item) by constant work as an author, a critic of books, pictures, and politics, a public speaker, and a social reformer, including the function of the wirepuller and committee man, as well as of the theorist and Utopian. All this had nothing to do with music; yet, in my musical criticism, it made all the difference between an execrable amateur and a reasonably competent workman. I was enormously helped as a critic by my economical studies and my political practice, which gave me an invaluable comprehension of the commercial conditions to which art is subject. It is an important part of a critic's business to agitate for musical reforms; and unless he knows what the reforms will cost, and whether they are worth that cost, and who will have to pay the bill, and a dozen other cognate matters not usually included in treatises on harmony, he will not make any effective impression on the people with whom the initiative rests—indeed he will not know who they are. Even his artistic verdicts will often be aimed at the wrong person. A manager or an artist cannot be judged fairly by any critic who does not understand the economic bearings of profits and salaries. It is one thing to set up an ideal of perfection and complain as long as it is not reached; but to blame individuals for not reaching it when it is economically unattainable, instead of blaming the conditions which make it unattainable; or to blame the wrong person—for instance, to blame the artist when the fault is the manager's, or the manager when the fault is the public's—is to destroy half your influence as a critic. All the counterpoint or literary brilliancy in the world will not save a critic from blunders of this kind, unless he understands the economics of art.

I need say no more as to the accomplishments of a musical critic, because I have already brought myself face to face with an economic difficulty in my own path. The emoluments of a musical critic are not large. Newspaper proprietors offer men from a pound a week to five pounds a week for musical criticism, the latter figure being very exceptional, and involving the delivery of a couple of thousand words of extra brilliant copy every week. And, except in the dead season, the critic must spend most of his afternoons and evenings, from three to midnight, in concert rooms or in the opera house. I need hardly say that it is about as feasible to obtain the services of a fully-qualified musical critic on these terms as it would be to obtain a pound of fresh strawberries every day from January to December for five shillings a week. Consequently, to all the qualifications I have already suggested, I must insist on this further one—an independent income, and sufficient belief in the value of musical criticism to sustain you in doing it for its own sake whilst its pecuniary profits are enjoyed by others. And since this condition is so improbable in any given case as to take my subject completely out of the range of the practicable, I may as well stop preaching, since my sermon ends, as all such sermons do, in a demonstration that our economic system fails miserably to provide the requisite incentive to the production of first-rate work.

2. Some Instruments and How to Play Them

The Star, 8 March 1889

Before I hurry away to St James's Hall to hear the Bach Choir and Joachim, I must snatch a moment to reply to the numerous correspondents who have been struck by my recent remarks as to the salutary effects of wind-instrument playing. It is impossible to answer all their questions in detail, but a few general observations will cover most of the cases.

First, then, as to the constantly recurring question whether the practice of musical instruments is likely to annoy the neighbors. There can be no doubt whatever that it is; and when the man next door sends in to complain there is no use in quarreling over the point. Admit promptly and frankly that the noise is horrible, promise to cease practising after half-past twelve at night, except when you have visitors; and confess that if he in self-defence takes up another instrument you will be bound to suffer in turn for the sake of his health and culture as he is now suffering for yours. This is far more sensible and social than to place the bell of your instrument against the partition wall and blow strident fanfares in defiance of his nerves, as I foolishly did when a complaint of the kind was made to me. But I was little more than a boy at the time, and I have never since thought of it without remorse.

As to my correspondent who inquires whether there is such a thing as "a dumb French horn," analogous to the "dumb piano" used for teaching children to finger the keyboard, I am happy to be able to assure him that no such contrivance is needed, as the ordinary French horn remains dumb in the hands of a beginner for a considerable period. Nor can anyone, when it does begin to speak, precisely foresee what it will say. Even an experienced player can only surmise what will happen when he starts. I have seen an eminent conductor beat his way helplessly through the first page of the Freischütz overture [by Weber] without eliciting anything from the four expert cornists in the orchestra but inebriated gugglings.

The amateur will find, contrary to all his preconceptions, that the larger the instrument the easier it is to play. It is a mistake to suppose that he has to fill the instrument with expired air: he has only to throw into vibration the column of air already contained in it. In the German bands, which were dispersed by the Franco-Prussian war, mothers of households used to observe with indignation from the windows that these apparently lazy and brutal foreigners always placed the burden of the largest instrument on the smallest boy. As a matter of fact, however, the small boy had the easiest job; and I recommend amateurs to confine themselves to the tuba or bombardon [bass tuba], the chest-encircling helicon [spiral bass tuba played encircling the player's head and resting on the shoulder], the ophicleide [keyed brass instrument similar to the tuba, or at most the euphonium [a smaller, mellower form of the tuba]. The euphonium is an extraordinary sentimental instrument, and can impart a tender melancholy to the most ferocious themes. The accents of the Count di Luna, raging to inflict *mille atroci spasimi* on Manrico, in the last act of [Verdi's] Trovatore, are bloodcurdling. Transcribed for the euphonium in a military band selection they remind you of the Maiden's Prayer [song by Polish composer Tekla Badarzewska-Baranowska].

Of course, you will not take my advice. You are bent on learning the flute or the cornet. As to the flute I do not greatly care: you will get tired of it long before you can play *Ah! non giunge* [from Bellini's *Sonnambula*], even without variations. But the cornet is a most fearful instrument, and one with which self-satisfaction is attainable on easy terms. The vulgarity of the cornet is incurable. At its best—playing *pianissimo* in heavenly sweet chords scored by Gounod [1818–1893], or making the sword motive heard, in the first act of [Wagner's] Die Walküre—it is only pretty. But in trumpet parts it is simply perdurable. Yet there is no getting rid of it.

Two cornet performancers have left an abiding memory with me. One was M. Lévy's variation on Yankee Doodle, take *prestissimo*, with each note repeated three times by "triple tonguing." This was in the open air, at the inauguration of Buffalo Bill; and it was preceded by spirited attempt on the part of Madame Nordica [American soprano, 1857–1914] to sing The Star Spangled Banner to an entirely independent accompaniment by the band of Grenadier Guards. The other was The Pilgrim of Love, played by an itinerant artist outside a public house in Clipstone-street, Portland Place. The man played with great taste and pathos; but, to my surprise, he had no knowledge of musical etiquette, for when, on his holding his hat to me for a donation, I explained that I was a member of the press, he still seemed to expect me to pay for my entertainment: a shocking instance of popular ignorance.

I dwell on the cornet a little, because in my youth I was presented by a relative with absolutely the very worst and oldest cornet then in existence. It was of an obsolete rectangular model, and sounded in B flat with the A crook on. Its tone was unique; my master—an excellent player, of London extraction—once described it as "somethink 'ellish"; and he did it no more than justice. I never come across Scott's line [from "Marmion" 1808], "Oh, for a blast of that dread horn," without thinking of it. After devastating the welkin with this remarkable instrument for some months, I was told that it would spoil my voice (perhaps in revenge for having had its own spoiled); and though I had not then, nor ever have had, any voice worth taking care of, I there and then presented the cornet as a curiosity to my instructor, and abandoned it for aye. It turned his brain eventually; for he afterwards spread a report that I was mad.

I believe that a taste for brass instrument is hereditary. My father destroyed his domestic peace by immoderate indulgence in the trombone; my uncle played the ophicleide—very nicely, I must admit—for years, and then perished by his own hand. Some day I shall buy a trombone myself. At the Inventions Exhibition Messrs Rudall and Carte displayed a double-slide trombone, which I felt insanely tempted to purchase. Of the merits of this instrument I was, and am, wholly ignorant, except that I inferred that its "shifts" were only half as long as on the ordinary trombone; and I ascertained that its price was 13 guineas. If ever I have so vast a sum at my command I shall probably buy that trombone, and ask Herr Richter to engage me for the next concert at which the Walkürenritt [Ride of the Valkyrie] or Les Francs-Juges [overture to an unfinished opera by Berlioz] is in the program.

By the bye, I do not agree with Musigena that Mr Manns [conductor, 1825–1907] keeps his brass too quiet at the Crystal Palace. I admire two things at Sydenham: the brass and Mr

41

Manns himself. The strings are often snappish and mechanical, the wood wind stolid; but the brass is generally noble. I have never heard the statue music in Don Giovanni more finely played than at Mr Manns' centenary recital of that masterpiece; and this is as much as to say that Mr Manns feels for the trombone like Mozart and myself. But I certainly believe that the time is approaching when it will be admitted that the doubling, trebling, and quadrupling of the strings which has taken place in the modern orchestra requires a proportional multiplication of the wind instruments to balance them. In spite of the splendors of the Boehm flute, it is often lost in passages where the old flute used to tell when violins were less numerous. For ensemble playing there ought to be at least six bassoons instead of two. And though I never want Mr Manns' trombones to play four times as loud—the trombone being a tender plant that must not be forced—I sometimes want twelve trombones instead of three. This would satisfy Musigena, though it would run into money.

But I must not leave my inquiring amateurs without a word for those who most deserve my sympathy. They are people who desire to enjoy music socially: to play together, to explore the riches of concerted chamber music for mere love of it, and without any desire to expand their lungs and display their individual virtuosity. Yet they are too old to learn to fiddle, or, having learnt, cannot do it well enough to produce tolerable concord. Their difficulty is, fortunately, quite easy to solve. The instrument for them is the concertina: not the Teutonic instrument of the midnight Mohock, but the English concertina of Wheatstone. I presume Wheatstone and Co. are still flourishing in Conduit Street, although Mr Richard Blagrove [composer and concertina player, 1826–1895] and his quartet party have not been much in evidence lately. You can play any instrument's part on a concertina of suitable compass, the B flat clarinet being most exactly matched by it in point of tone. The intonation does not depend on you any more than that of a pianoforte. A good concertina is everlasting: it can be repaired as often as a violin. It costs from 16 guineas for a treble to 24 for a contra-brass.

3. Fine Strokes of Comedy

The World, 15 February 1893

I do not know how far the matter is worth mentioning, but music is dying out in London. The Monday Popular and Ballad concerts go on from mere force of habit; the Crystal Palace concerts will begin again next Saturday, because they rashly promised to do so last year; oratorios are solemnized at the usual intervals in the Albert Hall; Sarasate [Spanish violinist, 1844–1908] goes and Joachim [Austrian violinist, 1831–1907] comes; and Mr Henschel's band is heard twice a month as usual. It is true that early February is not exactly the height of the musical season, and that this year the light opera houses produced their novelties much earlier in the year than is customary.

But when all allowances are made, it must be admitted that things for the moment are slack; and I have once or twice thought of raising an Unemployed Deadheads' agitation, and calling on the Government to at once set on foot a series of Relief Concerts, at which these unhappy people may pass their afternoons and evenings. The Abolition of Piecework for critics would be a prominent plank in the program of such an agitation; for even a critic must live, and if the agents will not give concerts and recitals, the critics will be driven to invent them; that is the long and short of it.

A man cannot go on repeating what he has said a thousand times about the way the Monday Popular quartet played Haydn in G, No. 12 of Opus 756, or about Santley [1834–1922] as Elijah [oratorio by Mendelssohn]. I turn in desperation to the musical journals, and my hopes rise as I see the words "Ig-nornant Misstatement." But it is actually not G. B. S. this time; somebody else, I suppose, has made a remark sufficiently obvious to shake the foundation of make-believe on which "art" of the usual professional type is built. The tenants of that fashionable edifice are always protesting that I am an impudent pretender to musical authority, betraying my ignorance, in spite of my diabolical cunning, in every second sentence. And I do not mind confessing that I do not know half as much as you would suppose from my articles; but in the kingdom of the deaf the one-eared is king.

The other evening I was looking into a shop window in Oxford-street, when a gentleman accosted me modestly, and, after flattering me with great taste and modesty into an entire willingness to make his acquaintance, began with evident misgiving and hesitation, but with no less evident curiosity, to approach the subject of these columns. At last he came to his point with a rush by desperately risking the question "Excuse me, Mr G. B. S., but do you know anything about music? The fact is, I am not capable of forming an opinion myself; but Dr Blank says you dont, and—er—Dr Blank is such a great authority that one hardly knows what to think." Now this question put me into a difficulty, because I had already learnt by experience that the reason my writings on music and musicians are so highly appreciated is, that they are supposed by many of my greatest admirers to be a huge joke, the point of which lies in the fact that I am totally igno-rant of music, and that my character of critic is an exquisitely ingenious piece of acting, undertaken to gratify my love of mystification and paradox.

From this point of view every one of my articles appears as a fine stroke of comedy, occasionally broadening into a harlequinade, in which I am the clown, and Dr Blank the policeman. At first I did not realize this, and could not un-derstand the air of utter disillusion and loss of interest in me that would come over people in whose houses I incautiously betrayed some scrap of amateurish enlightenment. But the naïve exclamation "Oh! you do know something about it, then" at last became familiar to me; and I now take particular care not to expose my knowledge. When people hand me a sheet of instrumental music, and ask my opinion of it, I carefully hold it upside down, and pretend to study it in that position with the eye of an expert. When they invite me to try their new grand piano, I attempt to open it at the wrong end; and when a young lady of the house informs me that she is practising the cello, I innocently ask her whether the mouthpiece did not cut her lips dreadfully at first. This line of conduct gives enormous satisfaction, in which I share to a rather greater extent than is generally supposed. But, after all, the people whom I take in thus are only amateurs.

To place my impostorship beyond question I require to be certified as such by authorities like our Bachelors and Doctors of music—gentlemen who can write a Nunc Dimittis in five real parts, and know the difference between a tonal fugue and a real one, and can tell you how old Monteverdi was on his thirtieth birthday, and have views as to the true root of the discord of the seventh on the supertonic, and devoutly believe that *si contra fa diabolus est*. But I have only to present myself to them in the character of a man who has been through these dreary games without ever discovering the remotest vital connexion between them and the art of music—a state of mind so inconceivable by them—to make them exclaim:

Preposterous ass! that never read so far
To know the cause why music was ordained,
[*The Taming of the Shrew*, III, i]

and give me the desired testimonials at once. And so I manage to scrape along without falling under suspicion of being an honest man.

However, since mystification is not likely to advance us in the long run, may I suggest that there must be something wrong in the professional tests which have been successively applied to Handel, to Mozart, to Beethoven, to Wagner, and last, though not least, to me, with the result in every case of our condemnation as ignoramuses and charlatans. Why is it that when Dr Blank writes about music nobody but a professional musician can understand him; wheras the man-in-the-street, if fond of art and capable of music, can understand the writings of Mendelssohn, Wagner, Liszt, Berlioz, or any of the composers?

Why, again, is it that my colleague William Archer, for instance, in criticizing Mr Henry Arthur Jones's play the other day, did not parse all the leading sentences in it? I will not be so merciless as to answer these questions now, though I know the solution, and am capable of giving it if provoked beyond endurance. Let it suffice for the moment that writing is a very difficult art, criticism a very difficult process, and music not easily to be distinguished, without special critical training, from the scientific, technical, and professional conditions of its performance, composition, and teaching. And if the critic is to please the congregation, who want to read only about the music, it is plain that he must appear quite beside the point to the organ-blower, who wants to read about his bellows, which he can prove to be the true source of all the harmony.

Some weeks ago, in speaking of the lecture and viol concert given by Mr Arnold Dolmetsch [musician and instrument maker, 1848–1940] before the conference of the Incorporated Society of Musicians, I seized the opportunity to put in a protest on behalf of opera-goers against the horrible custom of playing the prelude to the tenor air in the first act of

Les Huguenots [opera by Meyerbeer] on the *viole d'amour [a six- or seven-stringed instrument like the violin, with sympathetic strings, used in the baroque period]*, and then returning to the ordinary viola, with detestable effect, for the obbligato. Mr Dolmetsch, who is giving viol concerts on alternate Tuesdays at Barnard's Inn, Holborn, promises to bring a viole d'amour, tuned for playing this obbligato, to his next concert on the 14th, and to say something on the subject. I hope the upshot will be to get the obbligato played at the opera as Meyerbeer meant it to be played. The difference to the singer, who would be coaxed into the dulcet style, instead of having his teeth set on edge and his worst shouting propensities stirred up, would be considerable, and the difference to the audience incalculable.

I see that Mr Lunn [composer and organist, 1831–1899] is not quite convinced that he and I mean the same thing by the *coup de glotte*. But it is clear from his last utterance on the subject that we do. Marchesi's "sudden and energetic drawing together of the lips of the glottis an instant before expiration commences" is exactly what I mean, and what I object to. I never heard Titiens [1831–1877] sing Hear ye, Israel; so I will take it on Mr Lunn's authority that she used to attack the allegro with a coup de glotte on the I, I am He that comforteth [arias from *Elijah* by Mendelssohn], although Titiens was certainly not a coup de glottist in her ordinary practice. I myself, in the very rare instances when I pronounce the word "I" in a self-assertive mood, may sometimes attack it with a coup de glotte; but I always regret it the moment the sound strikes my conscience, which, in my case, as in that of all musical critics, is situated in my ear.

But when Mr Lunn goes on to say that if Titiens had not used the coup de glotte she must "inevitably" have produced the sentence as "Hi! Hi! am He that comforteth," I can only assure him that he is wrong on the point of fact. If Titiens had been an Academy pupil, with no power of distending and bracing her pharynx, and helplessly dependent on a carefully cultivated method of bleating with the vocal cords alone, then undoubtedly she could not have produced any vowel whatsoever without a coup de glotte, except by fairly gasping it into existence by a strong aspirate.

Being what she was, a practical dramatic singer, she could have attacked any vowel with a perfectly open glottis and without an aspirate, exactly as an organ flue-pipe attacks its note, or as I can attack a note in whistling, without closing my lips, by simply putting them in the proper position first, and then directing a stream of air through them. Now a flue-pipe is just as "natural" an instrument as a reed-pipe; and I will by no means admit that a vocal method based on the analogy of the reed mechanism is any more "natural," or "normal," or "spontaneous" than a method based on the analogy of the flue construction. Infants may, as Mr Lunn says, yell with a coup de glotte (the method of the yelling infant being instinctively vicious); but children croon or "sing to themselves" on the other plan; so I claim the child's evidence as on my side, though I attach no importance to it.

Consequently we may get rid of all discussion as to whether the coup de glotte reed-pipe method or the open glottis flue-pipe method is Nature's method. The question is, which of the two sounds better and wears better. The first point is a matter of taste: the second, a matter of experience and observation; and I declare for the flue-pipe on both issues.

Part II: Musical Theory

Shaw's reviews frequently have a theoretical element; and in his writing he sometimes focuses specifically on this, which distinguishes the following pieces, and qualifies them for a special section. Neither are reviews of any particular performance. One focuses mainly on musical history and musical development, the influence of one composer on others; the other on a musical instrument, its uses and abuses, comparing it to the introduction of printing in the knowledge of Shakespeare's plays and new developments in the theater, the importance of individuals learning to play this instrument—and the social problems associated with doing so in one's own home (as Shaw himself did). Both emphasize the moral and psychological significance of understanding and practising music, the importance of educating feeling (as opposed to university education of the intellect) and the proposition that music is the most focused of all the arts. Notably both also make reference to Wagner.

1. Mozart's Finality

The World, 9 December 1891

The Mozart Centenary has made a good deal of literary and musical business this week. Part of this is easy enough, especially for the illustrated papers. Likenesses of Mozart at all ages; view of Salzburg; portrait of Marie Antoinette (described in the text as "the ill-fated"), to whom he proposed marriage at an early age; picture of the young composer, two and a half feet high, crushing the Pompadour with his "Who is this woman that refuses to kiss me? The Queen kissed me! (Sensation)"; facsimile of the original MS. of the first four bars of *La ci darem* [aria from Mozart's *Don Giovanni*], and the like. These, with copious paraphrases of the English translation of Otto Jahn's great biography, will pull the journalists proper through the Centenary with credit. The critic's task is not quite so easy.

The word is, of course, Admire, admire, admire; but unless you frankly trade on the ignorance of the public, and cite as illustrations of his unique genius feats that come easily to dozens of organists and choirboys who never wrote, and never will write, a bar of original music in their lives; or pay his symphonies and operas empty compliments that might be transferred word for word, without the least incongruity, to the symphonies of Spohr [1784–1859] and the operas of Offenbach [1819–1880]; or represent him as composing as spontaneously as a bird sings, on the strength of his habit of perfecting his greater compositions in his mind before he wrote them down — unless you try these well-worn dodges, you will find nothing to admire that is peculiar to Mozart [1756–1791]: the fact being that he, like Praxiteles, Raphael, Molière, or Shakespear, was no leader of a new departure or founder of a school.

He came at the end of a development, not at the beginning of one; and although there are operas and symphonies, and even pianoforte sonatas and pages of instrumental scoring of his, on which you can put your linger and say "Here is final perfection in this manner; and nobody, whatever his genius may be, will ever get a step further on these lines," you cannot say "Here is an entirely new vein of musical art, of which nobody ever dreamt before Mozart." Haydn [1732–1809], who made the mould for Mozart's symphonies, was proud of Mozart's genius because he felt his own part in it: he would have written the E flat symphony if he could, and, though he could not, was at least able to feel that the man who had reached that pre-eminence was standing on his old shoulders. Now, Haydn would have recoiled from the idea of composing—or perpetrating, as he would have put it—the first movement of Beethoven's Eroica, and would have repudiated all part in leading music to such a pass.

The more farsighted Gluck [1714–1787] not only carried Mozart in his arms to within sight of the goal of his career as an opera composer, but even cleared a little of the new path into which Mozart's finality drove all those successors of his who were too gifted to waste their lives in making weak dilutions of Mozart's scores, and serving them up as "classics." Many Mozart worshipers cannot bear to be told that their hero was not the founder of a dynasty. But in art the highest success is to be the last of your race, not the first. Anybody, almost, can make a beginning: the difficulty is to make an end—to do what cannot be bettered.

For instance, if the beginner were to be ranked above the consummator, we should, in literary fiction, have to place Captain Mayne Reid [Scots-Irish American adventure novelist, 1818–1883], who certainly struck a new vein, above Dickens [1812–1870], who simply took the novel as he found it, and achieved the feat of compelling his successor (whoever he may be), either to create quite another sort of novel, or else to fall behind his predecessor as at best a superfluous imitator. Surely, if so great composer as Haydn could say, out of his greatness as man "I am not the best of my school, though I was the first," Mozart's worshipers can afford to acknowledge, with equal gladness of spirit, that their hero was not the first, though he was the best. It is always like that. Praxiteles, Raphael and Co., have great men for their pioneers, and only fools for their followers.

So far everybody will agree with me. This proves either that I am hopelessly wrong or that the world has had at least half a century to think the matter over in. And, sure enough, a hundred years ago Mozart was considered a desperate innovator: it was his reputation in this respect that set so many composers—Meyerbeer [1791–1864], for example—cultivating innovation for its own sake. Let us, therefore, jump a hundred years forward, right up to date, and see whether there is any phenomenon of the same nature in view today. We have not to look far. Here, under our very noses, is Wagner [1813–1883] held up on all hands as the founder of a school and the archmusical innovator of our age. He himself knew better; but since his death I appear to be the only person who shares his view of the matter. I assert with the utmost confidence that in 1991 it will be seen quite clearly that Wagner was the end of the XIX century, or Beethoven school, instead of the beginning of the XX century school; just as Mozart's most perfect music is the last word of the XVIII century, and not the first of the XIX. It is none the less plain because everyone knows that Il Seraglio [Mozart's opera Die Entführung aus dem Serail] was the beginning of the school of XIX century German operas of Mozart, Beethoven [1770–1827], Weber [1786–1826], and Wagner; that Das Veilchen is the beginning of the XIX century German song of Schubert [1797–1828], Mendelssohn [1809–1847], and Schumann [1810–1856]; and that Die Zauberflöte is the ancestor, not only of the Ninth Symphony, but of the Wagnerian allegorical music-drama, with personified abstractions instead of individualized characters as *dramatis persona*. But Il Seraglio and Die Zauberflöte do not belong to the group of works which constitute Mozart's consummate achievement—Don Juan [*Don Giovanni*], Le Nozze di Figaro, and his three or four perfect symphonies. They are XIX century music heard advancing in the distance, as his Masses are XVII century music retreating in the distance. And, similarly, though the future fossiliferous critics of 1991, after having done their utmost, without success, to crush XX century music, will be able to shew that Wagner (their chief classic) made one or two experiments in that direction, yet the world will rightly persist in thinking of him as a characteristically XIX century composer of the school of Beethoven, greater than Beethoven by as much as Mozart was greater than Haydn. And now I hope I have saved my reputation by saying something at which everybody will exclaim "Bless me! what nonsense!" Nevertheless, it is true; and our would-be Wagners had better look to it; for all their efforts to exploit the apparently inexhaustible wealth of musical material opened up at Bayreuth only prove that Wagner used it up to the last ounce, and that secondhand Wagner is more insufferable, because usually more pretentious, than even secondhand Mozart used to be.

For my own part, if I do not care to rhapsodize much about Mozart, it is because I am so violently prepossessed in his favor that I am capable of supplying any possible deficiency in his work by my imagination. Gounod [1818–1893] has devoutly declared that Don Giovanni has been to him all his life a revelation of perfection, a miracle, a work without fault. I smile indulgently at Gounod, since I cannot afford to give myself away so generously (there being, no doubt, less of me); but I am afraid my fundamental attitude towards Mozart is the same as his. In my small-boyhood I by good luck had an opportunity of learning the Don thoroughly, and if it were only for the sense of the value of fine workmanship which I gained from it, I should still esteem that lesson the most important part of my education. Indeed, it educated me artistically in all sorts of ways, and disqualified me only in one—that of criticizing Mozart fairly. Everyone appears a sentimental, hysterical bungler in comparison when anything brings his finest work vividly back to me. Let me take warning by the follies of Oulibicheff [biographer of Mozart, 1794–1858], and hold my tongue.

The people most to be pitied at this moment are the unfortunate singers, players, and conductors who are suddenly called upon to make the public hear the wonders which the newspapers are describing so lavishly. At ordinary times they simply refuse to do this. It is quite a mistake to suppose that Mozart's music is not in demand. I know of more than one concert giver who asks every singer he engages for some song by Mozart, and is invariably met with the plea of excessive difficulty. You cannot "make an effect" with Mozart, or work your audience up by playing on their hysterical susceptibilities.

Nothing but the finest execution—beautiful, expressive, and intelligent—will serve; and the worst of it is that the phrases are so perfectly clear and straightforward that you are found out the moment you swerve by a hair's breadth from perfection, whilst, at the same time, your work is so obvious, that everyone thinks it must be easy, and puts you down remorselessly as a duffer for botching it. Naturally, then, we do not hear much of Mozart; and what we do hear goes far to destroy his reputation. But there was no getting out of the centenary: something had to be done. Accordingly, the Crystal Palace committed itself to the Jupiter Symphony and the Requiem; and the Albert Hall, by way of varying the entertainment, announced the Requiem and the Jupiter Symphony.

The Requiem satisfied that spirit of pious melancholy in which we celebrate great occasions; but I think the public ought to be made rather more sharply aware of the fact that Mozart died before the Requiem was half finished, and that his widow, in order to secure the stipulated price, got one of her husband's pupils [Franz Xaver Süßmayr, 1766–1803], whose handwriting resembled his, to forge enough music to complete it. Undoubtedly Mozart gave a good start to most of the movements; but, suggestive as these are, very few of them are artistically so satisfactory as the pretty Benedictus, in which the forger escaped from the taskwork of cobbling up his master's hints to the free work of original composition. There are only about four numbers in the score which have any right to be included in a centenary program. As to the two performances, I cannot compare them, as I was late for the one at the Albert Hall.

The Jupiter Symphony was conducted by Mr Manns [conductor at the Crystal Palace, 1825–1907] in the true heroic spirit; and he was well seconded by the wind band; but the strings disgraced themselves. In the first movement even what I may call the common decencies of execution were lacking: Mr Manns should have sent every fiddler of them straight back to school to learn how to play scales cleanly, steadily, and finely. At the Albert Hall, there was no lack of precision and neatness; but Mr Henschel's reading was, on the whole, the old dapper, empty, *petit maître* one of which I, at least, have had quite enough. Happily, Mr Henschel [baritone, composer and conductor, 1850–1934] immediately redeemed this failure—for such it was—by a really fine interpretation of the chorus of priests from the Zauberflöte. This, with Mr Lloyd's [tenor, 1845–1927] delivery of one of the finest of Mozart's concert arias, Mr Norman Salmond's [baritone, 1856–1914] singing of a capital English version of Non più andrai [bass aria from Mozart's *Le Nozze di Figaro*], and the Crystal Palace Band's performance of the Masonic Dirge, were the successes of the celebration. I should add that Mr Joseph Bennett [music critic, 1831–1911], fresh from throwing his last stone at Wagner, modestly wrote a poem for recitation between the Requiem and the Symphony. He appeals to Mozart, with evidently sincere emotion, to accept his lines, in spite of any little shortcomings,

> Since tis from the heart they flow,
> Bright with pure affection's glow.

Perhaps Dr Mackenzie [Scottish conductor and composer, 1847–1935] or Dr Parry [symphonic and oratorio composer, 1848–1918], in view of a well-known observation of Beaumarchais ["that which is too silly to say may be sung," La Folle Journée, ou Le Mariage de Figaro, 1778], may set Mr Bennett's ode to music some of these days. Mr Herkomer [artist, 1849–1914], too, has helped by drawing a fancy portrait of Mozart. I have compared it carefully with all the accredited portraits, and can confidently pronounce it to be almost supernaturally unlike the original.

2. The Religion of the Pianoforte

The Fortnightly Review, February 1894

The other day somebody went to Rubinstein and said "Is the pianoforte a musical instrument?" That is just the sort of question people put nowadays. You call on the Prince of Wales to ask "Is England a republic?" or on the Lord Mayor with "Is London a city?" or on Madame Calvé [French soprano, 1858–1942] to take her opinion, as an expert, on "Is Cavalleria Rusticana [one-act opera by Mascagni] an opera?" In treating such questions as open ones you have already achieved a paradox; and even if the Prince of Wales should have the presence of mind to simply say No, and the Lord

Mayor and Madame Calvé, Yes, and have you immediately shewn out, still you are in a position to fill the contents bill of one of our weekly scrap papers with "Is England a republic?—What the Prince of Wales says"; and so sell off an edition to people who cannot bring themselves to think that the plain explanation of the mystery is that you are a foolish person.

Yet it will not do to reply to "Is the pianoforte a musical instrument?" by a simple Yes. That would be an understatement of a quite extraordinary case. The pianoforte is the most important of all musical instruments: its invention was to music what the invention of printing was to poetry. Just consider the analogy for a moment. What is it that keeps Shakespear alive among us? Is it the stage, the great actors, the occasional revivals with new music and scenery, and agreeably mendacious accounts of the proceedings in the newspapers after the first night? Not a bit of it. Those who know their Shakespear at all know him before they are twentyfive: after that there is no time—one has to live instead of to read; and how many Shakespearean revivals, pray, has an Englishman the chance of seeing before he is twentyfive, even if he lives in a city and not in the untheatred country, or in a family which regards the pit of the theatre as the antechamber to that pit which has no bottom? I myself, born of profane stock, and with a quarter-century of play-going, juvenile and manly, behind me, have not seen as many as a full half of Shakespear's plays acted; and if my impressions of his genius were based solely on these representations I should be in darkness indeed.

For what is it that I have seen on such occasions? Take the solitary play of Shakespear's which is revived more than twice in a generation! Well, I have seen Mr Barry Sullivan's Hamlet [1862], Mr Daniel Bandmann's Hamlet [1869], Miss Marriott's Hamlet [1864], Mr Irving's Hamlet [1864 and 1875], Signor Salvini's Hamlet [1876], Mr Wilson Barrett's Hamlet

[1884], Mr Benson's Hamlet [1890], Mr Beebohm Tree's Hamlet [1892], and perhaps others which I forget. But to none of
these artists do I owe my acquaintance with Shakespear's play
of Hamlet. In proof whereof, let me announce that, for all
my Hamlet-going, were I to perish this day, I should go to my
account without having seen Fortinbras, save in my mind's
eye, or watched the ghostly twilight march (as I conceive it)
of those soldiers who went to their graces like beds to dispute
with him a territory that was not tomb enough and conti-
nent to hide the slain. When first I saw Hamlet I innocently
expected Fortinbras to dash in, as in Sir John Gilbert's picture [1890], with shield and helmet, like a medieval Charles
XII., and, by right of his sword and his will, take the throne
which the fencing foil and the speculative intellect had let
slip, thereby pointing the play's most characteristically English moral.

But what was my first Hamlet to my first Romeo and Juliet,
in which Romeo, instead of dying forthwith when he took
the poison, was interrupted by Juliet, who sat up and made
him carry her down to the footlights, where she complained
of being very cold, and had to be warmed by a love scene,
in the middle of which Romeo, who had forgotten all about
the poison, was taken ill and died? Or my first Richard III.,
which turned out to be a wild *pot-pourri* of all the historical
plays, with a studied debasement of all the best word music
in the lines, and an original domestic scene in which Richard,
after feebly bullying his wife, observed "If this dont kill her,
she's immortal"? Cibber's Richard III. [adapted 1700] was, to
my youthful judgment, superior to Shakespear's play on one
point only, and that was the omission of the stage direction,
"Exeunt fighting," whereby Richmond and the tyrant were
enabled to have it out to the bitter end full in my view. Need
I add that it was not through this sort of thing, with five out
of every six parts pitiably ill acted and ill uttered, that I came
to know Shakespear?

Later on, when it was no longer Mr Blank's Hamlet and Miss Dash's Juliet that was in question, but "the Lyceum revival," the stage brought me but little nearer to the drama. For the terrible cutting involved by modern hours of performance; the foredoomed futility of the attempt to take a work originally conceived mainly as a long story told on the stage, with plenty of casual adventures and unlimited changes of scene, and to tightlace it into something like a modern play consisting of a single situation in three acts; and the commercial relations which led the salaried players to make the most abject artistic sacrifices to their professional consciousness that the performances is the actor-manager's "show," and by no means their own or Shakespear's: all these and many other violently anti-artistic conditions of modern theatrical enterprise still stood inexorably between the stage and the real Shakespear.

The case of Shakespear is not, of course, the whole case against the theatre: it is, indeed, the weakest part of it, because the stage certainly does more for Shakespear than for any other dramatic poet. The English drama, from Marlowe [1564–1593] to Browning [1812–1899], would practically not exist if it were not printed. To extend the argument to literature in general it is only necessary to imagine the nation depending for its knowledge of poetry and romance on the recitations of elocutionists and the readings with which some of our sects replace the "lessons" of the Church of England. Such a conception dies of its own absurdity. Clearly, the literature which the private student cannot buy or borrow to take home and puzzle out by himself may be regarded as, at best, in a state of suspended animation.

But what has all this to do with the pianoforte? Well, can anything be more obvious? I decline to insult the intelligence of the public by explaining.

Let me, however, do an unsolicited service to thousands of fellow creatures who are huddling round the fire trying to kill time with such sensations as they can extract from novels, not suspecting a far more potent instrument stands dumb by the wall, unthought of save as one of those expensive and useless pieces of show furniture without which no gentleman's drawing room is complete. Take a case by way of illustration. You are a youth, let us suppose, poring over The Three Musketeers, or some romance of Scott's. Now, in the name of all that is real, how much satisfaction do you get out of mere *descriptions* of duels, and escapes, and defiances, and raptures of passion? A good deal, you think (being young); but how if you could find a sort of book that would give you not merely a description of these thrilling sensations, but the sensations themselves—the stirring of the blood, the bristling of the fibres, the transcendent, fearless fury which makes romance so delightful, and realizes that ideal which Mr Gilbert has aptly summed up in the phrase "heroism without risk" [*The Mountebanks*, 1892]? Such a book is within your reach. Pitch your Three Musketeers into the wastepaper basket, and get a vocal score of Meyerbeer's Huguenots [1836]. Then to the piano, and pound away. In the music you will find the body and reality of that feeling which the mere novelist could only describe to you; there will come home to your senses something in which you can actually experience the candor and gallant impulse of the hero, the grace and trouble of the heroine, and the extracted emotional quintessence of their love.

As to duels, what wretched printed list of the thrusts in *carte* and *tierce* delivered by D'Artagnan [hero of Dumas' Three Musketeers, 1844] or Bussy d'Ambroise [tragic hero in play by Chapman, 1603] can interest the man who knows Don Giovanni's duel in the dark with the Commandant, or Romeo's annihilation of Tybalt (not Shakespear's, but Gounod's Romeo), or Raoul's explosion of courage on the brink of the fight in the Pré-aux-Clercs [opéra comique by Ferdinand Hérold, 1832]. And mark, it is only at the piano that that Pré-aux-Clercs fight is really fought out—that Maurevert comes out of the darkness with his assassins to back San Bris, and that Marcel, in extremity, thunders his *Ein' feste Burg* [hymn by Luther ("A mighty fortress is our God") set to music by Bach] at the door of the inn, and brings all the Huguenot soldiers tumbling out to the rescue with their rataplan. Go to the theatre for that scene, and there is no sense in what passes: Maurevert is cut; Marcel is cut; everything that makes the scene grow and live is cut, because the opera is so long that even with the fourth act omitted it is impossible to present it unmutilated without an ungentle-manly curtailment of the waits between the acts. Besides, it is a curious circumstance that operatic stage managers never read operas, perhaps because, since they never conceive cause and effect as operating in the normal way, the composer's in-structions would only lead them astray. At all events, we have Meyerbeer at the same disadvantage on the stage as Shake-spear.

Here I can conceive our Musketeer-loving youth interrupt-ing me with some impatience to explain that he cannot play the piano. No doubt he cannot: what of that? Berlioz [1803–1869] could not play the piano; Wagner could not play the piano; nay, I myself, a musical critic of European reputa-tion, *I* cannot play. But is any man prevented from reading Othello by the fact that he cannot act or recite? You need not be able to play your Huguenots: if you can read the notes and bungle over them, that is sufficient. This only leads our youth to put his difficulty more precisely: he cannot even read the notes. Of course not; but why? Because he has never discovered that they are worth learning. Pianism has been presented to him as a polite accomplishment, the object of which is to give pleasure to others—an object which has not been attained, he has observed, in the case of his sisters. To him, therefore, I seem to propose that he shall, in pure and probably unsuccessful altruism, spend so many hours a day for a year over Czerny's, Plaidy's, or Cramer's exercise in order that he may be able to play Beethoven's Pathetic Sonata slowly and awkwardly, but note-accurately, to the manifest discomfort and disturbance of all within earshot.

Now, he does not care two straws about the Pathetic Sonata, and would not spend twelve hours, much less twelve months, over Czerny [pianist and teacher, 1791–1857] to save all Beethoven's works from destruction, much less to oblige me. Therefore, though he will learn to smoke, to skate, to play billiards, to ride, to shoot, to do half a dozen things much more difficult than reading music, he will no more learn his notes than a sailor will learn ploughing. Why should he, since no pleasure can come of it for himself? As to giving pleasure to others, even sisterless youths know, first, that there are not ten men in Europe among the most gifted and arduously-trained professionals whose playing gives pleasure to enough people to fill St James's Hall; and second, that the effect of ordinary amateur playing on other people is to drive them almost mad. I learnt my notes at the age of sixteen or thereabouts; and since that time I have inflicted untold suffering on my neighbors without having on a single occasion given the smallest pleasure to any human being except myself. Then, it will be asked, Why did I begin? Well, the motive arose from my previous knowledge of music. I have been accustomed all my life to hear it in sufficing quantities; and the melodies I heard I could at least sing; so that I neither had nor desired any technical knowledge. But it happened one day [1873, when his mother left Dublin for London] that my circumstances changed, so that I heard no more music. It was in vain now to sing: my native woodnotes wild—just then breaking frightfully—could not satisfy my intense craving for the harmony which is the emotional substance of music, and for the rhythmic figures of accompaniment which are its action and movement. I had only a single splintering voice; and I wanted an orchestra.

This musical starvation it was that drove me to disregard the rights of my fellow lodgers and go to the piano. I learnt the alphabet of musical notation from a primer, and the keyboard from a diagram. Then, without troubling Czerny or Plaidy [pianist and teacher, 1810–1874], I opened Don Giovanni and began. It took ten minutes to get my fingers arranged on the chord of D minor with which the overturn commences; but when it sounded right at last, it was worth all the trouble it cost. At the end of some months I had acquired a technique of my own as a sample of which I may offer my fingering of the scale of C major. Instead of shifting my hand by turning the thumb under and fingering CDEFGABC – 12312345, I passed my fourth finger over my fifth and played CDEFGABC – 12345454. This method had the advantage of being applicable to all scales, diatonic or chromatic; and to this day I often fall back on it. Liszt [1811–1886] and Chopin [1810–1849] hit on it too; but they never used it to the extent that I did. I soon acquired a terrible power of stumbling through pianoforte arrangements and vocal scores; and my reward was that I gained penetrating experiences of Victor Hugo and Schiller from Donizetti 1797–1848], Verdi [1813–1901], and Beethoven [1770–1827]; of the Bible from Handel [1685–1759]; of Goethe from Schumann; of Beaumarchais and Molière from Mozart; and of Mérimée from Bizet [1838–1875], besides finding Berlioz an unconscious interpreter of Edgar Allan Poe. When I was in the schoolboy-adventure vein, I could range from Vincent Wallace [Irish composer, 1812–1865] to Meyerbeer; and if I felt piously and genteelly sentimental, I, who could not stand the pictures of Ary Scheffer [Dutch Romantic painter, 1795–1858] or the genteel suburban sentiment of Tennyson and Longfellow, could become quite maudlin over Mendelssohn and Gounod.

And, as I searched all the music I came across for the sake of its poetic or dramatic content, and played the pages in which I found drama or poetry over and over again, whilst I never returned to those in which the music was trying to exist ornamentally for its own sake and had no real content at all, it followed that when I came across the consciously perfect art work in the music dramas of Wagner, I ran no risk of hopelessly misunderstanding it as the academic musicians did. Indeed, I soon found that they equally misunderstood Mozart and Beethoven, though, having come to like their tunes and harmonies, and to understand their mere carpentry, they pointed out what they supposed to be their merits with an erroneousness far more fatal to their unfortunate pupils than the volley of half-bricks with which they greeted Wagner (who, it must be confessed, retaliated with a volley of whole ones fearfully well aimed).

Now, in this fragment of autobiography, what is it that stands as the one indispensable external condition of my musical culture? Obviously, the pianoforte. Without it, no harmony, no interweaving of rhythms and motives, no musical structure, and consequently no opera or music-drama. But on the other hand, with it nothing else was needed, except the printed score and a foreknowledge of the power of music to bring romance and poetry to an enchanting intimacy of realization. Let a man once taste of the fruit that brings that knowledge, and no want of technical instruction will prevent him from doing what I did, if only he can get access to a piano and ten shillings' worth of cheap editions of operas and oratorios. I had not the key of the instrument, but I picked the lock by passing my ring finger over my little finger, driven as I was to that burglarious process by my craving for the booty within. It was easier than learning to read French; and how many of us learn to read French merely to satisfy our craving for a less reticent sort of novel than England produces! It is worth anyone's while to do likewise for the sake of Meyerbeer, Gounod, and Verdi alone—nay, for the sake of Offenbach and the Savoy operas [Gilbert and Sullivan]. For one must not affright people of moderate capacity by promising them communion with the greatest men, whom they are apt to find dry.

On the other hand, let me not lead those older and abler souls to whom the heroics of Verdi, the seraphic philanderings of Gounod, and the pseudo-historical effect-mongering of Meyerbeer are but children's entertainments, to suppose that there is no music at their level. Music is not always serenading Jessica and Lorenzo [as in *The Merchant of Venice*]: it has higher business than that. As one of those swaggering bronzes from the furniture shops—two cavaliers drawing their swords at oneanother from opposite ends of the mantelpiece—is to a statue by Praxiteles, so is an opera by Meyerbeer to one by Mozart. However you may despise romantic novels, however loftily you may be absorbed in the future destiny of what is highest in humanity, so that for mere light literature you turn from Dante to Goethe, or from Schopenhauer to Comte, or from Ruskin to Ibsen—still, if you do not know Die Zauberflöte, if you have never soared into the heaven where they sing the choral ending of the Ninth Symphony, if Der Ring des Nibelungen is nothing to you but a newspaper phrase, then you are an ignoramus, however eagerly you may pore in your darkened library over the mere printed labels of those wonders that can only be communicated by the transubstantiation of pure feeling for musical tone. The greatest of the great among poets, from Eschylus to Wagner, have been poet-musicians: how then can any man disdain music or pretend to have completed his culture without it?

Thus to the whole range of imaginative letters, from the [W. S. Gilbert] Bab ballads to [Shelley's] Prometheus Unbound, you have parallel range of music from [Gilbert and Sullivan's] Trial by Jury to [Wagner's] Tristan und Isolde, conveying to your very senses what the other could only suggest to your imagination. Only, to travel along this higher range rather than along the lesser one, you must use your piano.

This is the mission of the pianoforte, to assert which adequately is such an answer to "Is the pianoforte a musical instrument?" as will send the questioner away an abashed idiot.

Now let us consider the drawbacks to culture by pianoforte as opposed to culture by ordinary reading. To begin with, people do not read aloud; consequently half a dozen persons can sit in the same room and enjoy six different books by the light of the same lamp. Imagine these people going to six pianos and simultaneously striking up The Mikado, Dinorah [Meyerbeer, 1859], Faust [Goundod, 1859], Aïda [Verdi, 1871], Fidelio [Beethoven, 1805], and Götterdämmerung [Wagner, 1876]. Nay, imagine them doing it, not in the same room, but even in the same house, or in the same square, with the windows open in summer! In German towns they have a music curfew, and will not let you play after a stated hour in the evening. When Liszt was teaching at Weimar, playing the pianoforte with the window open was a public misdemeanor punishable by fine. The only wonder is that the piano is permitted at all except in lighthouses and other detached residences. At present unmusical people get used to the noise of a piano just as they get used to the noise of cabs clattering past; but in the end the pianos will make most people musical; and then there will be an end of the present anarchic toleration. For just in proportion as you like bungling on a piano yourself does the bungling of others offend and disturb you. In truth, just as the face a man sees when he looks in the glass is not his face as his neighbor sees it, so the music we hear when we play is not what our neighbors hear.

I know no way out of this difficulty just at present. We cannot go back to the clavichord unless we listen to it through a microphone; for though you can play Bach fugues on a clavichord, you cannot play *Suoni la tromba* [from Bellini's opera *I Puritani*], or *Di quella pira* [from Verdi's opera *Il Trovatore*], or the Rákóczy March, or the Ride of the Valkyries—at least, not to your heart's content. Even good playing and good pianos are eternally impossible. For the laws of nature forbid good playing with our keyboard, which defies the human hand and only gives us the run of the twelve keys on condition that they are all perceptibly out of tune. And the laws of nature equally seem, so far, to decree that the pianoforte string which gives the most beautiful tone and the pianoforte action which gives the most perfect touch will not last; so that if you get an ideal piano at a cost of some hundreds of pounds, in five years you will want a new one. But you are far more likely, as the income-tax returns prove, to be compelled to put up with a twentyfive pound piano on the three years' system; and though excellent French pianets (considering) are to be had at that price, the ordinary British householder prefers a full-sized walnut piano of the sort that justifies the use of dynamite.

Thus we appear to be driven to this lamentable alternative: either to give up the best part of our culture or else make it a curse to the people downstairs or next door. We seem hardly to have the right to hesitate; for now that the moral basis of pianism as a means of giving pleasure to others is exploded, and shewn to correspond to the exact opposite of the facts of the case, it appears to be our plain duty to forbid amateur music altogether, and to insist on romance and poetry being restricted to their silent, incomplete, merely literary expression.

But this, I submit, we dare not do. Without music we shall surely perish of drink, morphia, and all sorts of artificial exaggerations of the cruder delights of the senses. Asceticism will not save us, for the conclusive reason that we are not ascetics. Man, as he develops, seeks constantly a keener pleasure, in the pursuit of which he either destroys himself or develops new faculties of enjoyment. He either strives to intensify the satisfaction of resting, eating, and drinking, the excitement and exercise of hunting, and the ardor of courtship, by "refining" them into idleness, gluttony, dipsomania, hideous cruelty, and ridiculous vice, or else he develops his feeling until it becomes poetic feeling, and sets him thinking with pleasure of nobler things. Observe, if you please, the order of development here: it is all-important, as I shall shew, even at the cost of a digression. It is feeling that sets a man thinking, and not thought that sets him feeling. The secret of the absurd failure of our universities and academic institutions in general to produce any real change in the students who are constantly passing through them is that their method is invariably to attempt to lead their pupils to feeling by way of thought.

For example, a musical student is expected to gradually acquire a sense of the poetry of the Ninth Symphony by accumulating information as to the date of Beethoven's birth, the compass of the *contra fagotto* [double bassoon], the number of sharps in the key of D major, and so on, exactly analogous processes being applied in order to produce an appreciation of painting, Greek poetry, or what not. Result: the average sensual boy comes out the average sensual man, with his tastes in no discoverable way different from those of the young gentleman who has preferred an articled clerkship in a solicitor's office to Oxford or Cambridge. All education, as distinct from technical instruction, must be education of the feeling; and such education must consist in the appeal of actual experiences to the senses, without which literary descriptions addressed to the imagination cannot be rightly interpreted. Marriage, for instance, is admittedly an indispensable factor in the education of the complete man or woman. But in educational institutions appeals to the senses can only take the form of performances of works of art; and the bringing of such performances to the highest perfection is the true business of our universities.

This statement will surprise nobody but a university man. Fortunately there is no such thing as an absolutely pure specimen of that order. If it were possible to shut off from a boy all the influence of home, and to confine him absolutely to public-school life and university life, the resultant pure product of what we call "education" would be such a barbarous cub or insufferable prig as we can only conceive by carefully observing the approaches to these types which are occasionally produced at present. But such a complete specialization is not possible. You cannot wholly shut art out now, even with the assistance of modern architects. Though my name is to be found on the books of no Oxford college, I have enjoyed all the real education which the university has to offer by simply walking through the university and looking at its beautiful old quadrangles. I know fairly-educated Oxford men—though, to be sure, they are all truants and smugglers, connoisseurs of the London theatres and galleries, with pictures, pianofortes, and beautiful things of one kind or another in their rooms, and shelves upon shelves of books that are never used as textbooks.

I remember conversing once [in March 1892] with the late Master of Balliol [Benjamin Jowett], an amiable gentleman, stupendously ignorant probably, but with a certain flirtatious, old-maidish frivolity about him that had, and was meant to have, the charm of a condescension from so learned a man. In Oxford he was regarded as a master educator. I would ask what right he had to that distinction in a country where Hallé [husband of violinist Norman-Neruda, 1819–1895] had made, and was conducting, the Manchester band; where August Manns, with Sir George Grove [founding editor of *Grove's Dictionary of Music*, 1820–1900], had created the Crystal Palace orchestra; and where, Richter [conductor, 1843–1916] was teaching us what Wagner taught him? Sir Frederick Burton [Pre-Raphaelite painter, 1816–1900], as master of the National Gallery, Sir Augustus Harris [1852–1896], as master of the Royal Italian Opera, were and are worth to England, educationally, forty thousand Masters of Balliol. Which is the greater educator, pray—your tutor

69

when he coaches you for the Ireland scholarship or Miss Janet Achurch when she plays Nora [1889] for you? You cannot witness A Doll's House without *feeling*, and, as an inevitable consequence, thinking; but it is evident that the Ireland scholarship would break up Oxford unless it could be won without either feeling or thinking. I might give a thousand illustrations, if space permitted, or if criticism of the university system were my main purpose instead of my digression.

Taking it, then, as established that life is a curse to us unless it operates as pleasurable activity, and that as it becomes more intense with the upward evolution of the race it requires a degree of pleasure which cannot be extracted from the alimentary, predatory, and amatory instincts without ruinous perversions of them; seeing, also, that the alternative of "high thinking" is impossible until it is started by "high feeling," to which we can only come through the education of the senses—are we to deliberately reverse our Puritan traditions and aim at becoming a nation of skilled voluptuaries? Certainly. It may require some reflection to see that high feeling brings high thinking; but we already know, without reflection, that high thinking brings what is called plain living. In this century the world has produced two men—Shelley [1792–1822] and Wagner—in whom intense poetic feeling was the permanent state of their consciousness, and who were certainly not restrained by any religious, conventional, or prudential considerations from indulging themselves to the utmost of their opportunities. Far from being gluttonous, drunken, cruel, or debauched, they were apostles of vegetarianism and water-drinking; had an utter horror of violence and "sport"; were notable champions of the independence of women; and were, in short, driven into open revolution against the social evils which the average sensual man finds extremely suitable to him. So much is this the case that the practical doctrine of these two arch-voluptuaries always presents itself to ordinary persons as a saint-like asceticism.

If, now, relieved of all the apprehensions as to the social safety of allowing the world to make itself happy, we come to consider which of the arts is the most potent to this end, we must concede that eminence to music, because it alone requires for its enjoyment an artistic act on the part of its reader, which act, in its perfection, becomes such an act of re-creation as Wagner found in Liszt's playing of Beethoven's sonatas. There is no need in this account to set up the musician above the painter, the masterbuilder, or the sculptor. There are points at which all rivalry between the arts vanishes. When you are looking at the Turner [Romantic painter, 1775–1851] watercolors in the National Gallery, the poetic feeling which they so exquisitely and sufficingly express completely delivers you from that plane on which mere hero worshipers squabble as to whether the painter or the composer of music is the better man. Nonetheless, in the National Gallery the feeling is expressed by the painter and not by you, although your feeling, too, struggles for expression, sometimes almost painfully. You stand dumb, or at best you turn to your neighbor and say "Pretty, aint it?" of which remark most art criticism is but an elaboration.

Now suppose the feeling were aroused, not by a picture, but by a song! At once your tongue is loosed: you sing the song, and thereby relieve one of your deepest needs—strange as that may sound to people who sing songs solely to gain the applause of others. Further, you gain by practice the power of expressing feeling, and with that power the courage to express it, for want of which power and courage we all go miserably about today, shrinking and pretending, misunderstanding and misunderstood, making remarks on the weather to people whose most nourishing sympathy or most salutary opposition we might enjoy if only we and they could become fully known to each other by a complete self-expression. Music, then, is the most fecund of the arts, propagating itself by its power of forcing those whom it influences to express it and themselves by a method which is the easiest and most universal of all art methods, because it is the art form of that communication by speech which is common to all the race.

This music wisdom has been urged on the world in set terms by Plato, by Goethe, by Schopenhauer, by Wagner, and by myself. As a rule, when, in order to obtain concreteness, I couple my teachings with the name of any individual who enjoys opportunities of carrying out my ideas, he threatens me with legal proceedings, on the ground that I have taken him seriously. And indeed the commonsense of the country under present circumstances feels that to take music as seriously as religion, morals, or politics is clear evidence of malicious insanity, unless the music belongs to an oratorio. The causes of this darkness are economic. What is the matter with us is that the mass of the people cannot afford to go to good concerts or to the opera. Therefore they remain ignorant of the very existence of a dramatic or poetic content in what they call "classical" or "good" music, which they always conceive as a web of learnedly and heavily decorative sound patterns, and never as containing a delicious kernel of feeling, like their favorite Annie Laurie [Scottish song based on a poem by William Douglas, 1672–1748]. Consequently they do not crave for pianos; and if they did they could not afford to buy them, and would perforce fall back on the poor man's piano—the German concertina or accordion.

At the same time, our most gifted singers, instead of getting ten or fifteen pounds a week and a pension, have to be paid more than Cabinet Ministers, whose work turns them prematurely grey, or officers in the field, or musical critics. All this must be altered before any serious advance in culture can be effected. The necessity for change in the social structure is so pressing that it drives the musician into the political arena in spite of his own nature. You have Wagner going out in '48 with the revolutionists because the State declined to reform the theatre, just as I am compelled, by a similar obtuseness on the part of our own Government, to join the Fabian Society, and wildly masquerade as a politician so that I may agitate for a better distribution of piano-purchasing power.

If I were now to string all these points in their logical order on the thread of a complete argument, to prove that the future of humanity depends at present of the pianoforte, I should render my case repugnant to the British mind, which sensibly objects to be bothered with logic. But let me, in allowing the British mind to jump at its conclusion, please for a large construction for the word pianoforte. An organ, an harmonium, a vocalion, an eolion, an orchestrion, or any instrument upon which the full polyphony of an opera or symphony can be given, may obviously replace the pianoforte; and so far as the playing can be done, wholly or partly, by perforated cards, barrels, or other mechanical means of execution, by all means let it be so done. A fingering mechanism so contrived as to be well under the *artistic* control of the operator would be an unspeakable boon. Supply me with such a thing and I will make an end of Paderewski.

Finally, let no one suppose that because private readings and performances are better than nothing, they are therefore an efficient substitute for complete dramatic and orchestral representations. Far from it; they are makeshifts, and very miserable makeshifts too. In Italy, when you go from the picture gallery to the photograph shop, you are revolted by the inadequacy of the "reproductions" which turn Carpaccio's golden glow into sooty grime. At Bayreuth when, on your way back of an evening from the Festival Playhouse, you hear someone strumming a pianoforte arrangement of the overture to Die Meistersinger [Wagner, 1867], you wonder how the wretch can bear to listen to himself. Yet, after a few months in England, when you pull out your photograph, or sit down to the pianoforte score of Die Meistersinger, you are very pleasantly and vividly reminded of Carpaccio [Venetian painter, 1465–1526] or Wagner. Also, however diligently you may read your Shakespear or your Ibsen, you must date your full acquaintance with any work of theirs from the time when you see it fully performed on the stage as they meant you to. The day will come when every citizen will find within his reach and means adequate artistic representations to recreate him whenever he feels disposed for them. Until then the pianoforte will be the savior of society. But when that golden age comes, everybody will see at last what an execrable, jangling, banging, mistuned nuisance our domestic music machine is, and the maddening sound of it will thenceforth be no more heard in our streets.

Part III: Vocalists

Particularly in his early anonymous reviews, ghostwritten for Vandeleur Lee, Shaw focused on professional opera singers. This is a small exemplary selection from his numerous pieces titled "Vocalists of the Season" in The Hornet. *He subsequently continued to refer to these singers in his opera reviews, and although he wrote later pieces on them for* The Star *and* The World, *these were generally laments for their passing or leaving the London stage. It can be seen, however, the way these analyses of talent relate to Shaw's writings for* The Voice.

1. Men and Women of the Day

The Hornet, 6 June 1877

In one of our portraits this week our readers will recognize the features of Madame Christine Nilsson [Swedish soprano, 1843–1921]. We do not propose to give here a sketch of her personal history. Such details may be sought with justifiable interest in the case of statesmen, or those who enjoy what is called "the confidence of the nation," but with the private life of artists the public has no concern; and the landmarks in the professional career of a *prima donna* possess too wearisome a sameness to leave any impression on the memory. Therefore, we will confine ourselves to artistic considerations only, no less from the necessity of making our columns entertaining than in obedience to the rules of good taste.

Madame Nilsson is beyond question the most gifted of our leading *soprani*. This position she has made good, notwithstanding the most serious technical deficiencies, by the force of her inborn dramatic instinct and the charm of a voice whose beauty asserts itself in spite of a most destructive method of production, the effects of which are but too obvious towards the conclusion of her performance in those operas which demand constant and severe exertion from the representative of the heroine. Nor are her vocal circumstances without a parallel in her employment of her rare histrionic talents. Madame Nilsson possesses genius; but it is undisciplined genius. Her greatest impersonations, abounding as they do in passages of great power, are never quite consistently sustained throughout. Take, for instance, that in which she has won her brightest laurels: the operatic version of Goethe's Gretchen [in Gounod's *Faust*, 1859]. In the second act we expectantly await the appearance of the innocent and timid girl returning from prayer. Instead of this we see a self-possessed woman come forth with assured step, listen composedly to the overtures of a tenor whose nervousness is not always feigned, give him what is popularly called "his answer," and pursue her homeward way with a manner sufficiently suggestive of her ability to take the best possible care of herself to daunt even the cynical perseverance of Mephistopheles.

In the garden scene all this vanishes. Nothing could be more truthfully conveyed than the confusion in which she endeavors to hide the jewels she has put on from the eyes of Faust. Thenceforth, the charm of the impersonation increases. We are carried away in defiance of bad phrasing, breathing in awkward places, wilful trifling with the *tempo* to the destruction of all rhythm, and any other liberty which the impulsive audacity of the singer may suggest. Her acting at the death of Valentin, once witnessed, cannot easily be forgotten; and in the church scene she attains the highest tragic expression of which the part admits. The curtain falls and rises again on the prison scene, when we are astonished to find the capricious charm again absent, and as in the second act the ideal Gretchen replaced by the real Madame Nilsson.

Similar dramatic suspensions are noticeable in all her greatest parts. As Elsa in [Wagner's] Lohengrin, after sustaining the character admirably through three acts, she unaccountably loses ground in the fourth, and conveys an impression rather of obstinate sulkiness than distracting grief. As Valentine in [Meyerbeer's] Les Huguenots she absolutely excites antagonism by her bearing at first, and inspires little interest subsequently until the great duet of the fourth act, in which she rises to the occasion and fairly electrifies her audience. For the full evocation of her great powers, some task which exercises them to the utmost seems requisite. In those scenes, in attacking which the greatest artists must feel at a disadvantage, she achieves a brilliant victory. On lighter occasions she is merely *la prima donna assoluta*, a little spoiled perhaps by success. In such a temper she disdains conventionality, and occasionally evinces a patronizing appreciation of the performances of her colleagues that must be humiliating rather than flattering to them. However, if Madame Nilsson be fairly judged, it will be found that her faults are such as a little study and self-discipline may easily overcome, whilst her merits are of that rare type of which it is commonly said that they are born and not acquired, and which constitutes the arbitrary attribute which we call genius.

We couple a portrait of M. Faure [baritone, 1830–1914] with that of Madame Nilsson, not because we conceive that any analogy exists between their artistic talent, but because accident has associated them in some of their most celebrated impersonations. M. Faure's principles of stage conduct may be summed up thus: "Keep well to the front, and take your time." So successful has this line of action proved, that he has come gradually to be accepted by a sort of critical conventionalism as the greatest living operatic baritone. Nevertheless, the quality of his voice is not remarkable: he is a vocalist of the French school, and a bad one; and he is an essentially commonplace actor. His two most admired parts are Don Giovanni and Mephistopheles. The first affords the highest test, both vocal and histrionic, to which an artist can he subjected, and in it M. Faure fails. Of the second, a character about which more has been written than read, good taste and a dramatic instinct, which need be no more than superficial, are quite sufficient to ensure a respectable performance, and M. Faure's performance is eminently respectable, not to say occasionally a trifle dull. In less central parts, where brilliancy as an actor and attractive vocalization are not absolutely necessary—Nevers, in Les Huguenots, for instance—M. Faure is most satisfactory; and, indeed, there would not be two opinions respecting his great utility on the operatic stage were it not for the exaggerated encomiums which have been lavished on him, with no other effect than that of placing him in a false position and raising expectations which his gifts do not enable him to realize.

2. Vocalists of the Season

The Hornet, 13 June 1877

Madame Trebelli [Zélia Trebelli-Bettini: French mezzo-soprano, 1838–1892] has, as most of us know, been for many years the leading contralto of Mr Mapleson's [opera impresario, 1830–1901] opera company. To her exertions it is mainly due that at Drury Lane and the Haymarket the performances have generally an artistic value far above those at Mr Gye's house [Covent Garden, managed by Gye (1810–1878) since 1849]. It may sound rash to ascribe the superiority of a whole company to the merits of one member of it, but it must be considered that many of the fine impersonations to which we are accustomed at Her Majesty's are matched by the efforts of rival artists at Covent Garden. The talents of Mesdames Nilsson and Patti [Spanish coloratura soprano, 1843–1919], of MM. Faure and Graziani [1828–1901] preserve an equal balance in the estimation of the public; but with Madame Trebelli the scale turns. Possessing a voice of exceptional richness, and a finished style which only a classicist can fully appreciate, she is without a rival amongst contraltos or a superior amongst singers. We have artists who rely on inspiration only, and we have to condone their impure style and lack of technical skill in consideration of their rare natural gifts. Madame Trebelli alone combines the truest lyrical expression with a style and phrasing so perfect that the greatest virtuoso of the pianoforte or violin might profit by hearing her sing the works of Handel and Mozart. Her mastery of every detail displays a conscientious devotion to music and a subtlety of taste rarely met with. Her delivery of the English text in oratorio might put to shame the majority of our clerics. (How few foreign artists have paid us the compliment of conquering our language, even superficially!) She never trifles with her work: never betrays indisposition or indifference, and never unduly obtrudes her own personality, which nevertheless lends a charm to all her performances. In opera she is unsurpassed; and in the works of Mozart, particularly as Zerlina, Cherubino, &c. [characters in Mozart's *Don Giovanni* and *Le Nozze di Figaro*], she leaves all competitors (in the first-named part she has at least one distinguished one) far behind. Of her dramatic ability it suffices to say that she has given us the Cherubino of Mozart instead of that of Beaumarchais, and that in her Zerlina we have the coy tenderness which the music teaches, without a trace of the pert vulgarity which we too often see associated with this most beautiful part. An actress who can achieve such things will not be found wanting in the coarser melodramas illustrated by Verdi and his school. Madame Trebelli is peculiarly entitled to the respect and gratitude of musicians because, although gifted by nature with a voice and person in themselves sufficient to ensure a wide popularity, she has by assiduous attention added to them a technical perfection but rarely aimed at, and still more rarely achieved, by her colleagues. Such refinements, acquired in the face of the obtuseness of the multitude to their value, are the strongest proof of her love of art. It will always be a grateful task to pay a public tribute to the fame of an artist whose greatest excellences are unfortunately "caviare to the general."

3. Vocalists of the Season

The Hornet, 20 June 1877

Signor Nicolini [1834–1898, married to Adelina Patti] is one of the most popular of our operatic tenors. This description would have been but doubtfully appropriate some weeks ago, when it seemed as if we were about to indulge in one of our periodical bursts of indignation at his expense. At present, whether it is that we have learned from our great essayist [Thomas Babbington Macaulay] that such displays of feeling are ridiculous and misplaced; or that Signor Nicolini, like Orpheus, has charmed us from our moral pedestal by the sweetness of his numbers: the fact remains that his popularity has emerged unabated from the trial, and his hold of the many-headed derived fresh security from its temporary relaxation. Therefore, an expression of opinion as to his demerits as an artist cannot now be considered as taking him at a disadvantage. If it is retorted on us that generous and enlightened criticism should rather dwell on his merits, we reply that we have not yet discovered what his merits are.

Signor Nicolini is interesting as an exponent of a school of singing (if we may use the term) which has lately become popular, and which may be considered as a monument of the extraordinary gullibility of the world in matters musical. The education of a singer, according to the approved Italian method, has been facetiously described as consisting of two distinct processes: the destruction of the natural and the creation of the artificial voice. This is at least half true, for the first operation is generally accomplished to a nicety. Unfortunately, here the system breaks down; and the student (should he possess a robust constitution, and survive) finds himself thrown on the world without any voice, but with the consolation of being no worse off than most of his profession. So he cultivates his head voice, in which register he can sing florid music with tolerable fluency; pulls together any ruins of chest notes which he happens to retain; and so manufactures a compound sound which is neither the voice of man, woman, nor boy, and which inflicts exquisite pain on all listeners who can pretend to any purity of taste. Its common characteristics are an impure and unsteady tone, an uncertain pitch, an undignified expression, and a constant tremolo.

Nevertheless, the public listens, imputes its unpleasant sensations to ignorance, applauds and encores as only the very ignorant can do, and eventually has its judgment so corrupted by habit that legitimate vocalization becomes actually repugnant to its ear. Therefore, though we began by stating that Signor Nicolini is one of our most popular tenors, we had no intention of implying any artistic excellence on his part. Flattery itself could scarcely deem his voice an agreeable one, or his style and presence impressive. The list of his qualifications is soon exhausted. He has a competent knowledge of stage business, and fills up a blank in a cast when no one better is to be had. No more remains to be said. To expatiate further on his peculiarities would be neither a graceful nor an interesting task.

4. Vocalists of the Season

The Hornet, 27 June 1877

Signor Fancelli [1833–1887] is a fortunate man. He is a tenor with a voice. The time has been, and will be again, we hope, when no man could hold a leading position on the stage without varied artistic qualifications. At present a great deal of audacity, a little affectation, some judicious puffing, and sufficient lung power to make a noise at brief intervals for three hours or so complete the list of acquirements necessary for a *primo tenore*. If he be able to shout, he will do well to sing a bar or two occasionally in a light falsetto. The critics will fall into raptures over his exquisite management of the *mezzo voce*, and the public will follow the critics. If he cannot do this, he has only to be careful not to lapse into inoffensiveness. Critics are only human, and they will attribute their anguish whilst listening to the tenor to anything sooner than to his defects. If they can see no excellences, they will invent some.

For instance, it is easy to say that a singer "phrases" well, because so few know what phrasing means. A certain tenor of this season, who is the very worst singer we ever heard, had this accomplishment specially manufactured for him by critics who felt it to be their duty to admire him, and who were at a loss to see what they should admire him for. Yet his case was by no means an exceptional one. For men who desire a reputation in art for which they have nothing to shew, Italian opera in England opens the only suitable field. In a state of affairs such as we have hinted at, it is obvious that (since the public always retain their natural predilection for what is good, beneath their affected raptures at what is mere imposture) an artist who has any real qualifications has a much fairer opportunity than if he were surrounded by really gifted rivals. Such a qualification, and such an opportunity, Signor Fancelli possesses. He is not an actor, but what he does is done in earnest, and he sustains comparisons only with men who cannot act and who are not in earnest. There are exceptions, perhaps, but they are too few to affect him. He has a real voice, and a fine one, and in this respect he is about alone amongst our operatic tenors. Opera-goers hail him with delight as a relief from the hideous varieties of throaty vibration with which they have been surfeited. His tasks this season have been arduous, and he has discharged them ably, as far as his gifts permitted him. That he is above the vanity which disdains a small contribution to the completeness of a performance, he proved by undertaking the few bars in Otello sung by the gondolier passing without. The inevitable comparison with the two other tenors who figured in the cast proved immeasurably to his advantage. If Signor Fancelli's taste and histrionic power were only equal to his voice and sincerity of intention, we should have on our stage an accomplished singer and actor. As it is, we have a most useful artist, and one that we always hear with pleasure.

5. Madame Nilsson

The Dramatic Review, 30 May 1885
Unsigned

The Daily News interviewed Madame Christine Nilsson [also known as Countess de Casa Miranda from her 1887 marriage] the other day, and received many valuable wrinkles in *l'art d'être prima donna.* Old as the Daily News is, for ladies love unfit: the power of beauty it remembers yet. It found Madame Nilsson's geniality agreeably tempered by "the profound gaze of her great thoughtful blue eyes, just as the music of her vibrant and sympathetic voice is in contrast with the firm grasp of her hand revealing force and will beneath its dainty envelope." Madame Nilsson would appear to be a hard hitter with both hands; for beside the above comparatively cool reference, we find the D. N. ardently describing "the beautiful white hands held forth in greeting." And again, "She receives her visitor with a hearty shake of the hand, or rather hands; for with that charming vivacity which is one of her chief characteristics she extends both in sign of greeting." Happy Daily News! Those hands, it protests, receive no adequate expression in Cabanel's portrait of Madame Christine as Ophelia. "Probably the painter thought, and with some justice, that the intense vitality typified by the singer's hands would ill accord with the lilies and languors"—and so on. The fascinating members are, it appears, "neither childishly small, boneless, and nerveless, nor large and coarse, but well proportioned, handsome, capable-looking hands—evidently the hands of a person who can do something valid." They can, for instance, perceptibly affect the heart from which proceeds "the largest circulation of any liberal paper in the world."

After such a theme as these magnetic hands, quotations as to "the fair head covered with short curls of the hue known as *blonde cendré*," or "the great serious blue eyes which look calmly out with an 'equal-to-either-fortune' expression" (how admirably our great daily describes when its full powers are roused by a genuine emotional crisis!) would only tantalize the readers of the DRAMATIC REVIEW; whilst the information that Madame Nilsson has for several years past been "practising her voice" in the Belgrave Road would be an anti-climax.

Madame Nilsson's notions of training herself for her feats on the stage are the usual odd mixture of science and superstition. She repudiates stimulants and late hours, and when the infatuated Daily News remarked that it "thought champagne was good for soprani, and stout for contralti," she contemptuously declared that "conviviality meant strong drink, followed by bad singing." "The best and only thing to sing on" said Madame Nilsson, very truly "is the effect of a sound wholesome meal eaten some hours before. To drink a pint of liquid of any kind before singing is madness." (The D. N. had feebly intimated that if it were about to sing in an opera, it would imbibe a pint of stout, because it had heard that Malibran [French soprano, mezzo and contralto, 1808–1836] used to do so.) On the whole Madame Nilsson's habits go far to explain why she retains her enviable strength and grace unimpaired, whilst so many of her colleagues fall off, not to the shadow, but, quite on the contrary, to three times the bulk of their former selves.

Madame Nilsson's superstitions are few and harmless. Though she likes to play the violin, she denies herself that beneficial exercise because someone (who must be little short of another Daily News in his ideas of hygiene) told her that "the cramped attitude and powerful vibration might affect her singing in the evening." The reply to this is that you should not play the violin in a cramped attitude; and that the "powerful vibration" of the instrument is far less objectionable than that of the carriage in which Madame Nilsson takes the fresh air because—and here is another of her superstitions—she is afraid that exercise on horseback, in which she delights, would also interfere with her efficiency as a vocalist. If Madame Nilsson will only adhere to her early hours and sensible diet, she may fearlessly ride and play the fiddle to her heart's content. Neither practice is likely to do her anything but good.

The Royal Academy of Music are convening a public meeting on the subject of musical pitch. The particulars have not yet been announced; but the secretary, Mr John Gill, undertakes to send tickets of admission to musicians, physicists, and persons interested in music, provided they apply to him before two o'clock today.

Most good singers, who can use their middle and lower registers effectively, and who do not enjoy a high pitch for its own sake, would probably advocate a return to the old pitch of Mozart's time, at which the A on the second space of the treble staff gave 422 vibrations per second. The instrumentalists have incurred, and probably deserve, the odium of steadily forcing the pitch up since then. However that may be, the pitch did rise until a stand was made by the solemn proclamation at Paris in 1859 of A with 435 vibrations as the diapason normal. Even this was quarter of a tone higher than Mozart's. (The irresponsible amateur, in order to shew how much higher he can sing than the first singers of Don Giovanni, will tell you offhand that the pitch is two or three tones higher than it was a hundred years ago—but never mind him.) The French pitch did not mend matters in this country, where the Philharmonic pitch, adopted by Messrs Broadwood in tuning their concert grands, was as high as 455, four-fifths of a semitone higher than the *diapason normal,* and nearly a semitone and a third higher than Mozart's. The Steinways, in America, tune their pianofortes to a pitch even higher than this. The organs at the Albert Hall, the Crystal Palace, the Royal Academy of Music, St James's Hall, and the

Alexandra Palace are all up to Philharmonic pitch, or within a few vibrations of it. As altering the pitch of an organ is a costly process, there is not much likelihood of the forthcoming meeting doing anything more practical than vainly protesting against the misdeeds of the men who built these organs, and so deprived the Handel Festival of the services of Mr Sims Reeves [tenor, 1821–1900], who resolutely refuses to produce his high A with more than 435 vibrations per second.

6. Goodbye, Patti

The Star, 23 January 1889
Unsigned

Madame Patti kissed hands last night, in her artless way, to a prodigious audience come to bid her farewell before her trip to South America. The unnecessary unpleasantness of the most useful of Mr Louis Stevenson's novels makes it impossible to say that there is in Madame Patti an Adelina Jekyll and an Adelina Hyde; but there are certainly two very different sides to her public character. There is Patti the great singer: Patti of the beautiful eloquent voice, so perfectly produced and controlled that its most delicate *pianissimo* reaches the remotest listener in the Albert Hall: Patti of the unerring ear, with her magical *roulade* soaring to heavenly altitudes: Patti of the pure, strong tone that made God Save the Queen sound fresh and noble at Covent Garden: Patti of the hushed, tender notes that reconcile rows of club-loving cynics to Home, sweet Home. This was the famous artist who last night sang *Bell raggio* and Comin' thro' the Rye [Scottish ballad by Burns] incomparably. With Verdure Clad would also have been perfect but that the intonation of the orchestra got wrong and spoiled it. But there is another Patti: a Patti who cleverly sang and sang again some pretty nonsense from Delibes' Lakmé. Great was the applause, even after it had been repeated; and then the comedy began. Mr Ganz [pianist and conductor, 1833–1914], whilst the house was shouting and clapping uproariously, deliberately took up his *bâton* and started Moszkowski's Serenata in D. The audience took its cue at once, and would not have Moszkowski [Polish composer, 1854–1925]. After a prolonged struggle, Mr Ganz gave up in despair; and out tripped the *diva*, bowing her acknowledgments in the character of a petted and delighted child. When she vanished there was more cheering than ever. Mr Ganz threatened the *serenata* again; but in vain. He appealed to the sentinels of the greenroom; and these shook their heads, amidst roars of protest from the audience, and at last, with elaborate gesture, conveyed in dumb show that they dare not, could not, would not, must not, venture to approach Patti again. Mr Ganz, with well-acted desolation, went on with the *serenata*, not one note of which was heard. Again he appealed to the sentinels; and this time they waved their hands expansively in the direction of South America, to indicate that the *prima donna* was already on her way thither. On this the audience showed such sudden and unexpected signs of giving in that the *diva* tripped out again, bowing, wafting kisses, and successfully courting fresh thunders of applause. Will not some sincere friend of Madame Patti's tell her frankly that she is growing too big a girl for this sort of thing, which imposes on nobody—not even on the infatuated gentlemen who write columns about her fans and jewels. No: the queens of song should leave the coquetery of the footlights to the soubrettes. How much more dignified was [Romanian violinist, 1838–1911: married to Hallé] Madame Neruda's reception of the magnificent ovation which followed her playing of Bazzini's Ronde des Lutins!

It is unnecessary to say more of the rest of the program than that *E che! fra voi la tema* [Rossini, *Robert Bruce*, adapted Niedermeyer, 1846] brought back pleasantly the days when Mr Santley [actor, 1834–1922] trod the stage, and that [William

Vincent] Wallace's ridiculous Let me like a Soldier Fall [from the opera *Maritana*] was treated as it deserves, even though it was Mr Edward Lloyd's breast [tenor, 1845–1927] that "expanded to the ball." Miss Gomez [contralto, 1865–1922] made a very favorable impression by her singing of Sir Arthur Sullivan's Sleep, my love, sleep. Madame Patti, it may be added, looks very well and strong, and her voice is as good as ever.

7. The Passing of Trebelli

The World, 5 October 1892

The recent death of Trebelli must not pass without a word of comment in this column, more especially as so many of the obituary notices contain descriptions of her singing which are purely imaginary. In her best days her voice was extraordinarily rich in the middle. Her tribute to Bella Venezia in the opening chorus of Lucrezia Borgia [opera by Donizetti]:

> *Men di sue notti e limpido*
> *D'ogn' altro cielo it giorno,*

sounded better than a ripe plum tastes, though the phrase lies round the middle of the treble stave, altogether above the point at which ordinary singers have to leave their chest register, on pain of displacing and ruining their voices. She produced contralto effects in mezzo-soprano and transposed soprano parts more successfully than in contralto parts, in one of which—Amneris, in [Verdi's] Aida—she ground her lower notes so unmercifully for the sake of "dramatic effect" that their old rich purple-velvety quality vanished irrecoverably.

This was one of many exploits of hers which seemed to prove her natural judgment much inferior to her cultivated taste; but I am afraid the truth was that the public were so obtuse to her finest qualities as an artist, and so appreciative of claptrap, that she either lost faith in herself at times, or else gave up the struggle with the public in despair. At Her Majesty's, as Cherubino or Zerlina, she would sing *Voi, che sapete*, or *Batti, batti* [arias from Mozart's *Le Nozze di Figaro* and *Don Giovanni*], transposed, but without a note altered or a phrase vulgarized, only to find herself written of with much less enthusiasm than Pauline Lucca at Covent Garden, whose treatment of Mozart was—well, I have spent five minutes in trying to find an epithet both adequate and decorous; without success. On the other hand, when, as Maffio Orsini, she turned the *brindisi* into a bad joke by that never-to-be-forgotten shake of hers, which was certainly the very worst shake ever heard in an opera house (it used to get sharper and sharper by perceptible jerks), she was encored and applauded to the echo. She liked Maffio, as she liked Siebel, Urbain, Arsaces, and all parts which freed her from the tyranny of the petticoat, of which, like most sensible women, she was impatient. She never seemed to lose her fresh enjoyment of these parts.

Once, happening to be behind the scenes at the end of the prologue to Lucrezia, I saw her, the moment the curtain fell, throw herself in a transport of excitement into the arms of Titiens, though the two had played the scene together often enough to make it the most hackneyed piece of business in the world to them. Trebelli was at her best in the most refined and quiet class of work. It is quite a mistake to suppose that she fell short as an oratorio singer. I have never heard her singing of He shall feed His flock surpassed: her diction alone put many of her English colleagues to shame. Her Cherubino, her Zerlina, and her Rezia in Oberon [opera by Weber] were criticism-proof. Her Carmen [opera by Bizet] was, vocally, the most finished we have heard. In the tragic, passionate contralto parts in Verdi's operas she was not good: she played them out of imaginative ambition, just as she sang such things as Offenbach's *C'est l'Espagne* [from *Les Bovards*] out of high spirits; but the result was commonplace and, by contrast with her fine Mozartean work, vulgar.

Unlike her daughter, she was deficient in agility of vocal execution, and could not manage a shake. She had also a certain mannerism which affected her intonation, and made her one of the many great artists who are always the piquant shadow of a shade out of tune—flat as I judged it; though I confess that in very minute dissonances I cannot tell flat from sharp. She was, I should say, a much more cultivated musician than most of her colleagues; and she was an eminently goodlooking woman, with a ready smile that did full justice to her teeth. The collapse of the old *régime* at the opera caused the stage to leave her long before she was ready to leave the stage; and she was by no means worn out as a singer when physical infirmity, produced by a paralytic stroke which fell on her some years ago, created the vacancy which remained unfilled until Guilia Ravogli [1866–1940] came.

Criticism, of course, knows no gratitude and no regret; but I must say that if all the artists of the Titiens epoch [soprano, 1831–1877] had been as good as Trebelli, my occasional references to that dark age would be much less ferocious than they generally are.

Of the late Emil Behnke [1836–1892] I knew just enough to be able to say that his death is a considerable loss to teachers-in-training, speakers, and singers who find themselves stopped by a difficulty which they cannot get round. He was an exceedingly good demonstrator with the laryngoscope, and would shew you exactly what he wanted done instead of making more or less vague suggestions to your imagination. His scorn of the professors who tell you to sing from the head, or the throat, or the chest, or to pin your voice to your hard palate, was immense: he was justly proud of his ability to name with the exactitude of a watchmaker the movement and action he wished you to produce. He knew a great deal about the physical act of voice production; and his principal achievements were the relief of experienced singers from disabilities which their ordinary training had not overcome (or had created), and his cures of stammering.

Everybody who went to him learnt something, though nobody learnt everything from him; and even those who knew beforehand what he demonstrated to them with the laryngoscope knew it much better afterwards. He was always keenly interested in himself and his work, and would talk about it, rush into controversies about it, and denounce the ordinary commercial singing-master up hill and down dale with unabated freshness at an age which finds most professional men stale routineers. Needless to add, he was not a popular character in academic circles. As to his artistic capacity, I confess I had and have my doubts about it. Besides his scientific interest in voice production, he undoubtedly had a strong practical turn, and hated to hear voices spoiled or wasted or only half turned to account. He wanted to have every throat in first-rate working order.

But whether he had that passion for perfect beauty of vocal tone and perfect dignity and expressiveness of delivery in singing which is the supreme attribute of the greatest singers and teachers of singing, I do not know, though I guess with some confidence that he had little more than the ordinary appetite for them. He once "sang" the notes of the common chord for me when shewing me the action of lifting the soft palate. He then got me to "sing" the same notes whilst he observed that action in me. I use the inverted commas because laryngoscopic vocalism can only be called singing by courtesy: as a matter of fact we simply bawled the syllable "Haw" at oneanother in a manner which would have created the utmost consternation in the theatre or on the platform.

I remember being struck by the fact that though he seemed interested by my success in managing my soft palate, he did not make any comment on the extreme unloveliness of the noise with which I had responded to his invitation to sing, which he had not qualified by any allusion to the impossibility of my complying in the artistic sense under such conditions. The incident by itself proved nothing; but it put me on the track of further observations, which finally left me under the impression (possibly a mistaken one) that his authority was limited to the physical acts involved by ordinary voice production, and did not extend even to the modifications of those acts which have no reasons for their existence except purely artistic ones.

For instance, he had made an elaborate study of breathing, and could teach people to use their diaphragms; but I once heard a pupil of his who had her diaphragm under perfect control, and who yet blew away her voice in the most ineffective way as she sang, because she had not been taught to acquire that peculiar steadying and economizing of the air column which is the first condition of beauty of tone in singing. I am therefore sceptical as to Behnke's having ever trained a complete artistic singer or speaker; though many singers and speakers learnt a good deal from him. I was so convinced on the latter point that at the moment of his death I had arranged with him to take in hand a class of about twenty political speakers, some of whom had already acquired sufficient skill and experience to enable them to teach an ordinary elocution professor his business.

Perhaps the most important thing to make known about Behnke is, that though he elected to take his differences with the majority fighting instead of lying down, and so made enemies of many whose countenance is supposed to be indispensable to musical success, he prospered, as far as I am able to ascertain, quite as well as his more compliant rivals. Although his terms were higher than any but first-rate teachers can venture to ask in these days of Guildhall Schools and Royal Colleges, he was overworked. His Voice Training Exercises sold at the rate of over eight thousand copies a year;

and his Mechanism of the Human Voice got into a seventh edition, whilst the better advertized book which he wrote in collaboration with Dr Lennox Browne nearly doubled that record.

It may be, of course, that London, according to its custom with professional men, gave with one hand and took back with the other, and that all the return he got for his labor over and above his bare subsistence was the privilege of collecting money for his landlord, his servants, his tradesmen, and so forth. But this is the common lot of the orthodox and the heterodox alike. My point is that he had not to pay any more for his self-respect than less courageous men have to pay for being humbugs and nonentities. It is a mistake to be too much afraid of London merely because it is much stronger and much stupider than you are, just as it is a mistake to be too much afraid of a horse on the same ground. Behnke, I imagine, was shrewd and resolute enough to know this.

His death is a real loss; for on his weak side (as I judge him) he at least did no mischief, whilst on his strong side he undid a great deal. Besides, he ventilated his profession, which is, if I may say so in a whisper, rather a stuffy one.

Part IV: Opera and Operetta

Opera is the major focus for Shaw in his music criticism, and this selection may be significantly longer than the other categories, but this mirrors the percentage of reviews that Shaw dedicated to opera. They have been selected to reflect his major interests. These range from estimates of a London opera company's season to reviews of new English operas, from mythic tragedies and historical pieces, to comic operas and operettas, including Gilbert and Sullivan. Since Shaw, even at the beginning of his career as a music critic, was concerned to promote the works of Richard Wagner, the selection of his reviews on Wagner have been set in a separate category.

In his reviews certain figures continually appear, among them an influential impresario, Carl Rosa, and such singers as Zélia Trebelli or Jean de Reszke. One of his recurrent themes is the appropriate language for opera, or the history of opera, while some reviews are based on operatic scores, not performances.

1. Pauline

The Hornet, 29 November 1876

Mr Cowen's Pauline was produced for the first time on Wednesday last, the 22nd November, by Mr Carl Rosa [impresario, conductor and founder of his own opera company, 1842–1889], in the presence of a large and favorably disposed audience. The book, by Mr Henry Hersee [translator and librettist, 1820–1896], is an adaptation of the late Lord Lytton's wellknown play [*The Lady of Lyons*] to operatic purposes, in compliance with the exigencies of which our old friend, Colonel Damas, has disappeared altogether, and the remaining characters ever and anon desert the smooth language of the original for verses for which the adapter in his preface has modestly disclaimed any poetic merit. In the musical illustration of the drama thus supplied, Mr Cowen [pianist, conductor, composer, 1852–1935] has had all the advantages which can be conferred by the indulgent attitude towards a young composer in whom they felt a national interest, a story of established popularity, the best artistic talent available in English opera, an orchestra and chorus of unusual excellence, and a conductor who spares no pains in the presentation of any work he undertakes.

Under these circumstances, it cannot be contended that Mr Cowen had not a fair field for his experiment as an operatic composer. We would be loth to bear hardly on so painstaking a musician as Mr Cowen is known to be, still more so to discourage a young musician who has come to the front amidst a dearth of native talent; but the fact remains that the music of Pauline possesses little originality, and displays an utter absence of dramatic faculty. The moment the composer quits the aria cantabile form, in which he has already achieved some renown, he betrays weakness, which sometimes verges on absurdity. The musical merit of the opera, therefore, depends principally on the songs with which it is liberally interspersed, and of these not one has any, save the slenderest, connexion with the drama, the words being of the ordinary type manufactured for ballads, and mostly without any bearing on the action.

The opera begins with an introduction consisting of a short *andante maestoso*, afterwards made use of in the ensemble of Act III., and a melody which also recurs in Claude Melnotte's famous description of his visionary palace at Como. On the rising of the curtain we find the widow Melnotte awaiting Claude's return from a *fête* outside her cottage. A chorus of villagers ensues, in which they hail the hero as their prince. When they retire, he expresses his passion in a song, One Kind Glance, sung by Mr Santley [1834–1932] in his usual finished style. It narrowly escaped an *encore*. We may add that the position adopted by the accomplished baritone, who sang the second verse with one foot placed on a chair, was by no means graceful, and interfered decidedly with his respiratory powers. In the awkward recitative, So do I scatter her image to the winds, in which Claude vents his indignation at the insult to his messenger, we have the first exemplification of the composer's means of delineating the more violent emotions, and we hail with relief the advent of a melody which for a few notes seems to be the familiar Auld Robin Gray, but which develops into a pretty duet of mutual consolation between mother and son. On the entrance of Glavis and Beauseant, the act concludes unhappily with a *trio* for the three men, which is the worst feature in the act. Apart from its barrenness as a musical composition, it is scored in a grandiose style, that, applied to the paltry situation of a plot against a scornful girl, is simply absurd.

Act II, which takes place in the garden of M. Deschapelles, opens with a ballet and chorus, commonplace and thinly instrumental, the harp being conspicuous by its abuse. Although the incident of Claude's cool disposal of the snuffbox and ring lent by his tempters seems hardly susceptible of musical treatment, Mr Cowen has embodied it in a sestet, which fairly preserves the humor of the original. In the scene which follows, Damas's challenge of the pretended prince's Italian is ingeniously replaced by a sneering request from Beauseant that Claude will try a guitar for him, on which artless pretext Claude accordingly favors us with Inez was beautiful, an effective song with a pretty pizzicato accompaniment. The description of the palace at Como is preserved *verbatim* from the original play, and the composer has successfully translated it into melody. The scene would be charming but for the unpleasant recitative, Oh false one, which follows. The concluding duet is spoiled by a monotonous accompaniment for the harp, of which instrument we have had already more than enough. A lively song for Glavis in nine-eight time, Love has Wings, was redemanded; and the act closed with a wedding march and chorus, which present no special features for criticism.

The third act, at Melnotte's cottage, begins with a song, From its mother's nest, which will probably be heard again on the concert platform. It was excellently sung by Miss Yorke [Josie Jones: American soprano, born 1853], who received a hearty *encore*. It is a pity that Mr Cowen has seen fit to injure this pretty song by the tasteless flute passages at the end of each verse. The scene between Claude and Pauline, on her discovery of his real station, contains an air, From my first years, and a charming duet, Yet, ere I go, which is the gem of the opera, and stands in agreeable contrast to the crude *agitato* passages with which it is surrounded. The intrusion of Beauseant is unhappily treated. It is difficult to judge the effect of his duet with Pauline, inasmuch as Miss Gaylord [American soprano, 1855–1894] and Mr Celli [bass-baritone, 1842–1904] sang flat throughout. The entrance of Claude to the rescue is illustrated by mock-heroic drum passages, which are but a sorry compensation for the fine stroke of character achieved by Lord Lytton in furnishing the "moun-tebank" with an empty chair. After a very unattractive air—I was tempted to crime,—sung by Claude, the act ends with a tolerably effective *ensemble* constructed on the opening bars of the introduction. In the *entr'acte* which precedes Act IV., we again hear the melody of the duet, Yet, ere I go, this time as a violin solo. We were scarcely prepared for the treatment it received at the hands of so able an artist as Mr Carl Rosa's leader, who played it flat from beginning to end. The most noteworthy numbers of the last act are a song, conventional in type, delivered by Miss Gaylord with much feeling, and a very pretty chorus of bridesmaids, Blooming and bright.

The orchestral portion of the opera displays little judg-ment. The effect is frequently impoverished, owing partly to excursions into the higher octaves, where the volume of tone is necessarily thin. We have already alluded to the injudi-cious use of the harp—a fault which has prevailed amongst our composers since the production of M. Gounod's Faust, where the instrument is employed with such exquisite effect. But exactly as in Faust the harp is introduced with a sparing hand, and always well-supported, so in Pauline, and other works of the same calibre, it is lavishly used throughout the score, and frequently left to bear the entire burden of the ac-companiment. As with the voice, so with the orchestra, Mr Cowen is most successful when his theme is some simple air, which is usually allotted to the oboe or violin. When he at-tempts passionate recitative or dramatic effect, the intention is not realized, or [results in] an indulgence in passages so ca-cophonous that they can only be accounted for as mistaken efforts at originality, colored, perhaps, by a little Wagnerian affectation.

Miss Julia Gaylord impersonated the scornful Lady of Lyons with the greatest success, displaying unexpected pathos in the last two acts. Her singing was marked by real feeling, and though sometimes uncertain in intonation, owing to defective method, was, on the whole, most creditable to her. Miss York's Widow Melnotte was all that could be desired, and was received with enthusiastic applause throughout. Mrs Aynsley Cook [Harriett Farrell Payne, 1833–1894: actress and vocalist, member of a famous theatre/pantomime family] as Madame Deschappeles, was, as she always is, thoroughly efficient. Mr Santley's performance of the part of Claude was even and finished, the success of many of the songs being mainly due to his artistic rendering of them. Mr Turner, as Glavis, the better to convey the foppishness of the character, adopted the unaccountable expedient of moving about as though his ankles were tied together. The effect was sufficiently ridiculous. The ungrateful part of Beauseant fell to the lot of Mr Celli, who appeared in various costumes, now revengeful in a "Hardress Cregan" walking suit [taken from Boucicault's *The Colleen Bawn*], and anon Satanic in pink satin. We are the more sorry to observe Mr Celli's melodramatic propensities, as we believe that with some study in the right direction, and his constant reference to his favorite part of Mephistopheles, he is capable of becoming a good actor. After each act, composer and artists were called before the curtain, and the librettist also appeared to receive the congratulations of the audience. Finally, a brief *ballet d'action* was performed by the conductor and composer, in which Mr Carl Rosa felicitated Mr Cowen in dumb show on the success of his work, and Mr Cowen mutely testified his conviction of how much that success was due to the exertions of Mr Carl Rosa.

2. English Opera

The Hornet, 6 December 1876

The English opera season is at length over. For a time, at least, theatre-going lovers of music must be content with the brassy delights of pantomime and the affecting symphonies which accompany the development of transformation scenes. Mr Carl Rosa has started on a provincial tour, which will, we hope, prove as successful as his season has been. During that season he has not hesitated to depart from managerial precedent so far as to keep his promises, and he has fairly carried out his program of discarding the star system and aiming at excellence of *ensemble*. For this he deserves our gratitude, rather than the reproaches with which he has been assailed for enlisting Mr Santley as "a star," and for excluding Mozart's operas from his repertory. Cavillers would do well to bear in mind that avoiding the star system does not mean engaging none but second-rate artists. When an *impresario* offers us an impoverished orchestra, incompetent subordinates, and defective *mise en scène* in order to meet the sensational terms of popular *prime donne* [*prima donnas*]: then we have just cause for complaint. But Mr Carl Rosa has not done this. On the contrary, his company is in all respects improved since the accession of Mr Santley.

As to the clamorers for Mozart, their importunity practically amounts to asking for a display of weakness in the production of works which demand all the highest qualifications which the most gifted artists can bring to their work. We have had an opera of Wagner's [*Der fliegende Holländer*] very creditably produced; we have had Fidelio, which some—notably those who speak of Mozart's works as trifles—declare the greatest of operas; we have had Pauline, specially written by one of our own composers; and if we are not satisfied, Mr Carl Rosa is not to blame in the matter.

The only special event of the closing week was a morning performance of Faust, for the benefit of the society for the relief of distressed Americans, the part of Marguerite being undertaken for this occasion by Madame Van Zandt [American soprano, 1858–1919], who, like the other artists, volunteered her services. Under these circumstances, a minute criticism of the lady's performance would be uncalled for. It will suffice to say that, with the exception of a trifling hitch in the church scene, she sang the music correctly, and achieved a floral success. We would suggest, however, that in future the persons who kindly undertake to throw bouquets should study the score beforehand, and offer their tributes at the proper opportunities. On Wednesday last, bouquets dropped promiscuously throughout the performance, and one, bearing a message of peace and charity, fell most inappropriately into the hands of Mephistopheles. The military band in the fourth act played strepitously—most offensively so, indeed. Mr Ludwig [Irish baritone, 1847–1923], who appeared as Valentin, effectually spoiled his song by delivering the words with a strong foreign inflexion: an affectation which cannot be too strongly reprehended. In other respects, the cast was the same as usual, Miss Yorke being conspicuous by her meritorious impersonation of Siebel.

On Tuesday, the 28th ult., Cagnoni's opera The Porter of Havre [opera semiseria, 1871, title in Italian *Papà Martin*] was performed before a rather limited audience. This pretty opera holds a position somewhat analogous to that of Marta [spelled *Martha*, opera by Flotow]. It is not great, but it is never disagreeable. It contains some beautiful numbers, the orchestration (in the style of Meyerbeer) is solid, and the plot, though absurdly constructed, is entertaining. Above all, in some of its scenes are familiar pictures of home life—impossible on the Italian stage—the power of presenting which is one of the most charming attractions afforded by English opera.

The last two nights were devoted to Fidelio and The Water Carrier [*Les deux journées, ou Le porteur d'eau* by Luigi Cherubini, 1800]. The association of these is the more appropriate as it gives us an opportunity of tracing the extent to which Beethoven followed Cherubini—his acknowledged model—in the structure of his only opera. As performed by the Carl Rosa company, the dialogue is retained according to the intention of the composers, and we escape the recitative impertinences with which Balfe [Irish composer, 1808–1870] and others have vulgarized these works for representation on the Italian stage.

3. Bach and Don Pasquale

The Hornet, 18 April 1877

On Wednesday, the 11th inst., the Bach choir—following their precedent of last year—gave a performance of the Mass in B minor, at the St James's Hall. In order that the Kyrie might be heard without interruption, the audience were invited to be seated at ten minutes before eight, an arrangement which the majority signified their appreciation of by arriving punctually at ten minutes past. The work was, however, listened to with attention; and the number who availed themselves of the pause before the Agnus Dei to leave the hall was, despite the great length of the Mass, unusually small. Considering the difficulties presented to an amateur chorus by the complicated polyphonic construction of Bach's music, the performance was a fairly satisfactory one. A few of the numbers dragged a little, and in all an extreme caution was evident, which interfered with that spontaneity which is essential to the full effect of massive choral works.

On the other hand, the choir displayed a praiseworthy accuracy and sense of the importance of their task. Many of the numbers of the Credo, which forms the grandest portion of the service, were followed by loud applause. Madame Lemmens-Sherrington [soprano, 1834–1906] and Madame Patey [contralto, 1842–1894] sang with their customary efficiency, the masterly duet Et in unum Dominum [from Bach's *Hohe messe in h-Moll* BWV 232], &c. being rendered with particular success. Signor Foli [Alan James Foley: bass, 1837–1899] was, as usual, in difficulties with his articulation, a peculiarity which the Latin language seems to render additionally prominent. Mr Cummings [1831–1915] sang the tenor music as he sings always, which was, doubtless, gratifying to admirers of his voice and style.

The numerous obbligati were well played as a rule, the difficult one to the Quoniam, for the horn, and that for the violin to the Benedictus, executed by MM. Wendtland [horn] and Straus [Austrian violinist, 1835–1899], deserving particular notice. The exception was the flute-playing of Mr Svensden, which was sharp throughout. As we have noticed the same want before with this artist, we are forced to conclude that it arises not from accidental circumstances, such as variation of temperature, but either from defective ear or an unhappy craving to be conspicuous at any cost. Herr Otto Goldschmidt [conductor and composer, 1829–1907, married to Swedish soprano Jenny Lind] conducted, and was warmly received by his choir.

At the Royal Italian Opera, on Thursday last, Mlle Marimon (who was announced for the part of Norina in Don Pasquale) was unable to appear. Mlle Smeroschi [lyric soprano, also called Carolina Smerowsky-Carbone], who took her place, acted with considerable spirit; but her favorite expedient of accomplishing executive difficulties by dashing at them was only occasionally successful, and proved an indifferent substitute for the finished roulade of perhaps the best vocalist on the stage. Her intonation is sometimes incorrect; but generally speaking she filled the part with tolerable success. Unfortunately, in an opera like [Donizetti's] Don Pasquale — in which everything depends on the excellence of four principal singers — something more than this is required to sustain the interest to the end of the three acts.

The honors of the performance fell to the lot of M. Capoul [tenor, 1839–1924], whose grace and fervor secure the approval of his audience in spite of his vicious French method of pro-

ducing his voice. His rendering of the familiar Com' è gentil
was the only encore of the evening. Signor Ciampi was the
Don, and he conducted his impersonation according to the
approved traditions of the Italian buffo style. That is to say,
he sang as little as possible, and talked as much as possible,
in a flat and brawling tone, sufficiently disagreeable in itself,
but quite irritating when uttered interjectionally during the
airs of the other characters. We do not know what effect an
Italian *buffo* produces on most cultivated Englishmen—we
can only speak for ourselves; but we imagine it might find a
parallel if [the English comedians] Mr Harry Paulton or Mr
J.L. Toole could be induced to perform in their characteristic
style to a polite Roman or Florentine audience. Signor Co-
togni [baritone, 1831–1918] as Malatesta, was operatic in the
same sense in which we speak of an actor as "stagey." He
sang correctly but with a powerful *tremolo*, and discharged
the necessary stage business efficiently. The choruses were
given with vigour and precision, but, as the wont of choruses
is, without refinement.

Signor Bevagnani [harpsichordist and conductor,
1841–1903] conducted. There are two conductors at Covent
Garden, and probably neither considers himself responsible
to the public for the shortcomings of the orchestra. The fact
remains that the band is intolerably coarse, continually
drowning the singers' most strenuous efforts in the *tuttis*, and
destitute of delicacy in the lighter passages. For the credit
of the house, the artists, and the conductors we trust that
one of the largest and most fully appointed of our orchestras
will not be permitted to rank also as the worst. We have
witnessed more interesting performances than that of Don
Pasquale on Thursday; but it was on the whole, a respectable
one. The attendance was so numerous as to give ample
promise of a busy season.

Signor Gayarré [Spanish tenor, 1844–1890] appeared as
Raoul in [Meyerbeer's] Les Hugenots on Saturday to a

tremendous house. He sang tamely at first, but in the duel septet and the grand duo with Valentine, he roused his audience to enthusiasm. His acting, however, was by no means up to the mark. Mlle Bianchi [Bertha Schwartz: 1855–1947] did fairly as the Queen, but her scale-singing is defective. Mlle d'Angeri [soprano, 1853–1907] was as usual.

4. Opera and Empty Bravado

The Hornet, 13 June 1877

The operatic events of the past week have not been specially interesting. On the 5th [Verdi's] Rigoletto was produced at Her Majesty's, with Signor Galassi [baritone, 1845–1904] in the title role. His impersonation was highly satisfactory. His earnestness and remarkable voice secure his success in parts which do not require great delicacy of treatment. Signor Talbo [Hugh Talbot: Irish tenor, 1845–1899], who appeared as the Duke, rather overacted his part, and spoiled La donna e mobile by concluding on a weak B natural. His preference for his higher register is, however, excusable, as it is the best part of his voice. He bids fair to be a useful singer. Mlle Valleria [1848–1925] was the Gilda, and Madame Trebelli a perfect Maddalena.

On Thursday Mlle Chiomi again appeared as Lucia [title role of Donizetti's *Lucia di Lammermoor*]. She would do well to bear in mind that excessive energy can never convert stage business into acting. Her voice is somewhat hard, and the upper notes are usually flat, which is caused by defective method rather than incorrect ear. She marred the first scena by a profusion of antiquated ornament. Mlle Chiomi's attractive appearance is, however, a strong point in her favor. Signor Fancelli was again successful as Edgardo; and Signor Rota, as Enrico, proved himself a master of the art of shouting. He also displayed his perseverance as a gesticulator by incessantly moving his right arm to and fro after the un-sightly fashion of an amateur violinist.

On the 5th inst. Mr Henry Ketten [Hungarian and French, 1848–1883] gave a pianoforte recital at the St James's Hall. The system of modern virtuosi is remarkable. Let any man ob-tain some favor from the public as a player or singer, and straightway he concludes himself competent to entertain an audience for three hours by his unaided exertions. He gen-erally finds himself mistaken. Even Herr Rubinstein's hearers are sometimes fain to cry "Hold, enough!" and he can play in several styles. Mr Ketten can only play in one, and that not a very agreeable one. He is unable to render a simple melody in the cantabile style, being simply an instrument of percussion. He plays rapidly, but inaccurately; and his use of the pedal is abhorrent to an educated ear. Under these circumstances his choice of Beethoven's prodigious sonata, Op. 106 (with in-cidental preludes by Henry Ketten) was an empty bravado, which, we trust, he will not repeat. A chaconne of Handel's and Bach's Italian concerto were steadily executed, and a few of the player's own compositions were favorably received. Mr Ketten's muse is, at any rate, prolific, his Serenade Espagnole being marked Op. 60.

5. On Opera in Translation

The Hornet, 8 August 1877

A not very brilliant season has been succeeded by a week of absolute stagnation, musically speaking. Impresarios, artists, and audiences have vanished from amongst us in quest of new singers, new triumphs, and such health as can be gained from the mountain winds of Switzerland, or the more eco-nomical atmosphere of the rearward apartments of appar-ently deserted premises. The critics are divided between op-eratic retrospects and the prospects of English opera during the autumn and winter with Mr Carl Rosa. We have so low an opinion of the merits of Italian opera in this country, and so steady a conviction that its downfall is only a question of time and musical culture, that we turn willingly to the rival enterprise which has relieved us from the absurdity of being the only music-patronizing nation in the world which systematically tolerates opera delivered in a foreign tongue. And, be it remembered, not in the language for which the music was written, but in a vile Italian substitute for the original French or German libretto.

Those persons who object to English versions on the score of their literary demerits are presumably unacquainted with the Italian language, or they would scarcely assert the superiority of the translations which we hear so maltreated by German, Spanish, Swedish, French, Irish, and American artists at our opera houses. The few Italian singers, mostly of minor importance, do even less justice to their native tongue than the foreigners, pronouncing their recitatives in a species of gabble which we can scarcely identify with the musical language which we have heard declaimed by Signor Salvini [Italian actor, 1829–1915]. In other countries the artists pay their audiences the compliment of mastering their speech, and presenting them with an intelligible and most enjoyable entertainment. The pre-eminence of Italian as the language of song has been urged to the serious detriment of opera in this country. English is the only tongue capable of enlisting the sympathy of the Englishman. It is far nearer to the German, in which the greatest operas have been written, than Italian; and it is also capable of greater variety of inflexion and expression. It is more amenable to musical requirements than French. Once cultivated on the lyric stage, an example would be constantly before the public which might perhaps modify the corruption which the unfortunate vowel experiences in London. But these are secondary matters.

The great point is that English is our national tongue, and, therefore, the only one which should be tolerated in our national opera houses. When we are at last roused to draw comparisons between the dreary emptiness of the evening spent in Covent Garden or the Haymarket, listening to performances which are foreign in heart and form, and the familiar and sympathetically rendered versions which excite the enthusiasm of shilling galleries for even Wagner, it is certain that we should as soon think of going to hear Mr Irving in a German translation of Hamlet as to an Italian opera. After this hint of our views, we need scarcely add that Mr Carl Rosa has our warmest wishes for the success of the enterprise which he has inaugurated with so much energy.

It is said that Herr Chandon [bass, 1838–1903] has been engaged by Mr Mapleson [1830–1901, singer under the name of Enrico Mariani, then opera impresario and manager of the Lyceum Theatre, Her Majesty's Theatre, and Theatre Royal Drury Lane] for the season of 1878. He will be remembered by visitors to the Wagner Festival of last May as a steady singer with a strong baritone voice of more resonance than quality, and withal somewhat coarse in his style. But he will appear to greater advantage when no longer contrasted with Herr Karl Hill [bass, 1831–1893], whose taste and expressive delivery might render the least severe critic fastidious.

A series of ten operas in English is in course of production at the Crystal Palace, by the Rose Hersee Opera Company. The list of vocalists is not particularly attractive, but there are materials for some pleasant performances, nevertheless.

6. Opera in Italian

The Saturday Musical Review, 22 February 1879;
Unsigned

If any man, having nothing else to do, will take the trouble
to scan the charges for admission to the Court, the Prince of
Wales's, or any of our first-rate theatres, and compare them
with the tariff of either of our opera houses, he will find a
difference sufficiently startling to raise the question whether
the prices exacted by the managers are justified by their expenses or by the superior gratification derivable from their
entertainments. The commercial aspect of opera is necessarily dependent on the esthetic, which involves, not only the
propriety of lyric drama as a musical form, a consideration
which the public have long since settled for themselves; but
the common sense question whether to visit Her Majesty's or
Covent Garden Theatre in the season be really a profitable
way of spending an evening.

As we believe that for many years past no speculator in
opera in England has been pecuniarily successful during any
extended period, we feel justified in concluding that the present system is as little satisfactory to the managers as to their
patrons. There are several reasons for this on the surface. The
large salaries paid to the artists, the necessity for a complete
orchestra, the chorus, and the employment of a conductor,
and other functionaries who have no place in the economy of
ordinary theatres, contribute to swell the expenses of an operatic company beyond those of any other scheme for the entertainment of the public. Yet if we consider the high prices
charged, and the great capacity of the houses used; if we allow
for the exaggerations which the gossips of the press delight to
indulge in, of the salaries of the leading singers, and compare
the number of such singers with the host of debutantes, and
others whose appearance is only explicable on the ground

that they pay heavily for the privilege of performing; if we bear in mind that the works produced have either survived their copyright, or been stolen from the composers by advantage of law, and are produced with little rehearsal save what they obtain at the public expense on subscription nights; and if we refer to the perfection of detail achieved elsewhere in return for much lower prices, the conviction will be forced on us that our Italian opera is pecuniarily unremunerative, simply because it is esthetically monstrous. We shall not attempt within our space to exhaust the prolific subject of its defects, but something we are bound to say in justification of our opinion that things are not as they should be on our lyric stage.

The function of dramatic music is to express the emotion which accompanies the action of a play, which play as a primary and indispensable requisite should be completely intelligible to the audience, down even to the minutest details of the dialogue. The degree in which any opera dispenses with this condition marks the degree in which it descends beneath the highest models; and the extent to which the listener can be content with a broad outline of the argument is the extent to which he may be looked on as one with a sensual relish for sweet sounds, instead of an intelligent perception of music. To the fact that out of a hundred persons who attend an opera from other than social reasons, not more than ten propose to themselves anything further than the gratification of this lower harmonic appetite, is due the existence in England of so ludicrous an anomaly as opera in Italian; for, be it observed, out of the many works which our Swedish, German, French, and American artists sing in bad Italian, only a few were originally written in that language; and these few are the least meritorious, and at the present time, happily, the least popular. The first requisite for the true appreciation of opera being thus denied to us, and that for no satisfactory reason, we are naturally indifferent to the acting of scenes which we cannot easily follow. The laws of supply and demand are as potent in the theatre as elsewhere; and, consequently, we have at our opera houses a system of gesticulation so unmeaning, so impotent to excite even derisive mirth, that the ghastliest and most ludicrous traditions of the old melodramatic stage would, if revived, be more tolerable to us. Even the few artists who are capable of better things only escape momentarily from the false atmosphere generated by their own thoughtlessness and the ignorance of the public, when the power of the composer dominates artist and audience, and conquers in spite of every disadvantage. Nor do the public seem to be offended by this false conventionalism. Praise which would sound exaggerated if applied to our greatest actors, is lavished in chamber, clique, and column, on the shallowest French charlatanry and the dreariest Italian buffoonery. Aspirants whose demerits are such as should debar them from participation in a piece performed by amateurs, are permitted to appear in the most responsible parts, and often meet with considerable encouragement. And hereby we have arrived at this: that with musical enthusiasts amongst us sufficiently numerous to crowd concert rooms where the loftiest abstract music prevails, our opera houses are abandoned to followers of fashion who feel no higher interest than a personal favoritism which is never based on artistic appreciation. For this evil the critical press is in part responsible. A comparison of the musical criticism in vogue with that concerning literature or the graphic arts will suffice to mark its degradation, the inevitable result of the timidity of critics who can only judge one performance by reference to another, and are unable to handle their subject with the certainty conferred by knowledge, or the independence which springs from resolute truthfulness.

The truth is that Italianized opera in England is aristocratic in the worst sense. It has become effete because it has never appealed to the people. Its audience has worn evening dress and kept late hours so long that its vitality has escaped; its power of discerning between sensational sham and true power has become confused; and it applauds with palsied hands spiritless desecrations of Mozart, or dodders feebly over the music of the future, so much louder and more stimulating than the music of the past. Whatever we may think of Wagner, we owe him thanks, inasmuch as he has taken fashionable opera by the throat, and shaken the old paralytic shrewdly. He has given us works that must be performed, with words that must be understood. One of these works, welcomed with enthusiasm in English, was treated with indifference when it was reproduced in Italian guise—a good sign, pregnant with the hope that we may yet see a popular performance of—let us say Don Giovanni—good enough to edify the people, to educate the critics, and to justify our national culture.

7. Palmy Days at the Opera

The Magazine of Music, January 1886;
Unsigned

When old-fashioned people deplore the decadence of the modern theatre, and regret the palmy days of the drama, superstitious ones are apt to take the desirability of palminess for granted, without troubling themselves to ascertain the exact conditions which constituted it. On inquiry, we are led to infer that long runs, elaborate scenery and dresses, efficient performance of minor parts, and prose dialogues, are degenerate; but that prompters, changes of program every night, poster playbills printed in blue color that adheres to everything except the flimsy paper, and "historical" costumes—i.e. costumes belonging to no known historic epoch—are palmy. Between the merits of these things, the young London playgoer can hardly judge; for he has no experience of palminess.

There are many persons of culture still under thirty who are familiar with the palmy flat, vanishing from the scene with the scene-shifters' heels twinkling at its tail; who have touched the orchestra palisade from the front row of a palmy stall-less pit; who have seen the creations of Shakespear enter and quit the scene to the strains of Handel; and whose fingers have been a sorry sight after smudging the playbill for three hours. But these experienced critics are from the country, and began their play-going careers whilst palminess and stock companies still lingered there, as they do, perhaps, to this day. But the West Londoner, who only visits first-class theatres, has only one way of studying palminess. He must go to the opera, where he will soon get quite enough of it to convince him that the theatre in John Kemble's time, when it was carried on much as Italian opera is now, had quite enough drawbacks to reconcile a reasonable man to the changes which have since taken place.

There are no long runs at the opera. Faust is played one night, and Lucia the next; Lohengrin follows, and so on. Here is a splendidly palmy training for the singers. No stagnation in one play for three hundred nights, until the characteristics of his part fasten themselves upon the actor as mannerisms, never afterwards to be got rid of. No rusting of one's powers of study by disuse, nor dawdling in drawing rooms when one should be busy with the divine art at rehearsal. No season passing away without a single performance of one of Mozart's operas, as seasons so often pass without a representation of Shakespear's plays. Development of powers in their fullest variety, by constant alternation of tragedy and comedy, classicism and romanticism, Italianism and Germanism; leading, of course, to enormous superiority of the lyric to the ordinary actor.

At this point it becomes somewhat obvious that the palmy theory lacks experimental verification. On the ordinary stage, crippled as it is supposed to be by long runs, everyone is

expected to act; and the more important characters are expected to act very well. At the opera the tenor is not expected
to act at all; and the baritone, though admittedly an eminently dramatic figure, would not, if he condescended to spoken dialogue, stand the smallest chance of being allowed to
play Rosencrantz at a revival of Hamlet at the Lyceum or
Princess. And if, by bringing strong private influence to bear,
he succeeded in getting cast for Bernardo, and attempted, at
rehearsal, to apply to that part the treatment which gained
general admiration for his Conte di Luna, he would undoubtedly be at once conveyed, under restraint, from the stage to
bedlam. Fancy a Don Felix or a Benedick at any West End
theatre exhibiting the manners of an average Don Juan or
Count Almaviva! Conceive any respectable dramatic company daring to act that great and neglected work of Molière's,
Le Festin de Pierre [originally titled *Don Juan*, and the inspiration for Mozart's *Don Giovanni*], as our opera singers usually
act the masterpiece which Mozart founded on it. Yet musical critics frequently speak of the dramatic power and tragic
intensity of the latest and absurdest [Donizetti's] Lucia or
[Verdi's] Traviata in terms which no sober critic of the kin-
dred profession ever applies to the most skillful achievements
of Mrs Kendal [actress and theatre-manager, 1848–1935].

But, then, the variety of resource, the freedom from mannerism—from [Dickensian] Middlewickism! Unhappily that
has not come off yet. Operatic actors, so far from being free
from mannerisms, wholly substitute mannerisms of the fee-
blest sort for acting; and as for variety of resource, there is not
a penny to choose between an average *prima donna*'s treatment of any two of her parts, however dissimilar in conception. Her Lady Henrietta is exactly the same as her Marguerite; her Marguerite [from *Faust*, opera by Gounod] is not
distinguishable by a deaf man from her Juliet, except by her
dress and wig; and her Semiramis [opera by Rossini] is only a
swaggering Juliet. Even the few singers, male or female, who

are specially celebrated for their acting, would be celebrated for their deficiency if they were placed in an equally prominent position in drama, judged by the standard set by Ristori and Salvini.

As to the development of "study," or the power of learning new parts by constant change of program, it is to be noted that wheras the power of prompting and of taking a prompt during actual performance is becoming a lost art at our theatres, opera singers never venture before an audience without a prompter in the middle of the stage to pilot them through their business. As there is no possibility of sufficient rehearsal, it is part of their qualification, as it still is of the actor in the remote places where the palmy system is still rampant, to get through a part in which they are not even letter-perfect, much less note and letter-perfect. Who has ever heard an opera go absolutely without a hitch, except it was a very new opera which had been recently the subject of special effort in preparation, or a very old one played by a company of veterans? How many singers, when they have once picked up enough of their part to get through it without disgrace by dint of watching the prompter, ever give any further study to its details? At the ordinary theatres a hitch is as exceptional an occurrence as the forgetting of the Lord's Prayer, or the benediction by a Dean. Our actors gain both study and practice from long runs. It is true that they are condemned too often to play for months shallow and characterless parts which they get to the bottom of in a week; but that is the fault of the abject condition of the drama in England, and not of the system of long runs, which gives artists time to get thoroughly inside their parts, and frees them during considerable periods from daily rehearsals, to dawdle in the drawing room if they like, but also to study in the library, the picture gallery, the museum, the gymnasium, or the concert room, as their bodily or mental wants may suggest. The old system of a changed program every night and a hurried rehearsal every day meant insufficient time to prepare one's part, and no time at all to prepare oneself for playing it. To the actor as to other men, leisure means light. He may not always make a good use of his leisure; but in that case he will eventually succumb to competition of the men who do.

As to the advantage of having performances of the greatest operas each season, it may be admitted that a few great works are included in the narrow and hackneyed repertory of our opera houses; but it must at the same time be asked whether such performance as they get is in any sense worthy of them. Don Giovanni is certainly kept before the public; but in what plight? With fine movements omitted in the second act; with the *recitatives* gabbled through in a manner which could not be adequately described without the employment of abusive epithets; and with most of the parts played so as to inspire a faint wonder as to whether ten or twenty more earnest rehearsals, followed by a run of a hundred nights, would suffice to reveal them to the players. When this is all we can do for Don Giovanni we had better keep it on the shelf, as we now keep Shakespear when we have not time to take due trouble with him. The actor who knows one part, and consequently one play thoroughly, is superior to the actor who can scramble with assistance through a dozen. The one gets into the skin of one character: the other only puts on the clothes of twelve. One impersonation is worth more than many impostures. Long runs mean impersonations: palminess means imposture. Let us rejoice over the departure of the palmy days of the theatre.

8. The Don Giovanni Centenary

The Pall Mall Gazette, 31 October 1887
Signed "By our Special Wagnerite"

When I was requested by the Pall Mall Gazette to attend the centenary concert recital of Don Giovanni on Saturday last at the Crystal Palace, I felt strongly disposed to write curtly to the Editor expressing my unworthiness to do justice to the beauties of XVIII century opera. However, I was by no means sure that the Editor would have appreciated the sarcasm (editors, as a class, being shocking examples of neglected musical education); and, besides, I was somewhat curious to hear the performance. For though we are all agreed as to the prettiness of Mozart's melodies, his *naïve* touches of mild fun, and the touch, ingenuity, and grace with which he rang his few stereotyped changes on the old-fashioned forms, yet I have observed that some modern musicians, in the face of a great technical development of harmony and instrumentation, and an enlargement even to world spaciousness of our views of the mission of art, yet persist in claiming for Mozart powers simply impossible to a man who had never read a line of Hegel or a stave of Wagner. I am not now thinking of the maudlin Mozart idolatry of M. Gounod, whom I of course do not consider a great musician; but rather of the unaccountable fact that even Richard Wagner seems to have regarded Mozart as in some respects the greatest of his predecessors. To me it is obvious that Mozart was a mere child in comparison with Schumann, Liszt, or Johannes Brahms; and yet I believe that I could not have expressed myself to that effect without considerable risk of contemptuous abuse, if not of bodily violence.

So I resolved finally to venture hearing poor old Rossini's pet *dramma giocosa*. Before starting, I took a glance at the score, and found exactly what I expected—commonplace

melodies, diatonic harmonies and dominant discords, ridiculous old closes and half-closes at every eighth bar or so,
"florid" accompaniments consisting of tum-tum in the bass
and scales like pianoforte finger studies in the treble, and a
ludicrously thin instrumentation, without trombones or clarinets except in two or three exceptionally pretentious numbers; the string quartet, with a couple of horns and oboes,
seeming quite to satisfy the Mozartian notion of instrumentation. These are facts—facts which can be verified at any
time by a reference to the score; and they must weigh more
with any advanced musician than the hasty opinions which I
formed at the concert when in a sort of delirium, induced, I
have no doubt, by the heat of the room.

For I am bound to admit that the heat of the room produced a most extraordinary effect upon me. The commonplace melodies quite confounded me by acquiring subtlety,
nobility, and dramatic truth of expression; the hackneyed diatonic harmonies reminded me of nothing I had ever heard
before; the dominant discords had a poignant expression
which I failed in my own compositions to attain even by
forcibly sounding all the twelve notes of the chromatic scale
simultaneously; the ridiculous cadences of half-closes came
sometimes like answers to unspoken questions of the heart,
sometimes like ghostly echoes from another world; and the
feeble instrumentation—but that was what warned me that
my senses were astray. Otherwise I must have declared that
here was a master compared to whom Berlioz was a musical
pastrycook. From Beethoven and Wagner I have learned that
the orchestra can paint every aspect of nature, and turn im-
personal but specific emotion into exquisite sound. But an
orchestra that creates men and women as Shakespear and
Molière did—that makes emotion not only specific but personal and characteristic (and this, mind, without clarinets,
without trombones, without a second pair of horns): such
a thing is madness: I must have been dreaming. When the

trombones did come for a while in a supernatural scene at the end, I felt more in my accustomed element; but presently they took an accent so inexpressibly awful, that I, who have sat and smiled through Liszt's Inferno with the keenest relish, felt forgotten superstitions reviving within me. The roots of my hair stirred; and I recoiled as from the actual presence of Hell. But enough of these delusions, which I have effectually dispelled by a dispassionate private performance at my own pianoforte. Of the concert technically, I can only say that it was practically little more than a rehearsal of the orchestral parts.

9. Jean De Reszke's Romeo

The Star, 17 June 1889

It was instructive to compare the effect of the thoroughly prepared representation of Gounod's Romeo and Juliet on Saturday with that of the scratch performance of Don Giovanni two nights before. In every sort of merit that an opera can have, Don Giovanni is as superior to Romeo as a sonnet by Shakespeare to a sonnet by Adelaide Procter; yet on Thursday the house was bored and distraught, wheras on Saturday it was alert and interested. Everything on the stage had been thought about and practised: everybody there was in earnest and anxious. The result was that an opera with an established reputation for tedium became engrossing where another opera, with an established reputation for inexhaustible variety and vivacity, had just fallen flat. Many persons went about asking why Romeo had never been a success before. The question implied too much; for, after all, the opera has had its measure of success in the past. Further, it is quite true that the work is monotonous in its mood. One greatly misses the relief which Mephistopheles gives to Faust. No doubt when you first fall under the spell of the heavenly melody, of the exquisite orchestral web of sound colors, of the unfailing dignity and delicacy of accent and rhythm, you certainly do feel inclined to ask whether the people who disparaged the work were deaf. Not until you have had your fill of these, and have realized that there is nothing more coming, do you begin to look at your watch. On Saturday the watch would have come out sooner and oftener but for M. Jean de Reske [Polish baritone, then tenor, 1850–1925]. He is an artist who cannot be described in a few words. Though a highly intelligent one at his best, he has moments of *naïveté*—not to say stupidity—which seems to run in his gifted family. Again, though he does everything with a distinction peculiar to himself, there is an exasperatingly conventional side to his posing and playing across the footlights. And though he has the true dramatic instinct, and does really throw himself into his part, yet he is not consistently an actor: for instance, no human being—except perhaps a sexton—ever entered a tomb at midnight in the fashion illustrated by him in the fifth act on Saturday night. I do not believe in ghosts; but if I had occasion to visit a mausoleum, even in the daytime, I should not come bounding into it. Under such circumstances one refrains from gamboling until one's eyes get accustomed to the dim light. The charm of De Reske lies in the beauty of his voice, his sensitively good pronunciation, and the native grace and refinement of his bearing, all of which make his manliness, his energy, and his fire quite irresistible. The charm of the man may be separated from the interest in his performance, which is created almost entirely by his declamation. In the pretty duet, the Madrigal which practically begins Romeo's part, he did not make much effect; but when he exclaimed "O douleur! Capulet est son père; et je l'aime!" the effect was electric. At the end of the balcony scene his half-whispered "Adieu, jusqu'à demain—jusqu'à demain," will surely be remembered by many a woman in the audience. His acting in the duel scene, uneven as it was, was convincing; and he rose to eloquence in the scene which follows the sentence of exile from the Duke: a scene newly written by Gounod. Madame Melba [Australian soprano with vocal range of 2½ octaves, 1861–1931] may thank her stars that she had so good a Romeo to help her out in the last two acts. At one or two points in the balcony scene she sang with genuine feeling; and in the tragic scenes she was at least serious and anxious to do her best. In the first act, however, she was shrill and forward, the waltz *arietta* coming out with great confidence and facility, which I think Madame Melba mistook for art. Her fresh bright voice and generally safe intonation are all in her favor at present. Mlle Jeanne de Vigne phrased *Que fais-tu, blanche tourterelle* nicely, and would have got an *encore*—which she evidently wanted badly—had she been content with the simple run up to C and down again of which Gounod made such a perfect ornament. But she *would* try to improve the final phrase; and as her taste is not quite as fine as Gounod's, the *encore* was nipped in the bud, which I think served her right. Madame Lablache [Emilie Glossop de Méric-Lablache: French mezzo, 1830–1901] had, of course, no trouble with the part of the nurse. Mr Winogradow [Mikhail Vinogradov, Russian baritone], as Mercutio, shewed all the symptoms of a short life and a merry one as a singer. No man can, without wrecking his voice, sing on the plan of delivering every note with the utmost possible intensity and vehemence. Unless Mr Winogradow pulls in at once, and learns to get at least nine out of ten of his effects quietly, Covent Garden will soon know him no more. M. Montariol [French tenor, 1859–1894] (Tybalt) was as good as his word, as far as improving the ensemble went, though he should have done this without saying anything about it. He played his second-rate party like a first-rate artist, just as he has occasionally played first-rate parts like a second-rate artist. Also he fenced so perfectly that Romeo was able to go for him quite recklessly; and this, of course, is the explanation of the nonsense about his condescending to play Tybalt. If he had not Brer Jean would now be awaiting his trial for manslaughter. M. Séguin [French bass-baritone, 1854–1942] also helped materially by playing Capulet. But the honors among the basses went, of course, to Edouard de Reske [baritone, 1853–1917], who had tremendous time of it as Friar Laurence. The family *naïveté* already hinted at peeped out in such brilliant readings as *Dieu, qui fit l'homme à ton image*, delivered in the stentorian manner of masterbuilders when they seek the ear of a bricklayer on a very high scaffold, and the magic word *femme* marked by sudden subsidence to a tenderly respectful *pianissimo*. But the marriage service and the potion scene delighted the audience; and a special cheer was always received for Frère Edouard when the rest, having passed before the curtain, left him—he coming last—for a moment in sole possession of the proscenium.

10. Trovatore and the Huguenots

The World, 4 June 1890

Last week I mildly suggested that the usual combination of a new *prima donna* with an old opera was a little hard on the critics. The words were still wet from the pen when I received a stall for Madame Tetrazzini's first appearance as Leonora in [Verdi's] Il Trovatore. Now a subscription night Trovatore is a dreadful thing. This is not an explosion of Wagnerian prejudice. I know my Trovatore thoroughly, from the first drum-roll to the final chord of E flat minor, and can assert that it is a heroic work, capable of producing a tremendous effect if heroically performed. But anything short of this means vulgarity, triviality, tediousness, and failure; for there is nothing unheroic to fall back on—no comedy, no spectacle, no symphonic instrumental commentary, no relief to the painful flood of feeling surging up repeatedly to the most furious intensity of passion; nothing but love—elemental love of cub for dam and male for female—with hate, jealousy, terror, and the shadow of death throughout. The artists must have immense vital energy, and a good deal of Salvini's skill in leading up to and producing a convincing illusion of terrible violence and impetuosity, without wrecking themselves or becoming ridiculous. At no point can the stage manager come to the rescue if the artists fail. Mr Harris has secured the success of [Meyerbeer's] Les Huguenots, Faust, [Wagner's] Die Meistersinger, and [Rossini's] William Tell by drill and equipment, costume and scenery; but for Il Trovatore he can do nothing but pay band, conductor, and principals, let them loose on the work in his theatre, and sit looking at them, helpless. Unless, indeed, he were to go down next day and read out the unfavorable press notices to them, emphasizing the criticism with the homely eloquence of which he is a master.

On Saturday week Trovatore was batoned by Bevignani, concerning whom some of my fresher colleagues came out last winter (in dealing with the Promenade Concerts at Her Majesty's) with the goodnatured and entirely novel idea that he is a superb conductor—rather an important secret to have kept itself for twenty years if there is really anything very serious in it. The conductor at Covent Garden ought to be nothing less than the greatest in the world; and the truth is that Mr Harris's three conductors, with all their considerable merits, would not, if rolled into one, make a Richter or a Faccio [Italian composer and conductor, 1840–1891]. Therefore I am not going to trifle with an old and sincerely respected public acquaintance by joining in the latest chorus of "Good old Bevignani." I shall even venture to ask him why he takes an impulsive *allegro* like *Mal reggendo* at an easy andante, and whether he really thinks Verdi meant *Perigliarti ancor* as an allegretto when he marked it *velocissimo*? But worse things than these befell Verdi. The young bloods of the string band, nursed on the polyphony of Wagner and Brahms, treated the unfortunate Trovatore as mere banjo work. They relieved the tedium of their task by occasional harmless bursts of mock enthusiasm, usually ending in a smothered laugh and a relapse into weariness, until they came to the hundred and forty bars, or thereabouts, of slow and sentimental *pizzicato* to the tune of *Si la stanchezza* in the prison scene. This proved too much for their sense of duty. Languishing over their fiddles, they infused a subtle ridicule into their toneless "pluck-pluck, pluck-pluck" that got the better of my indignation. It was impossible to help laughing. But why had not Bevignani shewed these young gentlemen that there is room for their finest touch and most artistic phrasing in Verdi's apparently simple figures of accompaniment, and that a band which cannot play a simple prelude of nine common chords with even the prosaic virtue of simultaneous attack, much less with the depth and richness of tone upon which the whole effect depends, is not in a position to turn up its nose at Italian opera, or any other style of instrumental composition? As for the poor silly public, it yawned and looked at its watch, quite ready to vote Verdi empty, stale, and played out, but incapable of suspecting perfunctoriness and tomfoolery in a precinct where evening dress is indispensable.

As to the singing, there was a tenor who was compendiously announced as "Signor Rawner [Polish tenor, 1858–1930], who has created so great a sensation in Italy," and who is undoubtedly capable of making an indelible mark anywhere. I listened expectantly for *Deserto sulla terra*, knowing that if the sensationist were a fine artist, his interpretation of its musical character would surround it with illusion, making it come from among the trees in the moonlight, soft, distant, melancholy, haunting; wheras, if he were the common or Saffron Hill Manrico, he would at once display his quality by a stentorian performance in the wing, putting all his muscle and wind into a final B flat (substituted for G), and storming

London with that one wrong note alone. My suspense was short. Signor Rawner, knowing nothing about the musical character of the serenade, but feeling quite sure about the B flat, staked his all on it; and a stupendous yell it was. It is said that he can sing D; and though he mercifully refrained from actually doing so, I have not myself the smallest doubt that he could sing high F in the same fashion if he only tried hard enough. As may be inferred, I do not like Signor Rawner, in spite of the sensation he has created in Italy: therefore let me not do him the injustice of pushing my criticism into further detail. Madame Tetrazzini [1871–1940], with her tip-tilted nose, her pretty mouth, her ecstatic eyes, her delicately gushing style, and the intense gratitude of her curtsy whenever she brought down the house, did very well as Leonora, though I would suggest to her that *D'amor sull' ali rosee* might have been encored had she chosen her breathing places with some regard for the phrasing, and either restored Verdi's *cadenza*, or at least omitted that flagrant pianoforte sequence (G, B, A, G, &c.) from the one she substituted.

As Valentine in The Huguenots she did not improve on her first attempt. Her Italian tremolo and stage hysteria were so intensified that but few of her notes had any definite pitch; whilst her playing was monotonously lachrymose from end to end. When she sings in the manner of a light soprano, and so steadies her voice for a moment, everybody is pleased; but when she becomes "dramatic" the charm vanishes. And yet you cannot get these Italian ladies to believe this. The more we shew by our encouragement of Miss Nordica [American soprano, 1857–1914], Miss Russell [1864–1935], and Miss Macintyre [1865–1943], and by our idolatry of Madame Patti [coloratura, 1843–1919] with her eternal Home, Sweet Home, that our whole craving is for purity of tone and unwavering accuracy of pitch, the more our operatic visitors insist on desperately trying to captivate us by paroxysms of wobbling. Remonstrance, in English at least, is thrown away on them.

For example, although Ravelli [tenor, born 1848], who appeared as Elvino on Thursday, is no Rubini [Italian bel canto tenor, 1794–1854], yet the delight of the house at escaping from the detested *tremolo*, and hearing some straightforward, manly singing, was so extravagant, that he was recalled uproariously three times.

Miss Russell's Violetta [character in Verdi's *La Traviata*], a part in which the *tremolo* rages throughout Europe worse than the influenza, is a triumph of good singing. Hard as it is to drag me to Covent Garden oftener than my bare duty requires, I would go again to hear her sing *Parigi, o cara* [from *La Traviata*] as she sang it on Saturday last. Madame Fursch-Madi [Victorine Fource: 1847–1894] has not Miss Russell's youth and beauty, but she never wobbles and never fails. The idolized De Reszkes sing like dignified men, not like male viragos. But do you suppose that Madame Tetrazzini or Signor Rawner will take the hint, or that Dufriche [baritone, born 1848: director at the Met, 1908], the St Bris of Tuesday week, will cease to discount the beautiful quality of his voice by a laborious *vibrato*? Not a bit of it: they will only wonder at the simplicity of our insular taste, and modestly persist in trying to teach us better.

The Huguenots, admirably rehearsed, goes without a hitch. Ybos [Guillaume Ibos, French tenor, 1860–1952], another new tenor, with a much better forehead and brow (to put the point as delicately as possible) than the usual successor to Mario, appeared as Raoul; and though he did not attempt the C sharp in the duel septet, any more than Madame Tetrazzini ventured on the chromatic run through two octaves in the fourth act, he came off with honor, in spite of the shyness which hampered his acting. In the absence of a first-rate *basso profundo*, Edouard de Reszke was forced to repeat the double mistake of relinquishing the part of St Bris, which fits him to a semitone, and taking that of Marcel, which lies too low for him. He has to alter the end of the chorale, and to produce the effect of rugged strength by an open brawling tone which quite fails to contrast with the other bass and baritone voices as Meyerbeer intended. D'Andrade [baritone, 1859–1921], too, whose voice is only effective (I had almost said only tolerable) when he is singing energetically between his upper B flat and G, repeatedly transposes passages an octave up, quite ruining the variety and eloquence of Never's declamation in the conspiracy scene. It is hardly necessary to add that every artist brought his or her own *cadenza*; but as none of them were quite so accomplished as Meyerbeer in this sort of composition, they only spoiled the effect they might have produced by sticking to the text. All these drawbacks notwithstanding, the performance reached a high degree of excellence; and the instrumental score was played (under Bevignani) with great spirit and accuracy.

Madame Gerster [Hungarian soprano, 1855–1920] has grown mightily since June 1877. Her columnar neck and massive arms are now those of Brynhild rather than Amina; and I am afraid that her acting, though it was touchingly good, did not reconcile the Philistines to the incongruity. I see, too, that the comparative ineffectiveness of her *Ah! non giunge* [*La Sonnambula*], and a certain want of ringing quality in her extreme upper notes, are being cited as results of the loss of voice which placed her for awhile in the position of George Eliot's *Armgart* [the title of a poem featuring a *prima donna*, published in *The Legend of Jubal and Other Poems*, 1874]. But the *Ah! non giunge* fell equally flat in 1877; and her Astrifiammante in that year shewed exactly the same want of the delicate tintinnabulation which was so enchanting in Di Murska's singing of *Gli angui d' inferno* ["der Hölle Rache" from *Die Zauberflöte*]. I could detect no falling off that the lapse of fourteen years does not account for; and the old artistic feeling remained so unspoiled and vivid, that if here and there a doubt crossed me whether the notes were all reaching the furthest half-crown seat as tellingly as they came to my front stall, I ignored it for the sake of the charm which neither singer nor opera has lost for me. The pre-eminent claims of Covent Garden again compel me to leave the concerts aside for the moment; but next week St James's Hall and its legion pianists shall have their due without fail.

11. Signor Lago's Opera Season

29 October 1890

Signor Lago's enterprise at Covent Garden looked unpromising on the first night. The opera was Aïda: but the artists were nervous and unwelcomed; the dresses misfitted horribly; the chorus of Egyptian priests looked more like a string of sandwich-men than ever; the carpenters' department was so short-handed that the audience whistled "We wont go home till morning" and the Marseillaise whilst the last scene was being built; and there was a perfect plague of interruption from a contingent of Italians, who insisted on shouting Brava, and drowning the orchestral endings of all the songs by premature applause, in spite of smoldering British indignation. And Bevignani, as I hinted last week, did no more for Verdi than barely keeping the band and the singers together. In vain such written entreaties as *p p p p p, estremamente* piano, and the like appealed to him from the score: the bluff *mezzo forte* never varied two degrees the whole evening. For *crescendos* we had undignified little hurry-scurries of *accelerandos*; and for the deep rich flood of harmony, which should sometimes make itself felt rather than heard through the silence, and sometimes suffuse everything with its splendor, we had shallow, blaring street music and prosaic *mezzo forte* as aforesaid. Once or twice the real Verdi color glowed for a moment through the fog: for instance, in the accompaniment for three flutes in the fourth act; but that was due solely to the initiative of the players. When the conductor's guidance was needed, as it was very conspicuously by the gentleman who played the *obbligato* to *Gia i sacerdoti adunanzi* [from Verdi's *Aida*] on a saxophone, and who quite missed the pathetic dignity of its tragic measure, the conductor galloped placidly after him as if the saxophone were doing all that could reasonably be expected of it. As to the majestic but tremendously grave and self-contained address of the captive Ethiopian King to his Egyptian conqueror, I turn in despair from Bevignani to Galassi [baritone, 1845–1904], and ask him to consider the words—to listen for a moment to the music—and then to say whether he really considers that Verdi intended Amonasro to behave like a bedlamite Christy Minstrel. When one remembers Faccio and the Scala orchestra, it is hard to have to go back to the drum-slammings and blarings and rantings of the bad old times, which can only be mended now by their survivors, Signori Bevignani and Galassi among others, taking warning by the bankruptcy in which they ended. I hoped that fairer treatment might have awaited Il Trovatore; but I am afraid I shall appear smitten with Bevignanophobia if I dwell on what actually occurred. Whether the conductor had made a bet that he would get through the opera in the shortest time on record or not, I do not know: certain it is that the concerted music was taken at a speed which made all artistic elaboration, all point, all self-possession, even bare accuracy, impossible. Bevignani only drew rein once, and that was when, at the end of the first scene of the second act, his eye suddenly caught the word *velocissimo* in the score. At first the slipping, scrambling, and bewilderment of the artists amused me; then I became indignant; and at last the continual jarring and baulking got on my nerves, so that I fled, exhausted and out of temper. But for the relief afforded by the solos, during which the band followed the singers, I should not have held out so long. And I need hardly add that the burden of my grumbling as I went home was that it is all very well to appeal to the critics to encourage cheap opera, but that opera without artistic interpretation is dear at any price, and will soon drive the eighteenpenny god back to the Lyric, where Audran [French composer, 1840–1901] as handled by Mr Caryll [Félix Marie Henri Tilkin: 1861–1921] seems a great composer in comparison with Verdi as handled by Bevignani, who should really devote himself for the future to English oratorio.

On Monday night there was a vast improvement. Arditi [Italian composer and conductor, 1822–1903], as alert as the youngest man in the band, and, what is more, quite as anxious, conducted Les Huguenots, which only needs a little better stage-management to be as presentable as it is in the summer season. For instance, when Marcel enters in the Pré-aux-Clercs scene, and the Catholics insist that he shall take off his hat, whilst the Huguenot soldiers maintain that he is right to keep it on, it is hardly reasonable in the Catholics to remain covered whilst the soldiers carefully take off their helmets, under a vague impression that somebody ought to do something of the sort. I am no bigot, and have never complained of the Catholics first joining in the Rataplan Chorus, with its gibes at i Papisti, and then returning to the bosom of their church for the Ave Maria. Still I do not think that these things should be done when there is no musical gain thereby. Perhaps I am inconsistent; but it is odd how one strains at a gnat and swallows a camel at Covent Garden. In Il Trovatore, for instance, it seemed quite natural to me that a horde of bloodthirsty feudal retainers should break into a convent yard without causing the assembled nuns to exhibit the faintest concern; because, after all, the thing occurs every season. But when the gypsy blacksmiths the other night deposited a glowing bar with its red-hot end on a wooden chair, where it lay during the rest of the act without either cooling itself or damaging the furniture, I could not help feeling that the illusion of the scene was gone.

On the pecuniary prospects of Signor Lago's enterprise I have only to say that if it fails, the failure will be due to the superstition that the primary function of Italian opera is to provide a means of passing the evening for a clique of deadheads in evening dress. The Covent Garden house is a vast auditorium to which hosts of people would willingly pay from two to five shillings a head to be admitted. But these persons would drive out the deadhead, and cause his stalls and boxes to be replaced by plebeian chairs or even benches. On the other hand, ten "commercial gents," each with his missis or young woman, at two shillings a head, would bring in £2 solid cash (*non olet!*) into the treasury; wheras the one languid deadhead, who keeps them out at present, brings nothing. As to that crow's nest in the roof, where you can now swelter and look at the crowns of the performers' hats for eighteenpence, that is not cheap: it would be dear at a shilling: sixpence is the proper price for such a place. It seems to me that Signor Lago, like all his forerunners in this direction, is trying to sit down between two stools. A cheap imitation of the regular fashionable season is impossible. It never pays to charge exclusive prices except when the West End guarantees the inevitable loss for the sake of the exclusiveness. Let me clinch the argument with one statistical fact. Only thirtynine out of every thousand of us die worth as much as £300, including the value of every stick and shred we possess. The moment you propose to do without the West End subsidy this fact forces you back to Drury Lane prices, no matter what the "traditions" of your entertainment may be.

Signor Lago's vocal artists are by no means ill selected. If he were as lucky in his stage managers and conductors as in his singers, his performances would be rather better all round than three out of four of last season's subscription nights. Perotti [Julius Prott: German tenor, 1849–1901] is a vigorous and intelligent tenor, prompt and to the point with his stage business to a degree which contrasts very favorably with Jean de Reszke's exasperating unpunctuality and irresolution, and gifted with ringing high notes of genuine tenor quality. And if he would but reconsider his pink-and-white makeup, and tone down the terrible smile with which he expresses amorous sentiments, he would escape those incongruous reminiscences of the ballet which one or two passages of his Raoul evoked. Giannini [tenor, 1868–1948] is unsuited to heroic parts, much as Mr Tupman [Dickens' *Pickwick Papers*] was unsuited to the costume of a bandit. He can shout high notes without wobbling; but he has so far shewn absolutely no other qualification for his eminent position. The sisters Giulia and Sofia Ravogli [1865–1910] are two children of nature who have, by dint of genuine feeling for their art, contrived to teach themselves a great deal; but their Tuscan is full of nasal and throaty intonations abhorred of the grand school; and they indulge in unheard-of *naïvetés* (especially Giulia—Sofia has more *savoir faire*) when they come out of their parts to acknowledge applause, which they are apt to do at the most absurd moments. Further, they trust to luck rather than to skill for getting over florid difficulties; and their metrical sense is particularly untrained: they hardly ever sing a scale with the accents on the right notes. Giulia, the worse offender in this respect also, sang *Strida la vampa* [from *Il Trovatore*] as if every two bars of the three-eight time were one bar of common time. These are matters, fortunately, admitting of remedy. The main point is that Giulia thinks out her parts for herself and acts them courageously and successfully. Her Azucena was a striking performance, though I advise her to give up such little originalities, new but not true, as frankly presenting herself as a fine young *contadina* of eighteen, and laughing ironically as she repeats *Strana pieta! Strana pieta!* [also from *Trovatore*]. Her voice is an ample mezzo-soprano, a little hollow and disappointing in the lower registers, where one expects the tone to be rich, but sympathetic all over, and very free and effective at the top. Sofia is a soprano, with much less spontaneity of utterance and dramatic expression, though she, too, feels her business strongly. Her voice, too, is smaller: indeed, it is hardly enough, used as she uses it, for so large a theatre. She was nervous in Aïda and overweighted in Trovatore; so that she cannot be said to have done much more than hold her own; wheras her sister has made a decided success. Madame Stromfeld [soprano Stromfeld-Klamrzynska, Aleksandra: 1859–1946] who appeared as Marguerite de Valois in Les Huguenots, is blonde, plump, and over thirty. She has a phenomenal range upward, and is apparently a highly cultivated musician and experienced singer. It is a pity to have to add that the freshness of the voice is gone, except at the top, where some of the more impossible notes are remarkably brilliant. Mlle Maria Peri, aided by youth, screamed her way through Valentine, barely holding the C in the duet with Marcel for half its appointed duration, and occasionally forcing her chest register up to middle A, a fourth higher than she can afford, if she wishes to keep her voice. And here I must drop the Opera for this week, as I have other matters to record.

Sarasate [Spanish violinist, 1844–1908], set up by the autumn holiday, left all criticism behind him at his first concert on Saturday week. He also left Mr Cusins behind by half a bar or so all through the two concertos, the unpremeditated effects of syncopation resulting therefrom being more curious than delectable. Bertha Marx [1859–1925] gave a recital on Thursday. It was very brilliant, and brilliant in a sympathetic way; but O, Miss Bertha, if you would only mix just a little thought with the feeling now and then! Essipoff [1851–1914] gave her first concert at Steinway Hall on the same evening. I see that Mr Kappey is going to give a lecture today (Tuesday) at the Chelsea Town Hall on military music. I hope he will, with Colonel Shaw-Hellier's assistance [4th Dragoon Guards, Commandant of the Royal Military School of Music], succeed in wakening people up to the importance of having plenty of good wind bands among us. That is the sort of music that really attracts the average Briton to take up an instrument himself.

12. Jack-Acting

The World, 17 December 1890

One cannot but admire Mr Richter Temple's independence and enterprise in trying back to Gounod and Molière as a relief to Cellier [conductor and composer of *Dorothy*, Lucy Shaw's opera: 1844–1891] and Stephenson [dramatist (pen name Bolton Rowe) and librettist of *Dorothy*: 1839–1906]. His Mock Doctor company, however, shews how superficial are the accomplishments of the artists (save the mark!) who run about the country in light-opera companies. To perform all the latest works in their line no very great technical skill is needed: good looks, a certain felicity of address, and suffi-cient natural aptitude for music qualify any young person to play principal parts. At the Savoy we are highly amused by what we indulgently call the acting; but we have only to pro-nounce the magic word Molière, and think of the Théâtre Français, to recognize at once that this "acting" is nothing but pure tomfoolery—"jack-acting," the Irish call it—wittily turned into a stage entertainment by Mr Gilbert.

I was at the gala performance of The Gondoliers the other night, and noticed two things: first, that the music was much more familiar to the band than to the composer, who con-ducted on that occasion; and second, that the representation did not involve a single stroke of skilled stage-playing. Mr Frank Wyatt's [singer and theatre manager, 1852–1926] success as the Duke of Plaza-Toro does not afford the faintest pre-sumption that he could manage three minutes of Sganarelle: Mr Courtice Pounds [1862–1927] and Mr Wallace Brownlow [baritone, 1861–1919] might win unbounded applause as Marco and Luiz a thousand times without knowing enough to enable them to walk half across the stage and make a bow in the character of Leandre. I do not say this as an advocate of the French system: I have always maintained that the English actor who grows his own technique is much to be preferred to the drilled French actor with his borrowed regulation equipment. But if the finished English actor's original art is better than the French actor's conventional art, the Frenchman has still the advantage of the Englishman who has "gone on the stage" without any conception of art at all—who has not only an untrained body and a slovenly tongue, but who, having walked and talked all his life without thinking about it, has no idea that action and speech are subjects for artistic culture. Such innocents, though they do not find engagements at the Garrick or the Haymarket, unfortunately get before the public in light opera very easily, if only they can achieve anything that will pass for singing. Indeed, I need not confine the statement to light opera.

The vulgarities and ineptitudes of Carl Rosaism pass unrebuked at Drury Lane, although, if the culprits were only actors, Mr Harris would scornfully recommend them not to venture north of the Surrey or west of the Pavilion until they had made themselves commonly presentable. Light opera gets the best of it; for all the pleasantest, funniest, and most gifted novices get snapped up by the Savoy, the Gaiety, the Prince of Wales's, and the Lyric, leaving the second-rate aspirants to the provinces for rough wear in grand opera (in English) or lighter work on tour with comic operas, according to their robustness and capacity. Under these circumstances I do not blame Mr Temple for failing to find a company capable of handling The Mock Doctor [a play by Henry Fielding, 1732] with the requisite skill and delicacy. No doubt he has done the best he could; but the result is not satisfactory. And I must say, even making the largest allowance for the incapacity of the performers, that I cannot see why so much of the concerted music should be absolutely discordant. It is always possible to be at least smooth and tuneful. Surely Mr Temple could obtain a more musicianly performance of that sextet if he cared enough for it to assert his authority. Still, on Thursday last, when I dropped unobtrusively into the pit, the audience, put in good humor by the irresistible flavor of Molière which hangs about Kenny's libretto, were very willing to be pleased. If Mr Temple's enterprise fails, it will not be the fault of the piece.

Maurel's lecture was, as everybody by this time knows, a great success. That is to say, everybody was there, and everybody seemed delighted. Nevertheless, my private opinion is that very few of the audience appreciated the situation sufficiently to feel the least urgency in what Maurel had to tell them. A certain eminent dramatic critic [William Archer] whom I consulted as I left the Lyceum said, with the air of a man who does not wish to be unkinder than he can help, that the lecture was "free from paradox." By this he meant that it struck him as truistic, not to say platitudinous. Happy man! to have to deal with a department of art in which the petty warfare of the critic is fully accomplished, leaving him free to devote his energy to the demand for a higher order of subject now that there is no further question of the necessity for intelligent and unified treatment of that subject, no matter what its order may be. After his round of the Lyceum, the Princess's, Haymarket, the Criterion, the Alhambra, the Olympic, and Drury Lane this pampered scribe hears Maurel insisting that operatic actors should study the psychology of their parts, and that the designers of stage costume and scenery should aim at producing an appropriate illusion as to the place and period assigned by the dramatist to the action of the piece; and his only comment is "Who disputes it?" How I should like to see him doing six weeks Italian Opera without the option of a fine! There he would find only one period, "the past," and only two places, "an exterior" and "an interior." In costume the varieties might prove more definite and numerous. I have often seen Marta [spelled Martha, opera by Flotow], in which Queen Anne is introduced alive, with the ladies in early Victorian Archery Club dresses, the Queen's retinue in the costume of feudal retainers of the Plantagenet period, the comic lord as Sir Peter Teazle, the noblemen in tunics and tights from Il Trovatore, and the peasants with huge Bavarian hats beneath their shoulders, reminding one of the men in Othello's yarns. As to La Traviata, with Violetta in the latest Parisian confections, and Alfredo in full Louis XIV. fig, that is familiar to every operagoer. Yet this by itself might matter no more than the Venetian costumes in Paul Veronese's Marriage in Cana, if it were ignorance, naïveté, convention, poetic license, or anything but what it is: to wit, sheer carelessness, lack of artistic conscience, cynical conviction that nothing particularly matters in an opera so long as the singers draw good houses.

When a special effort has to be made in the case of a practically new work, such as Romeo, [Wagner's] The Mastersingers, or Othello [operas by Bellini, Wagner, and Verdi], the exception only brings the rule into more glaring prominence; and too often the exception is in point of scenography (as Maurel puts it) rather than of psychology: that is, the scenepainter and costumier, stimulated by lavish managerial expenditure, think out their part of the opera, whilst the principal singers and the stage manager (if there is one) jog along in their old grooves. Clearly, then, Maurel's appeal, granted that from a dramatic critic it would be a mere knocking at an open door, is in the opera house a sort of Childe Roland's blast on the slughorn.

So much I have said to spare the feelings of the dramatic critics. Now I may add privately to Maurel that average dramatic criticism here is simply confusion made articulate, expressing the critic's likes and dislikes unintelligently and therefore unsystematically. It is all very well to say to Maurel "Well, what then? We knew all this before you were born." Suppose Maurel were to produce a sheet of paper, in the manner of Mephistopheles producing his bond, and to say "In that case, oblige me by allotting a hundred marks to Mr Beerbohm Tree, or any other actor whom you have criticized, in such a manner as to shew the proportion between his technical, his psychological, and his scenographic accomplishments; and append an estimate of the allowance to be made for your idiosyncratic bias for or against him." How many dramatic critics would be able to do more than exclaim piteously with [Dickens'] Barnacle junior, "Look here: you have no right to come this sort of move, you know"? If these gentlemen as much as suspected the existence of half the things that I have to pretend to know all about, and that Maurel has actually to do, they would transpose their remarks a tone or so down at future performances.

For my own part, I have no fault to find with the lecture, except on a point of history. All that about the Dark Ages and the barbarous Middle Ages is a modern hallucination, partly pious, partly commercial. There never were any Dark Ages, except in the imagination of the Blind Ages. Look at their cathedrals and their houses; and then believe, if you can, that they were less artistic than we who have achieved the terminus at Euston and the Gambetta monument. And to think that Maurel, of all men—Maurel, who was an architect before he went over to the lyric stage—should believe such a thing! However, he does not really believe it; for instead of following it up in the sequel, he turned right round in his tracks, and practically assumed that art has been going to the deuce ever since the Renascence.

I have no other exception to take to the lecture or to the vocal illustrations. The rôle of lecturer was never better acted since lecturing began. As far as one man, limited by a peculiar vocal technique and a strongly marked meridional temperament, could make his case complete he made it complete. The Verdi *nuance* he utters as if he were native and to the manner born; the Wagnerian *nuance*, like the Mozartian, he has to translate; and intelligently and skilfully as the translation is done it is to me still a translation. Iago and Rigoletto, with their intense moods and swift direct expression, come to life in him; but Wolfram and Don Juan, with their yearning northern abstract sentiment flowing with endless inflexions, only find in him a very able proxy.

I must return to the subject of the Hallé orchestra to chronicle a magnificent performance of Berlioz's Fantastic Symphony. At present no London band can touch this work at all, because no London band has learnt it thoroughly. We can get the notes played, and we sometimes do; but, as in the case of the first movement of the Ninth Symphony, only confusion and disappointment come of the attempt. Now the Manchester band, knowing the work through and through, handles it with a freedom, intelligence, and spirit which bring out all its life and purpose, and that, too, without giving the conductor any trouble. It is especially to be hoped that the orchestral students of the Royal College of Music who had a turn at the Harold Symphony in St James's Hall two days before were at this concert. If so, it must have helped them to realize how completely they were beaten, in spite of the highly praiseworthy degree of skill they have attained in using their instruments, and the excellent drill they are getting in *ensemble* playing.

The singing of the Royal College pupils bore eloquent testimony to the fund of negative advice available at the institution. One could see with half an eye how earnestly the young vocalists had been told what not to do—as, for instance, not to press on the notes with their breath, not to force the tone, not to sing with effort, and so on. If the College only succeeds presently in securing some teacher who can also tell the pupils what to do, they will soon begin to shew signs of knowing how to sing. At present they seem to me to be hardly more advanced than M. Jourdain was in fencing after his instructor had informed him that the two main points in practising that art are—first, to hit your adversary, and second, to avoid being hit by him.

Mr Boscovitz's recital at Steinway Hall last week was unusually well worth hearing. He had a spinet and a harpsichord, both of them really fine instruments of their sort; and on them he played a number of old pieces, from Bull's Carman's Whistle to the Harmonious Blacksmith, occasionally repeating one, with detestable but interesting effect, on a Steinway grand, which is about as like a harpsichord as an oboe is like a Boehm flute, or a bassoon like a euphonium. If Mr Boscovitz repeats this recital, or lecture, he will do well to complete it by also using a clavichord, if he can get one, as well as by securing a double harpsichord for Bach's Italian Concerto. His omission of the last two movements from this work considerably astonished the audience, in whose powers of endurance he seemed suddenly to lose faith. The *pianos* and *fortes* marked by Bach can only be produced on a harpsichord with two manuals. If Mr Boscovitz cannot obtain such an instrument, he should explain the matter in defence of his own playing; for I confess I did not know what was wrong until Mr Fuller Maitland told me; and without this warning I should certainly have ignorantly pitched into Mr Boscovitz for not attending to Bach's directions.

13. A Non-Mozartian Don

The World, 13 May 1891

Ever since I was a boy I have been in search of a satisfactory performance of Don Giovanni; and I have at last come to see that Mozart's turn will hardly be in my time. I have had no lack of opportunities and disappointments; for the Don is never left long on the shelf, since it is so far unlike the masterpieces of Wagner, Berlioz, and Bach, that cannot be done at all without arduous preparation. Any opera singer can pick up the notes and tumble through the concerted pieces with one eye on the conductor: any band can scrape through the orchestral parts at sight. Last year and the year before, it was tried in this fashion for a night at Covent Garden, with d'Andrade as Don Juan, and anybody who came handy in the other parts. This year it has been recognized that trifling with Mozart can be carried too far even for the credit of the Royal Italian Opera.

At the performance last Thursday, the first three acts of the four (twice too many) into which the work is divided at Covent Garden shewed signs of rehearsal. Even the last had not been altogether neglected. In the orchestra especially the improvement was marked. Not that anything very wonderful was accomplished in this department: the vigorous passages were handled in the usual timid, conventional way; and the statue music, still as impressive as it was before Wagner and Berlioz were born, was muddled through like a vote of thanks at the end of a very belated public meeting. But the overture was at least attentively played; and in some of the quieter and simpler numbers the exhalations of the magical atmosphere of the Mozartian orchestra were much less scanty and foggy than last year, when I could not, without risk of being laughed at, have assured a novice that in the subtleties of dramatic instrumentation Mozart was the greatest master of them all. The cast was neither a very bad nor a very good one. Its weakest point was the Leporello of Isnardon. Lacking the necessary weight in the middle of his voice, as well as the personal force demanded by the character, he was quite unable to lead the final section of the great sextet, *Mille torbidi pensieri*, which, thus deprived of its stage significance, became a rather senseless piece of "absolute music." Again, in *O statua gentilissima*, he hardly seized a point from beginning to end.

Now if an artist has neither voice enough nor musical perception enough to interpret forcibly and intelligently such an obvious and simple dramatic transition as that which follows the incident of the statue nodding acceptance of the invitation to supper, he is not fit to meddle with Mozart. Isnardon certainly makes a considerable show of acting throughout the opera; but as he is only trying to be facetious—abstractly facetious, if I may say so—without the slightest feeling for his part, the effect is irritating and irrelevant. Such pieces of business as his pointing the words, *Voi sapete quel che fa*, by nudging Elvira with his elbow at the end of *Madamina*, almost make one's blood boil. Poor old Sganarelle-Leporello, with all his failings, was no Yellowplush [a caricature serialized in *Fraser's Magazine*, 1837–8]: he would not have presumed upon a familiarity of that character with Donna Elvira, even if she had been a much meeker and less distinguished person than Molière made her. There is one man in Mr Harris's company whose clear artistic duty it is to play Leporello; and he, unfortunately, is an arrant *fainéant*, whose identity I charitably hide under the designation of Brother Edouard, which, I need hardly add, is not that under which he appears in the bills. In Leporello he would have one of the greatest parts ever written, exactly suited to his range, and full of points which his musical intelligence would seize instinctively without unaccustomed mental exertion. And now that I have begun sketching a new cast, I may as well complete it. *Dalla sua pace* is not an easy song to sing; but if Jean de Reszke were to do it justice, the memory thereof would abide when all his Gounod successes were lapsed and lost.

With Giulia Ravogli [contralto, born 1866] as Zerlina, and the rest of the parts allotted much as at present, a tremendous house would be drawn. Nevertheless the tremendous house would be bored and kept late for its trains unless the representation were brought up to date by the following measures. Take a pot of paste, a scissors and some tissue paper, and start on the *recitativo secco* by entirely expunging the first two dialogues after the duel and before *Ah, chi mi dice mai*. Reduce all the rest to such sentences as are barely necessary to preserve the continuity of the action. Play the opera in two acts only. And use the time thus gained to restore not only the Don's song, *Metà di voi*, which Faure used to sing, but, above all, the last three movements of the second *finale*, thereby putting an end for ever to the sensational vulgarity of bringing down the curtain on the red fire and the ghost and the trapdoor. There are other suppressed pages of the score to be reconsidered—a capital song which gets Leporello off the stage after the sextet, a curiously old-fashioned tragic air, almost Handelian, for Elvira between *Là ci darem* and the quartet, and a comic duet for Zerlina and Leporello, one of the later Vienna interpolations, which, however, is a very dispensable piece of buffoonery.

To return to the actual Don Giovanni of Thursday last, I need say no more of Miss de Lussan, who does not grow more interesting as her voice loses freshness and sustaining power and her manner becomes perter and trickier, than that she is one of those Zerlinas who end *Batti, batti*, on the upper octave of the note written, as a sort of apology for having been unable to do anything else with the song. The effect of this suburban grace can be realized by anyone who will take the trouble to whistle Pop goes the Weasel with the last note displaced an octave.

I am sorry to add that alterations of Mozart's text were the order of the evening, every one of the singers lacking Mozart's exquisite sense of form and artistic dignity. Maurel [Victor Maurel, French baritone, 1848–1923], though he stopped short of reviving the traditional atrocity of going up to F sharp in the serenade, did worse things by dragging an F natural into the end of *Finch' han del vino*, and two unpardonable G's into the *finale* of the first ballroom scene, just before the final *stretto*, thereby anticipating and destroying the cli-

max *Odi il tuon* from the sopranos. Madame Tavary still clings
to that desolating run up and down the scale with which she
contrives to make the conclusion of *Non mi dir* ridiculous;
and Montariol, unable to evade *Il mio tesoro* by omitting it
like *Dalla sua pace,* did strange things with it in his desperation. His Ottavio was altogether a melancholy performance,
as he was put out of countenance from the beginning by being clothed in a seedy misfit which made him look lamentably
down on his luck. Mr Harris would not dream of allowing
such a costume to be seen on his stage in a modern opera; and
I must really urge upon him that there are limits to the application even of the principle that anything is good enough for
Mozart.

Maurel's Don Giovanni, though immeasurably better than
any we have seen of late years, is not to be compared to his
Rigoletto, his Iago, or, in short, to any of his melodramatic
parts. Don Juan may be as handsome, as irresistible, as adroit,
as unscrupulous, as brave as you please; but the one thing
that is not to be tolerated is that he should consciously parade
these qualities as if they were elaborate accomplishments instead of his natural parts. And this is exactly where Maurel
failed. He gave us a description of Don Juan rather than an
impersonation of him. The confident smile, the heroic gesture, the splendid dress, even the intentionally seductive vocal inflexion which made such a success of *Là ci darem* in spite
of Miss de Lussan's coquettish inanity, were all more or less
artificial. A Don Juan who is continually aiming at being Don
Juan may excite our admiration by the skill with which he
does it; but he cannot convince us that he is the real man. I remember seeing Jean de Reszke play the part when he had less
than a tenth of Maurel's present skill and experience; and yet
I think Mozart would have found the younger man the more
sympathetic interpreter.

It seems ungrateful to find fault with an artist who rescues
a great *rôle* from the hands of such ignoble exponents as the

common or Covent Garden Dons who swagger feebly through it like emancipated billiard-markers; but it would hardly be a compliment to Maurel to praise him for so cheap a superiority. And, indeed, there is no fault-finding in the matter. It is a question of temperament. When all is said, the fundamental impossibility remains that Maurel's artistic vein is not Mozartian. One or two points of detail may be mentioned. He was best in the love-making scenes and worst in those with Leporello, whom he treated with a familiarity which was rather that of Robert Macaire with Jacques Strop [from the 1885 comic opera *Ermine*] than of a gentleman with his valet. The scene of the exposure in the ballroom he played rather callously. Nothing in the score is clearer than that Don Juan is discomfited, confused, and at a loss from the moment in which they denounce him until, seeing that there is nothing for it but to fight his way out, he ceases to utter hasty exclamations of dismay, and recovers himself at the words *Ma non manca in me coraggio*. Maurel dehumanized and melodramatized the scene by missing this entirely, and maintaining a defiant and self-possessed bearing throughout.

And again, on the entry of the statue, which Don Juan, however stable his nerve may be imagined to have been, can hardly have witnessed without at least a dash of surprise and curiosity, Maurel behaved very much as if his uncle had dropped in unexpectedly in the middle of a bachelor's supper party. The result was that the scene went for nothing, though it is beyond all comparison the most wonderful of the wonders of dramatic music. But if the audience is ever to be cured of the habit of treating it as a sort of voluntary to play them out, it must be very carefully studied by the artist playing Don Juan, upon whose pantomime the whole action of the scene depends, since the statue can only stand with a stony air of weighing several tons, whilst the orchestra makes him as awful as the conductor will allow it. Since Maurel let this scene slip completely through his fingers, I do not see how he can be classed with the great Don Juans (if there ever were any great ones). The problem of how to receive a call from a public statue does not seem to have struck him as worth solving.

The Elvira (Madame Rolla), whose B flat at the end of her aria was perhaps the most excusable of all the inexcusable interpolations, was as good as gold, not indulging once in a scream, and relying altogether on pure vocal tone of remarkable softness. In *Mi tradi* she succeeded in being more pleasing than any Elvira I can remember except Di Murska, who understood the full value of the part and played it incomparably, like the great artist she was. Madame Rolla does not act with the force of Nilsson; and in the quartet she failed to bring off the effect at the end, where Elvira gets louder and angrier whilst the wretched Don gets more and more agitated by the dread of making a scene; but I think Maurel was a little unequal to the occasion here too. On the whole, Madame Rolla, whose voice reminds one somewhat of Marimon's, is a useful addition to the company. Mr Harris had better now turn his attention to achieving a really serious performance of Le Nozze di Figaro.

14. Incognita

The World, 12 October 1892

Now that we have five comic operas running, London perhaps feels satisfied. I, for one, do not want any more. Sufficient for me the privilege of living in the greatest city in the world, with five comic operas within easy reach, and not a symphony to be heard for love or money. However, it is a poor heart that never rejoices; and I have been doing my best to rejoice at the Royalty over The Baroness, and at the Lyric over Incognita. To Incognita especially I must be civil; for is it not financed by that great syndicate which has set about buying up the London press as the Viennese press has been bought up? Do not expect outspoken criticism from me in such days as these: I cannot afford it: I must look to the future like other journalists. Therefore the utmost I dare say against Incognita is that the more you see of it the less you like it, because the first act is better than the second, and the second much better than the third, which produces the effect of being the first act of some other comic opera. The piece has a plot turning upon some maze of Portuguese diplomacy; but I speedily lost my way in it, and made no attempt to extricate myself, though I was conscious of its boring me slightly towards the end of the performance. The music is quite Lecocquian: that is to say, it is cleverly scored, rises occasionally to the level of a really graceful *chansonette*, is mechanically vigorous in the *finales*, and calculatedly spirited in the frequent Offenbachian rallies, for which the old quadrille and galop prescription has been compounded with the old remorseless vulgarity.It is also Lecocquian in the speedy running dry of its thin fountain of natural grace and piquancy, and the eking out of the supply with machine-like *bouffe* music more and more as the opera proceeds. This remark does not apply to the third act, which is not by Lecocq at all, but by Mr Bunning, who, if I recollect aright, recently had a most tremendous tragic *scena* performed at the Crystal Palace by Mr Hamilton Clarke; and by the composer who conceals his identity under the exasperating name of Yvolde. I may add that the pretty stage pictures of the first act degenerate into the pecuniary garishness of the second in sympathy with the degeneration of the music; and with this I abandon all attempt at formal criticism, and proceed to discuss the affair at random.

To begin with Miss Sedohr Rhodes, she made all the usual American mistakes. First, by a well-worked battery of puff, she led us to expect so much from her that an angel from the spheres would have disappointed us; and then she arranged

an elaborate handing up of floral trophies across the footlights, in spite of the repeatedly proved fact that this particular method of manufacturing a success invariably puts up the
back of an English audience. I have never seen the American
flower show turned to good account by any prima donna except Miss Macintyre. One evening at Covent Garden, when
she was playing Micaela to the Carmen of an American dèbu-
tante, the two ladies appeared before the curtain simultaneously; and the contractor's men set to work at once to deliver
bouquets and wreaths. Carmen, overwhelmed with innocent
surprise at this spontaneous tribute from the British public,
gracefully offered a nosegay to Micaela, who quietly turned
her back and walked off the stage amid signs of thorough and
general approval which ought to have settled the question
of flowers or no flowers for all future American prima donnas. On Thursday night Miss Rhodes, though she entirely
failed to make herself first favorite on the merits of her performance, got so overloaded with trophies that she had to ask
Mr Wallace Brownlow to carry the last basket for her. He, being goodnatured, did not there and then inform her publicly
that he was not her florist's porter; but if he had done so he
would, I imagine, have had the entire support of the house.
The puffs and the flowers were the more ill-judged in Miss
Rhodes's case because she had exactly that degree of talent
which playgoers, with cheap generosity, like to discover and
encourage when it is modestly and friendlessly presented to
them, wheras if it be thrust pretentiously upon them as first-
rate, they delight in taking it down a peg.

When Miss Rhodes stepped out of her sedan chair in the
first act she was for a few moments a complete success; for,
with her delicate skin, fine contours, slender fragile figure,
small hands and feet, and perfect dress, she was sufficiently
near the perfection of the ladylike ideal of beauty. Unfortunately, it presently appeared that she not only looked like a
Court beauty, but sang like one. Her voice, thin, and with

a flexibility which is only a quality of its fault, could not be fitted by her warmest admirer with any stronger adjective than prettyish. In order to substantiate her pretensions as a vocalist, she had to attempt a florid vocal waltz which was much too difficult for her, and which was only encored from a chivalrous desire to console her for the opposition of a party of malcontents who were, I must say, musically in the right, though they would have done wiselier to have kept silent. Her dancing, again, was rather pretty, but not extraordinary. She speaks in the American dialect, which I do not at all dislike; but her diction, though passable, has all the amateurish deficiency in force and style which we tolerate so weakly in our operatic *prima donnas*. On the other hand, the assurance with which she carried off her part in spite of her want of technical grip, and the courage with which she faced the opposition from the gallery, shewed that she is not lacking in force of character. I therefore conclude that she will improve with experience up to a certain point. To pass that point she will require something of the genius for her profession which is displayed so liberally by Miss Jenoure, who quite fulfilled the promise of her performance in The Mountebanks [Alfred Cellier, libretto W. S. Gilbert, 1892]. Her singing, from the purely musical point of view, is commonplace enough; but her dancing and pantomime are capital. Mr Wallace Brownlow made a very decided hit as the hero. He is a vigorous and handsome young man of the type which Kemble made fashionable in "the palmy days"; his voice is a genuine baritone, of good tone all over his range; he sings with fire and feeling, without any suicidal shouting; and he has abundant freshness, virility, humor, and activity. What he lacks is training in speech and movement: he is always off his balance, and is therefore only comfortable when he is hard at work at some stage business or other; and his diction is rough and ready, audible and intelligible certainly, but no more artistic than the diction of the Stock Exchange. Happily, these are eminently remediable faults; and when they are vanquished, Mr Hayden Coffin will have a rival all the more formidable because of the wide difference of style between them.

The tenor is Mr John Childs, whose vigorous B flat will be remembered by the patrons of Carl Rosa. It is still in stentorian condition; and though Mr Childs has a strong provincial tendency to bawl occasionally (if he will pardon the expression) and to concern himself very little about his tone and style when using the middle of his voice, the *encore* he won for the catching soldier's song in the first act was the heartiest of the evening. The opera is so strongly fortified by a squadron of comedians of established drollery and popularity that a great deal of thin and childish stuff becomes amusing in their hands. Mr Monkhouse, who has gained remarkably within the last two years in quietude and refinement of play without losing an inch of the breadth of his humor, was seconded by Miss Susie Vaughan in a stale and odious duenna part which she contrived to make not only bearable, but for the most part genuinely funny. The attempt to double the harlequinade in the third act by the introduction of a second comic king (Mr Fred Kaye) and a second comic old woman (Miss Victor) was not a success. Mr Kaye [well-known actor, died 1913] was certainly laughable in his surpassingly silly character; but Miss Victor, who had really no function in the piece at all, and had been engaged solely that she might repeat the vulgar business of her part in Miss Decima—a part entirely unworthy of her—cannot be congratulated this time.

The whole third act, however, is such a desperate and obvious makeshift that it would be mere affectation not to accept it, with its serpentine dance, pastoral symphony with transformation scene, and comic turns for Mr Monkhouse as a gypsy girl, &c., as a brilliant variety entertainment. The band is good, as it usually is at the Lyric; and the chorus, though not up to the Savoy level of refinement, would pass with credit if some of the men could be induced to refrain from shouting. Finally, let me say that the Lord Chamberlain, by licensing the second act of Miss Decima, has completely cleared himself of all suspicion of Puritanical intolerance. When I saw the audience laughing at the spectacle of a father, in nightcap and bedgown, chuckling as he listened at the door of his daughter's bridal chamber, I could not help feeling how vast an advance we had made since last year, when all London was supposed to have shuddered with horror at the wickedness of that scene in Ibsen's Ghosts, where the mother in the drawing room overhears her son kissing the housemaid in the dining room.

Mr Cotsford Dick's Baroness, at the Royalty, is not so well staged as Incognita, the management having evidently been compelled to accept what recruits they could get for the rank and file in the face of a heavy competition. On the whole, they have made the best of their circumstances; and the opera gets a tolerable chance. The book, which begins as a burlesque of King Lear, and proceeds on the lines of the Who's who? pattern of farce, is funny enough, especially in the Turkish-bath scene, until the third act, in which the tangled threads of the plot are unravelled in a rather butter-fingered way. The fact is, Mr Cotsford Dick, who is his own librettist, takes matters too easily and genially to turn out distinguished work; but he always manages to keep on pleasant terms with his audience. The music is lively and pretty, with plenty of Cotsford-Dickian ballads, and much unblushing borrowings from [Gilbert and Sullivan's] The Mikado and Trial by Jury, not to mention a vocal waltz of which the honors are divided between Gounod and Weber. The verses I need not describe, as Mr Dick's powers in that field are familiar to all my readers. The cast has been selected with a view to having the music sung rather than to having the opera played. Miss Giglio, who makes a considerable display as a vocalist, and is evidently quite conscious of being able to sing the heads off most comic-opera *prima donnas*, hardly seems to know that speech and action on the stage are arts not a whit less important and less difficult than fluent vocalization. Mr William Foxon, too, though rather above the usual stage mark as a tenor singer, is, to speak plainly, such a stick that it is difficult to believe that he has ever seriously studied and practised the business of the stage with a competent instructor. The principal tenor, Mr Charles Conyers [1861–1896], is an agreeably robust and good-looking young gentleman, no great artist dramatically, but a pleasant singer of ballads. Mr Magrath, familiar to us as the old knight in Cosi fan tutte [opera by Mozart] and the venerable barber of Bagdad in Cornelius's opera, flashes out in The Baroness as a dark-eyed handsome youth who might serve the President of the Royal Academy as a model for a young Italian noble. He was much more nervous over this comparatively trivial job than he shewed himself in his former far more difficult exploits; and his air of melodramatic exaggeration was not always humorously intentional: there was a touch in it of that traditional penny-plain-and-twopence-colored style which has left so many promising young artists fit for nothing better than the boundless absurdities and artistic shams of "English Opera" in the provinces. His drinking song in the last act was loudly applauded; but it would have been a much greater success if it had been sung with the easy self-possession of a gentleman at a ball, and not with the heroic stress of John of Leyden's Versez in the last act of [Meyerbeer's] Le Prophête. I take Mr Magrath the more specially to task on this point because he has improved in every other respect, and is likely to have an honorable career if he shuns the burnt-cork path along which I have seen so many well-equipped aspirants go down to their destruction. The fun of the opera was kept up vigorously by Mr Lionel Brough, Mr Fred Emney, Mr George Grossmith, junior, and Mr Charles

Stevens, a comedian whom I last saw, if I mistake not, at Bristol, where he was for some years a leading member of Mr Macready Chute's company.

I am informed that three other comic operas are in contemplation, in addition to the five already in full swing. I can quite believe it. The one business notion that theatrical managers have is that when the bank flourishes, then is the time to make a run on it.

15. The Third Act of Ernani

The World, 2 November 1892

The young English composer is having a good time of it just now, with his overtures and symphonies resounding at the Crystal Palace, and his operas at the Olympic. Mr Granville Bantock's [composer, 1868–1946] Cædmar is an enthusiastic and ingenious piece of work, being nothing less than an adaptation of all the most fetching passages in Wagner's later tragic music-dramas to a little poem in which Tristan, Siegmund, Siegfried, Hunding, Isolde, and Sieglinde are aptly concentrated into three persons. The idea is an excellent one; for in the space of an hour, and within a stone's-throw of the Strand, we get the cream of all Bayreuth without the trouble and expense of journeying thither. There is also, for the relief of anti-Wagnerians, an intermezzo which might have been written by the late Alfred Cellier or any other good Mendelssohnian.

The plot, as I understood it, is very simple. A pious knight-errant wanders one evening into the garden of Eden, and falls asleep there. Eve, having had words with her husband, runs away from him, and finds in the sleeping warrior the one thing lacking to her: to wit, somebody to run away with. She makes love to him; and they retire together. Elves appear on the deserted stage, and dance to the strains of the intermezzo.

They are encored, not because the audience is particularly charmed, but because Cavalleria [Rusticana] has put it into its head that to recognize and encore an intermezzo shews connoisseurship. Then the pair return, looking highly satisfied; and presently Adam enters and remonstrates. Ten minutes later the knight-errant is the sole survivor of the three, whereupon he prays the curtain down.

The whole affair is absurdly second-hand; but, for all that, it proves remarkable musical ability on the part of Mr Granville Bantock, who shews a thorough knowledge of the mechanism of the Wagnerian orchestra. If Cædmar had been produced as a newly discovered work by Wagner, everyone would have admitted that so adroit a forgery implied a very clever penman. After Cædmar, Signor Lago put up the third act of [Verdi's] Ernani.

Strange to say, a good many people did not wait for it.

Just imagine the situation. Here is a baritone singer, Signor Mario Ancona [1860–1931], who has attracted general notice by his performance of Telramund in [Wagner's] Lohengrin and Alfonso in [Donizetti's] La Favorita. Signor Lago accordingly mounts a famous scene, the classic opportunity for lyric actors of the Italian school (baritone variety), a scene which is not only highly prized by all students of Italian opera, but which had its dramatic import well taught to Londoners by the Comédie Francaise when they crowded to see Sarah Bernhardt as Doña Sol, and incidentally saw Worms as Charles V. In the play Charles is sublime in feeling, but somewhat tedious in expression. In the opera he is equally sublime in feeling, but concise, grand, and touching in expression, thereby proving that the chief glory of Victor Hugo as a stage poet was to have provided libretti for Verdi.

Every opera-goer who knows chalk from cheese knows that to hear that scene finely done is worth hearing all the Mephistopheleses and Toreadors that ever grimaced or swaggered, and that when a new artist offers to play it, the occasion is a first-class one. Yet, when Cædmar was over there was a considerable exodus from the stalls, as if nothing remained but a harlequinade for the children and the novices. "Now this" thought I "is pretty odd. If these people knew their Ernani, surely they would stay." Then I realized that they did not know their Ernani—that years of Faust, and Carmen, and Les Huguenots, and Mefistofele, and *soi-disant* Lohengrin had left them ignorant of that ultra-classical product of Romanticism, the grandiose Italian opera in which the executive art consists in a splendid display of personal heroics, and the drama arises out of the simplest and most universal stimulants to them.

Il Trovatore, Un Ballo [*un ballo in maschera*], Ernani, &c. [all operas by Verdi], are no longer read at the piano at home as the works of the Carmen *genre* are, and as Wagner's are. The popular notion of them is therefore founded on performances in which the superb distinction and heroic force of the male characters, and the tragic beauty of the women, have been burlesqued by performers with every sort of disqualification for such parts, from age and obesity to the most excruciating phases of physical insignificance and modern cockney vulgarity. I used often to wonder why it was that whilst every asphalt contractor could get a man to tar the streets, and every tourist could find a gondolier rather above the average of the House of Lords in point of nobility of aspect, no operatic manager, after Mario vanished, seemed to be able to find a Manrico with whom any exclusively disposed Thames mudlark would care to be seen grubbing for pennies. When I get on this subject I really cannot contain myself. The thought of that dynasty of execrable impostors in tights and tunics, interpolating their loathsome B flats into the beautiful melodies they could not sing, and swelling with conceit when they were able to finish *Di quella pira* [aria from *Il Trovatore*] with a high C capable of making a stranded man-of-war recoil off a reef into mid-ocean, I demand the suspension of all rules as to decorum of language until I have heaped upon them some little instalment of the infinite abuse they deserve. Others, alas! have blamed Verdi, much as if Dickens had blamed Shakespear for the absurdities of Mr Wopsle [in *Great Expectations*].

The general improvement in operatic performances of late years has taken us still further away from the heroic school. But in due time its turn will come. Von Bülow, who once contemptuously refused the name of music to Verdi's works, has recanted in terms which would hardly have been out of place if addressed to Wagner; and many who now talk of the master as of a tuneful trifler who only half-redeemed a misspent life by the clever artificialities which are added in Aida and Otello to the power and freedom of his earlier works, will change their tone when his operas are once more seriously studied by great artists.

For the present, however, it is clear that if Signor Mario Ancona wishes to interest the public, he must depend on character parts instead of heroic ones. His offer of Charles V. could hardly have been less appreciatively received. This was certainly no fault of his own; for he sang the opening *recitative* and cavatina well, and the solo in the great sestet, *O sommo Carlo*, very well. As a piece of acting his performance was a trifle too Italian-operatic; his fold of the arms and shake of the head when Ernani insisted on being beheaded was overmuch in the manner of Mr Lenville [in *Nicholas Nickelby*]; and there was too constant a strain throughout, since even in the third act of Ernani there are moments which are neither stentorian nor sentimental. But one does not expect a revolution in operatic acting to be achieved in a single night, especially in a part which is, to say the least, somewhat inflated; and, on the whole, Signor Ancona was more dignified and sincere than any experienced opera-goer had dared to hope.

The applause at the end was only moderately enthusiastic; but this was largely due to the carelessness of the management, which, instead of providing a book of the triple bill, left the audience entirely in the dark as to what the Ernani excerpt meant, and tried to effect separate sales of vocal scores of Cædmar and shilling books of L'Impresario [opera by Mozart] to elucidate the rest of the program. After which you felt that Signor Lago deserved anything that might happen to him in the way of the performance falling flat.

And the chances of Ernani were not improved by the modesty of Charles's coronation arrangements, or by the unkempt staginess of the conspirators, or by the fact that though the music had been rehearsed sufficiently to secure accuracy, no attempt was made to color and enrich the sombre depths of the orchestra. As to the choristers, they were allowed to bawl away in the old slovenly, rapscallionly fashion, on the easy assumption that, if the time came right and the pitch right (or thereabouts), the quality of tone and style of delivery did not matter two straws. When will Signor Lago pay a visit to our comic-opera houses with their English choruses, and realize that Queen Anne has been dead for some time now?

Der Schauspieldirektor, in the version known as L'Impresario, of course put all the rest of the entertainment into the shade. Every number in it is a masterpiece. The quartet would make a very handsome finale for any ordinary opera; the overture is a classic; the air *Quando miro quel bel ciglio* will last as long as Pergolesi's *Tre giorni son che Nina*, or Gluck's *Che farò senza, Euridice?* How far its finest qualities are above our heads, both before and behind the curtain, I need not say. The overture was scrambled through post-haste in the old exhilarating slapdash style, expressive of the idea that Mozart was a rattling sort of drunkard and libertine, tempered by the modern and infinitely more foolish notion that he was merely a useful model of academic form for students.

Mr G. Tate sang *Quando miro* in the person of Mozart himself. To shew how thoroughly he grasped the character he altered the last phrase so as to make the ending more "effective," much as, if he were a sculptor instead of a singer, he might alter the tails of the Trafalgar Square lions by sticking them up straight in order to make *their* endings more effective. This public announcement on Mr Tate's part that he considers himself a better judge of how a song should end than Mozart is something that he will have to live down. Unless, indeed, the real explanation be that Mr Tate is too modest, and succumbed, against his own better sense, to the bad advice which is always thrust upon young artists by people who have all the traditional abuses of the stage at their fingers' ends, and know nothing about art. And that is why, on the boards as off them, eminence is only attained by those whose strength of conviction enables them to do, without the least misgiving, exactly the reverse of what all the non-eminent people round them advise them to do. For naturally, if these non-eminents knew the right thing to do they would be eminent.

Of the performance generally, I have only to say that it has been well prepared and is really enjoyable. Mlle Leila, who played Mlle Herz, has a naturally good voice, which has been somewhat squeezed and wire-drawn by an artificial method; but she managed to hold her own in her very difficult part, which is worth hearing not only for its own sake, but for the very fine Mozartian aria which she introduces when asked by the Schauspieldirektor (Mr R. Temple) to give a sample of her powers.

I have to chronicle the resumption of the Monday and Saturday Popular Concerts, and to congratulate Señor Arbos on his playing in the adagio of Beethoven's quartet in E flat (Op. 74) at the opening concert, and Mlle Szumowska on her neat handling of the last three movements of the Pastoral Sonata. The first movement came to nothing, perhaps because Mlle Szumowska had a cold, perhaps because she has not a pastoral turn. Mlle Wietrowetz succeeds Señor Arbos this week as first violin.

16. Verdi's Falstaff

The World, 12 April 1893

Easter has afforded me an opportunity for a look through the vocal score of Verdi's Falstaff, now to be had at Ricordi's for sixteen shillings, a price which must obviously be reduced before the opera can get into the hands of the amateur at large. I did not go to Milan to hear the first performance for several reasons, the chief being that I am not enough of a first-nighter to face the huge tedium and probable sickness of the journey from Holborn to Basle (the rest I do not mind) in order merely to knock at the tradesman's door of Italy, so to speak, and turn back after hearing an opera half murdered by La Scala *prima donnas* with shattering tremolos, and witnessing a Grand Old Man demonstration conducted for the most part by people who know about as much of music as the average worshiper of Mr Gladstone does of statesmanship. In short, being lazy and heavily preoccupied, I cried sour grapes and stayed at home, knowing that the mountain would come to Mahomet soon enough.

Let it be understood, then, that since I have not been present at a complete performance of Falstaff I do not know the work: I only know some things about it. And of these I need not repeat what has already been sufficiently told: as, for instance, that Falstaff is a music-drama, not an opera, and that consequently it is by Shakespear, Boïto, and Verdi, and not by Verdi alone. The fact that it is a music-drama explains the whole mystery of its composition by a man eighty years old. If there were another *Il balen* [aria from Verdi's *Il Trovatore*] or *La donna è mobile* [aria from Verdi's *Rigoletto*] in it, I should have been greatly astonished; but there is nothing of the sort:

PART IV: OPERA AND OPERETTA

the fire and heroism of his earlier works blaze up now only on strong provocation.

Falstaff is lighted and warmed only by the afterglow of the fierce noonday sun of Ernani; but the gain in beauty conceals the loss in heat—if, indeed, it be a loss to replace intensity of passion and spontaneity of song by fulness of insight and perfect mastery of workmanship. Verdi has exchanged the excess of his qualities for the wisdom to supply his deficiencies; his weaknesses have disappeared with his superfluous force; and he is now, in his dignified competence, the greatest of living dramatic composers. It is not often that a man's strength is so immense that he can remain an athlete after bartering half of it to old age for experience; but the thing happens occasionally, and need not so greatly surprise us in Verdi's case, especially those of us who, long ago, when Von Bülow and others were contemptuously repudiating him, were able to discern in him a man possessing more power than he knew how to use, or indeed was permitted to use by the old operatic forms imposed on him by circumstances.

I have noticed one or two exclamations of surprise at the supposed revelation in Falstaff of a "hitherto unsuspected" humorous force in the veteran tragic composer. This must be the result of the enormous popularity which Il Trovatore first and Aida afterwards attained in this country. I grant that these operas are quite guiltless of comic relief; but what about [Verdi's] Un Ballo, with its exquisitely lighthearted *E scherzo od e follia*, and the finale to the third act, where Renato is sarcastically complimented on his domestic virtue by the conspirators who have just shewn him that the Duke's veiled mistress, whom he is defending from them after devotedly saving the Duke's life, is his own wife. Stupidly as that tragicomic quartet and chorus has always been mishandled on our wretched operatic stage, I cannot understand anyone who knows it denying Verdi's gift of dramatic humor.

In the first act of Otello, the *stretto* made in the drinking song by Cassio when he gets drunk is very funny without being in the least unmusical. The grim humor of Sparafucile, the terrible ironic humor of Iago, the agonized humor of Rigoletto: these surely settled the question as to Verdi's capacity for Falstaff none the less because the works in which they occur are tragedies and not comedies. All that could be said on the other side was that Verdi was no Mozart, which was as idle as saying that Victor Hugo was no Molière. Verdi's vein of humor is all the more Shakespearean on that account.

Verdi's worst sins as a composer have been sins against the human voice. His habit of taking the upper fifth of the compass of an exceptionally high voice, and treating that fifth as the normal range, has a great deal to do with the fact that the Italian singer is now the worst singer in the world, just as Wagner's return to Handel's way of using the voice all over its compass and obtaining physical relief for the singer and artistic relief for the audience by the contrast of the upper and lower registers has made the Wagnerian singer now the best singer in the world. Verdi applied his system with special severity to baritones.

If you look at the score of Don Giovanni, you will find three different male voices written for on the bass clef, and so treated as to leave no doubt that Mozart, as he wrote the music, had a particular sort of voice for each part constantly in his head, and that one (Masetto's) was a rough peasant's bass, another (Leporello's) a ready, fluent, copious *basso cantante*; and the third a light fine baritone, the voice of a gentleman. I have heard public meetings addressed successively by an agricultural laborer's delegate, a representative of the skilled artisans, and a university man; and they have taught me what all the treatises on singing in the world could not about the Mozartian differentiation between Masetto, Leporello, and Don Giovanni.

But now please remark that there is no difference of range between the three parts. Any man who can sing the notes of one of them can sing the notes of the others. Let Masetto and the Don exchange characters, and though the Don will be utterly ineffective in the concerted music on Masetto's lower G's and B flats, whilst Masetto will rob the serenade of all its delicacy, yet neither singer will encounter any more impossibility, or even inconvenience, in singing the notes than Mr Toole would have in reading the part of Hamlet. The same thing is true of the parts of Bartolo, Figaro, and Almaviva in Le Nozze [Le Nozze di Figaro by Mozart]; of San Bris and Nevers in Les Huguenots; of Wotan and Alberich in The Niblung's Ring; and of Amfortas and Klingsor in [Wagner's] Parsifal. The dramatic distinction between these parts is so strong that only an artist of remarkable versatility could play one as well as the other; but there is practically no distinction of vocal range any more than there is a distinction of physical stature or strength.

But if we turn to Il Trovatore, we find two vocal parts written in the bass clef, of which the lower, Ferrando, is not a *basso profundo* like Osmin or Marcel, but a basso cantante like San Bris or Leporello; yet the baritone part (Di Luna) is beyond the reach of any normal basso cantante, and treats a baritone voice as consisting of about one effective octave, from G on the fourth space of the bass stave to the G above. In Il balen there are from two hundred and ten to two hundred and twenty notes, including the cadenza, &c. Barring five notes in the cadenza, which is never sung as written, only three are below F on the fourth line, whilst nearly one hundred and forty lie above the stave between B flat and the high G. The singing is practically continuous from end to end; and the strain on a normal baritone voice is frightful, even when the song is transposed half a tone as it usually is to bring it within the bare limits of possibility. Di Luna is in this respect a typical Verdi baritone; and the result has been that only singers with abnormally high voices have been able to sing it without effort.

As to the normal baritones who have made a speciality of bawling fiercely up to G sharp, they have so lost the power of producing an endurable tone in their lower octave, or of pitching its notes with even approximate accuracy, that they have all but destroyed the popularity of Mozart's operas by their occasional appearances as Don Giovanni, Figaro, &c. I have often wished that the law would permit me to destroy these unhappy wretches, whose lives must be a burden to them. It is easy to go into raptures over the superiority of the Italian master in vocal writing because his phrases are melodious, easily learned, symmetrical, and often grandiose; but when you have to sing the melodious well-turned phrases, and find that they lie a tone higher than you can comfortably manage them, and a third higher than you can keep on managing them for five minutes at a stretch (for music that lies rather high is much more trying than music that ventures very high occasionally), you begin to appreciate the sort of knowledge of and consideration for the voice shewn by Purcell, Handel, and Wagner, and to very decidedly resent Verdi's mere partiality for the top end of it.

Now comes the question, what sort of voice is needed for the part of Falstaff? Well, Ferrando and the Count di Luna rolled into one—Amonasro [king of Egypt in Verdi's *Aida*], in short. A rich *basso cantante*, who can knock out a vigorous high G and play with F sharp as Melba plays with B flat. Polyphemus in Handel's Acis and Valentin in Gounod's Faust might do it justice between them. Barely reasonable this, even at French pitch, and monstrous at Philharmonic pitch. And yet it is the fashion to say that Verdi is a master of the art of writing singable music.

The score is necessarily occupied to a great extent by the discourses of Falstaff, which are set with the most expert ingenuity and subtlety, the advance in this respect from the declamation of Charles V. in Ernani to that of Falstaff being as great as from Tannhäuser's to Parsifal's [operas by Wagner], or from Vanderdecken's to Hans Sachs's. One capital effect—the negative answers in the manner of Mr Chadband to the repeated questions as to what honor is—is, musically, a happy adaptation from Boïto's Mefistofele, and is, as far as I have discovered, the only direct Boïtoism in the work, though I imagine that Verdi has profited generally by having so fine an artist and critic as Boïto at his elbow when composing Otello and Falstaff. There are some amusing passages of instrumental music: for instance, a highly expressive accompaniment to a colossal drink taken by Falstaff.

During the abundant action and stage bustle of the piece we get a symphonic treatment, which belongs exclusively to Verdi's latest manner. Some tripping figuration, which creates perpetual motion by its ceaseless repetition in all sorts of ingenious sequences, as in Mendelssohn's *scherzos* or the *ws* to his concertos, is taken as the musical groundwork upon which the vocal parts are put in, the whole fabric being wrought with the most skilful elegance. This is a matter for some of our musical pundits to consider rather anxiously. For, if I had said ten years ago that Ernani was a much greater musical composition than Mendelssohn's Scotch symphony or any of his concertos, words could not have conveyed the scorn with which so gross an opinion would have been received. But here, today, is the scorned one, whom even Browning thought it safe to represent as an empty blusterer shrinking amid a torrent of vulgar applause from the grave eye of—of—of—well, of ROSSINI! (poor Browning!) falling back in his old age on the Mendelssohnian method, and employing it with ease and brilliancy.

Perhaps, when Verdi turns a hundred and feels too old for opera composition, he will take to concerto writing, and cut out Mendelssohn and Schumann in the pretty pattern work which the pundits love them for. Which will shew how very easy it is for a good musician, when he happens to be a bad critic, to admire a great composer for the wrong thing.

17. Utopian Gilbert and Sullivan

The World, 11 October 1893

Pleasant it is to see Mr Gilbert and Sir Arthur Sullivan working together again full brotherly. They should be on the best of terms; for henceforth Sir Arthur can always say "Any other librettist would do just as well: look at Haddon Hall"; whilst Mr Gilbert can retort "Any other musician would do just as well: look at The Mountebanks." Thus have the years of divorce cemented the happy reunion at which we all assisted last Saturday. The twain still excite the expectations of the public as much as ever. How Trial by Jury and The Sorcerer surprised the public, and how Pinafore, The Pirates, and Patience kept the sensation fresh, can be guessed by the youngest man from the fact that the announcement of a new Savoy opera always throws the middle-aged playgoer into the attitude of expecting a surprise. As for me, I avoid this attitude, if only because it is a middle-aged one. Still, I expect a good deal that I could not have hoped for when I first made the acquaintance of comic opera.

Those who are old enough to compare the Savoy performances with those of the dark ages, taking into account the pictorial treatment of the fabrics and calculi on the stage, the cultivation and intelligence of the choristers, the quality of the orchestra, and the degree of artistic good breeding, so to speak, expected from the principals, best know how great an advance has been made by Mr D'Oyly Carte in organizing and harmonizing that complex cooperation of artists of all kinds which goes to make up a satisfactory operatic performance. Long before the run of a successful Savoy opera is over Sir Arthur's melodies are dinned into our ears by every promenade band and street piano, and Mr Gilbert's sallies are quoted threadbare by conversationalists and journalists; but the whole work as presented to eye and ear on the Savoy stage remains unhackneyed.

Further, no theatre in London is more independent of those executants whose personal popularity enables them to demand ruinous salaries; and this is not the least advantageous of the differences between opera as the work of a combination of manager, poet, and musician, all three making the most of oneanother in their concerted striving for the common object of a completely successful representation, and opera as the result of a speculator picking up a libretto, getting somebody with a name to set it to music, ordering a few tradesmen to "mount" it, and then, with a stage manager hired here, an acting manager hired there, and a popular *prima donna*, comedian, and serpentine dancer stuck in at reckless salaries like almonds into an underdone dumpling, engaging some empty theatre on the chance of the affair "catching on."

If any capitalist wants to succeed with comic opera, I can assure him that he can do so with tolerable security if he only possesses the requisite managerial ability. There is no lack of artistic material for him to set to work on: London is overstocked with artistic talent ready to the hand of anyone who can recognize it and select from it. The difficulty is to find the man with this power of recognition and selection. The effect of the finer artistic temperaments and talents on the ordinary speculator is not merely nil (for in that case he might give them an engagement by accident), but antipathetic. People sometimes complain of the indifference of the public and the managers to the highest elements in fine art. There never was a greater mistake. The Philistine is not indifferent to fine art: he *hates* it.

The relevance of these observations will be apparent when I say that, though I enjoyed the score of Utopia more than that of any of the previous Savoy operas, I am quite prepared to hear that it is not as palatable to the majority of the human race—otherwise the mob—as it was to me. It is written with an artistic absorption and enjoyment of which Sir Arthur Sullivan always had moments, but which seem to have become constant with him only since he was knighted, though I do not suggest that the two things stand in the relation of cause and effect. The orchestral work is charmingly humorous; and as I happen to mean by this only what I say, perhaps I had better warn my readers not to infer that Utopia is full of buffooneries with the bassoon and piccolo, or of patter and tum-tum.

Whoever can listen to such caressing wind parts—zephyr parts, in fact—as those in the trio for the King and the two Judges in the first act, without being coaxed to feel pleased and amused, is not fit even for treasons, stratagems, and spoils; whilst anyone whose ears are capable of taking in more than one thing at a time must be tickled by the sudden busyness of the orchestra as the city man takes up the parable. I also confidently recommend those who go into solemn academic raptures over themes "in diminution" top go and hear how prettily the chorus of the Christy Minstrel song (borrowed from the plantation dance Johnnie, get a gun) is used, very much in diminution, to make an exquisite mock-banjo accompaniment. In these examples we are on the plane, not of the bones and tambourine, but of Mozart's accompaniments to *Soave sia il vento* in Cosi fan tutte and the entry of the gardener in Le Nozze di Figaro. Of course these things are as much thrown away on people who are not musicians as a copy of Fliegende Blätter on people who do not read German, wheras anyone can understand mere horseplay with the instruments.

But people who are not musicians should not intrude into opera houses: indeed, it is to me an open question whether they ought to be allowed to exist at all. As to the score generally, I have only one fault to find with Sir Arthur's luxurious ingenuity in finding pretty timbres of all sorts, and that is that it still leads him to abuse the human voice most unmercifully. I will say nothing about the part he has written for the unfortunate soprano, who might as well leave her lower octave at home for all the relief she gets from the use of her upper one. But take the case of Mr Scott Fishe [baritone, 1871–1898], one of Mr Carte's most promising discoveries, who did so much to make the ill-fated Jane Annie endurable.

What made Mr Fishe's voice so welcome was that it was neither the eternal callow baritone nor the growling bass: it rang like a genuine "singing bass"; and one felt that here at last was a chance of an English dramatic *basso cantante*, able to "sing both high and low," and to contrast his high D with an equally fine one an octave below. Unfortunately, the upper fifth of Mr Fishe's voice, being flexible and of excellent quality, gives him easy command (on occasion) of high passages; and Sir Arthur has ruthlessly seized on this to write for him an excessively specialized baritone part, in which we get not one of those deep, ringing tones which relieved the Jane Annie [comic opera by J. M. Barrie and Arthur Conan Doyle, music by Ernest Ford, 1893] music so attractively. I have in my time heard so many singers reduced by parts of this sort, in the operas of Verdi and Gounod, to a condition in which they could bawl F sharps *ad lib.* at high pressure, but could neither place a note accurately nor produce any tolerable tone from B flat downwards, that I always protest against vocal parts, no matter what voice they are written for, if they do not employ the voice all over its range, though lying mainly where the singer can sing continuously without fatigue.

A composer who uses up young voices by harping on the prettiest notes in them is an ogreish voluptuary; and if Sir Arthur does not wish posterity either to see the stage whitened with the bones of his victims or else to hear his music transposed wholesale, as Lassalle transposes Rigoletto, he should make up his mind whether he means to write for a tenor or a baritone, and place the part accordingly. Considering that since Santley retired from the stage and Jean de Reszke turned tenor all the big reputations have been made by *bassi cantanti* like Edouard de Reszke and Lassalle, and that all the great Wagner parts in which reputations of the same calibre will be made for some time to come are impossible to completely specialized baritones, I venture, as a critic who greatly enjoys Mr Fishe's performance, to recommend him to ask the composer politely not to treat him worse than Mozart treated Don Giovanni, than Wagner treated Wolfram, or than Sir Arthur himself would treat a clarinet. Miss Nancy McIntosh [American soprano, 1868–1954], who was introduced to us, it will be remembered, by Mr Henschel at the London Symphony Concerts, where she sang in a selection from Die Meistersinger and in the Choral Symphony, came through the trials of a most inconsiderate vocal part very cleverly, evading the worst of the strain by a treatment which, if a little flimsy, was always pretty. She spoke her part admirably, and, by dint of natural tact, managed to make a positive advantage of her stage inexperience, so that she won over the audience in no time. As to Miss Brandram, Mr Barrington (who by means of a remarkable pair of eyebrows transformed himself into a surprising compound of Mr Groschen and the late Sir William Cusins), Messrs Denny, Kenningham, Le Hay, Gridley, and the rest, everybody knows what they can do; and I need only particularize as to Miss Owen and Miss Florence Perry [1869–1949], who gave us some excellent pantomime in the very amusing lecture scene, contrived by Mr Gilbert, and set to perfection by Sir Arthur in the first act.

The book has Mr Gilbert's lighter qualities without his faults. Its main idea, the Anglicization of Utopia by the people boundlessly credulous as to the superiority of the English race, is as certain of popularity as that reference to England by the Gravedigger in Hamlet, which never yet failed to make the house laugh. There is, happily, no plot; and the stage business is fresh and well invented—for instance, the lecture already alluded to, the adoration of the troopers by the female Utopians, the Cabinet Council "as held at the Court of St James's Hall," and the quadrille, are capital strokes. As to the "Drawing Room," with débutantes, cards, trains, and presentations all complete, and the little innovation of a cup of tea and a plate of cheap biscuits, I cannot vouch for its verisimilitude, as I have never, strange as it may appear, been present at a Drawing Room; but that is exactly why I enjoyed it, and why the majority of the Savoyards will share my appreciation of it.

18. Half a Century Behind

The World, 25 October 1893

Comic opera is still trying to mend its luck, apparently with some success. The Mascotte has been transferred from the Gaiety to the Criterion, where Miss St John [1855–1912] still keeps it going with ease, though from the middle of the last act onwards it is certainly as crazy a piece of dramatic botchwork as the worst enemy of the human intelligence could desire. What it would be without the *prima donna* I dare not imagine; rather let me sit quietly in my stall and wonder whether Miss St John's next speech will be delivered in the prettiest serious manner of Miss Ellen Terry, or in cockney, Irish, or Yankee, as the mood of the moment may suggest. But, however it comes, it comes with genuine comic force; and the opera does not flag for a moment while Miss St John is on the stage. Her singing is as good as ever; and though her voice is a shade less fresh than it was twenty years ago, it is in much better condition than most voices are after twenty months' stage wear. Mr Wallace Brownlow is unfortunate in having to impersonate a youth who is accepted by a traveling dramatic company as a nimble comedian, which is exactly what he is not; but his singing pulls him through. Mr Conyers, the tenor, does not improve, the fault being, not his, but his method's. Mr Fred Emney is condemned to enact one of those zany kings of *opera bouffe* whose tyranny, I hope, must be as heavy on the player as on the audience. Miss Phyllis Broughton [actress, 1862–1926], rather at a discount in the earlier scenes, brought off her song and dance in the last act triumphantly; and Miss Mabel Love [dancer, 1874–1953], who with the natural expansion of her view of life has quite relaxed the tragic aspect which distinguished her in her teens, was left breathless by a double *encore* for a tarantella which was really a dance, and not one of the arrant impostures which have lately got into currency under the pretext of "skirt dancing."

Mr Hollingshead's venture at the Princess's is chiefly notable for the new departure downward in prices. Whether Miami [melodramatic opera based on J. B. Buckstone's *The Green Bushes*, 1845] succeeds or not, Mr Hollingshead is certainly sound in his economic reasoning. The notion that you can keep on increasing the supply of places of entertainment in London without affecting prices can only be defended on the hypothesis that the demand at the old prices far exceeded the supply. Considering that theatrical business has been falling off in all directions for some time past at the old prices, whilst the music halls, at lower prices, hold their own, the hypothesis seems contradicted by the facts. Obstinately high prices and obstinately high salaries on the one hand, with closing theatres and the most desperate precariousness of employment on the other, have been the rule for the last few years. It is not certain even that the theatres which have kept open have paid.

Actor-managers find "backers" to subsidize experiments with expensively mounted plays which are assumed to be successful because they are persisted in for some months; but in such cases there is no satisfactory evidence to shew that the backer has escaped a loss, much less come out with his capital intact, plus the ordinary interest on it. Meanwhile hundreds of half-crowns are paid every night at the pit-door by men who would pay five shillings for an orchestra or balcony stall if it were to be had so cheap; whilst hundreds of others stay at home or go to the music halls because theatre managers will not make them comfortable at a reasonable rate. Whether the stalls are always filled by persons who pay half a guinea apiece is best known to the managers.

My own observation leads me to suspect that, under circumstances of no more than ordinary attractiveness, is difficult to fill even three rows of stalls without the assistance of deadheads—and as I am a professional deadhead myself, I may perhaps be excused for hinting a doubt as to whether the tone given to the stalls by the courtiers of the boxoffice is so very much more elevated from the fashionable point of view than that which might be expected to prevail among plain persons good for hard cash to the extent of five shillings. On the whole, I agree cordially with Mr Hollingshead that there is room for his Volkstheater in London, and can testify, having tried the experiment, to the sense of economic satisfaction produced by a comfortable balcony stall costing a modest extravagance of three shillings.

At the same time, I must confess I do not in the least believe in the success of Mr Hollingshead's extraordinary freak of combining the most advanced arrangements before the curtain with an attempt to revive the Crummles repertory behind it. I daresay Miami will draw a certain number of veteran playgoers who will go to see [J.B. Buckstone's 1845 melodrama] Green Bushes again just as they might go to see their birthplace, or their old school, or anything else likely to

recall the sensations of "auld lang syne." Such gnawing plea-
sures reassure and freshen the man who fears that he has lost
his youthful power of feeling thoroughly maudlin. The veterans, combined with the devotees of Miss Violet Cameron
and Mr Courtice Pounds, will, no doubt, keep Miami going
for a time; but I am sceptical as to its enjoying any great vogue
on the strength of its artistic merits. The fact is, it has no such
merits, and never had.

I do not speak altogether as a modern: these eyes have seen
the great Céleste as Miami, and also as the heroine of a melodrama [J.S. Coyne's 1868 *The Woman in Red*] in which she
was eighteen in the first act, thirty in the second, forty in the
third, sixty in the fourth, and eighty in the fifth; after which
I came away wondering how old Madame really was, as she
had looked like a made-up old woman in the early stages,
and like a made-up young woman in the later ones, never
by any chance presenting a convincing appearance of being
near the age indicated by the dramatist. She was, I took it, a
clever lady who had taken the measure of that huge section of
the playgoing public which is enormously credulous of everything except the truth, highly susceptible to the instinctive
emotions, entirely uncritical as to the reasonableness of what
it is used to, and mutinously indisposed to face the painful
and unaccustomed exertion of thought or artistic perception,
though not without a certain practical shrewdness as to the
worth of its money, which makes it very necessary to give
good value for it in amusement, excitement, and, above all, in
that moral satisfaction produced by the spectacle of punish-
ment spread over crime like jam over butter.

The melodramas of Buckstone and the acting of Céleste
had no other purpose in the world that I could ever discover
beyond the exploitation of this stratum of the playgoing
world to the uttermost farthing. Considered in relation to
any other purpose, Green Bushes is foolish and Miami-
Céleste impossible. This is apparent to everybody now that

the purpose is no longer fulfilled, the falling-off in the efficiency of the play being due, not, I regret to say, to any elevation of the taste of its audience, but simply to a change of fashion in stage folly. Green Bushes now looks dowdy, and it is accordingly found out and cut by the very people who would sedulously chatter its praises in order to prove their culture if it were up to date in externals. This, I apprehend, is why Mr Hollingshead has not ventured to revive it as it originally stood. Instead, he has, by a happy thought, changed it into an opera, thereby securing for its absurdities the benefit of the unwritten law by which the drama which is sung is allowed to lag half a century behind that which is spoken.

If the experiment succeeds, we shall perhaps have The Wreck Ashore set to music by Mr Haydn Parry and revived. I shall not object, for Miami entertained me more than most comic operas do, the obvious reason being that Buckstone was a playwright without genius trying to be popularly sentimental, an attempt in which a man of ordinary sense and sympathy may attain a tolerable measure of success, wheras your modern comic opera librettist is mostly a man without brains trying to be clever, which is out of the question. This is the most that can be said for the Green Bushes basis of Miami; and I think that if Mr Hollingshead will rub the glamor of old times out of his eyes, and contemplate that last act gravely from the point of view of the rational stranger who never heard of Madame Céleste or Paul Bedford, he will agree with me that its day is happily past.

And before he changes that attitude, he might as well take the opportunity to forget that Grinnidge is a notoriously funny part, and Mr George Barrett a notoriously funny actor; so that, escaping for a moment from the foregone conclusion that Mr Barrett's Grinnidge is a screamingly funny performance, he may be able to give him a friendly hint that it is a noisy, slovenly business, unworthy of a comedian of Mr Barrett's standing. Mr Barrett himself, indeed, continues to intimate, by an expressive gag, that he considers the part an impossible one. All the more reason why he should take it quietly.

The cast does credit to Mr Hollingshead's judgment. Miss Jessie Bond did not appear on the night of my visit; but the lady who took her place sang pleasantly, and would no doubt have spoken equally well if she had frankly given up her hopeless attempt at a brogue. Miss Violet Cameron played Miami with a wholehearted loyalty to the management, which stopped at nothing but the firing off of a Martini rifle, a weapon unknown to Céleste and Fenimore Cooper. Her voice is in excellent preservation, sound and sympathetic in the middle, as a properly used voice of its age ought to be. Miami's songs are all encored; and the audience does not laugh at her when she is not singing, a fact which speaks volumes for Miss Cameron's earnestness. Miss Isabella Girardot celebrates the virtues and misfortunes of Geraldine in song; and Mr Courtice Pounds struggles bravely to avoid the throaty habits which seemed at one time likely to cost him his voice. The score, which was probably composed originally to some other libretto, is pretty in a well-established way, with plenty of bright and tender orchestral color; but it has been considerably shorn on the comic side, the numbers for Jack Gong and Grinnidge appearing only in the program—which, by the way, costs nothing, and is full of instruction and amusement. Miss Clara Jecks enters into the humors of the Mrs Gong, née Tigertail, much further than I could; but the opera is certainly none the heavier for her. Each act contains at least one effective *coup de théâtre* in the way of a *finale* or a dance. *Matinées* are promised of Cavalleria, Suppé's Galatea, Handel's Rinaldo (!), Dr Arne's Artaxerxes (good heavens!), and an original operetta by Mr Squiers, not to mention a Christmas play for children. I am sure I wish Mr Hollingshead every success.

I have said my say so often about Gounod, our XIX century Fra Angelico, that I need not add to the burden of the obituary notices that have been laid upon us since his death on Wednesday last. In his honor the program of the Saturday concert at the Crystal Palace was altered so as to include his Religious March and the overture to Mireille. The march was only nominally appropriate: it is, in truth, an uninspired affair, with a trio that would not surprise anyone in a second-rate comic opera. That exquisite little funeral march from Romeo, called Juliet's Last Sleep, would have been far better. Mireille was altogether charming: the beautiful smoothness of its lines and the transparent richness and breadth of its orchestral coloration were admirably reproduced by the Crystal Palace band. In the sixties the Parisian critics found it Wagnerian: nowadays the abyss of erroneousness—not to say downright ignorance—revealed by such an opinion makes one giddy.

After the Gounod numbers came an orchestral prelude to The Eumenides of Eschylus, by Mr W. Wallace, whose Passing of Beatrice made some mark last year. Like that work, it shewed that Mr Wallace knows how to use every instrument except the scissors. It is all that a young man's work ought to be, imaginative, ambitious, impetuous, romantic, prodigal, and most horribly indiscriminate. Mr Wallace's imagination is so susceptible, and his critical faculty so unsuspicious, that when he once gets exalted he will keep pegging away at a figure long after it has been worn threadbare, or he will remind you, in the thick of The Eumenides, of the bathers' chorus in Les Huguenots, because he cannot resist a few rushing bassoon scales. If every bar in the overture were as good as the best, it would be very good; and if every bar were as bad as the worst, it would be very bad: further than that I decline to go, as there is no saying what Mr Wallace would be at next if he were rashly encouraged. Mr Manns and the band covered themselves with glory in Schumann's first symphony, which was very welcome after Saint-Saëns' violin concerto in B minor, with its trivially pretty scraps of serenade music sandwiched between pages from the great masters. Miss Frida Scotta failed to interest me either in the concerto or in her own certainly very surprising technical skill. The vocal part of the concert was unusually strong, Miss Emma Juch very nearly vanquishing the difficulties of Softly Sighs, and shewing herself at any rate a highly cultivated singer; whilst Mr David Bispham attacked a still more difficult song—Purcell's Mad Tom—and was completely victorious.

19. Born-Again Italian Opera

The World, 23 May 1894

I have been to the Opera six times; and I still live. What is more, I am positively interested and hopeful. Hitherto I have had only one aim as regards Italian opera: not, as some have supposed, to kill it, for it was dead already, but to lay its ghost. It was a troublesome phantom enough. When one felt sure that it had been effectually squeezed out at last by French opera, or Hebraic opera, or what may be called operatic music-drama—Lohengrin, for instance—it would turn up again trying to sing *Spirto gentil* [from Donizetti's *La Favorita*] in the manner of Mario, raving through the mad scene in Lucia amid childish orchestral tootlings, devastating Il Trovatore with a totally obsolete style of representation, or in some way gustily rattling its unburied bones and wasting the manager's money and my patience.

The difficulty was to convince those who had been brought up to believe in it (as I was myself) that it was all over with it: they *would* go on believing that it only needed four first-rate Italian singers to bring the good old times back again and make the rum-tum rhythms, the big guitar orchestration, the florid cabalettas, the cavatinas in regular four-bar lines, the choruses in thirds and sixths, and all the rest of it swell out to their former grandeur and sweep Wagner off the boards. I have no doubt they believe it as devoutly as ever, and that if Mr Mapleson were to start again tomorrow, he would announce [Donizetti's] Lucia and Il Barbiere [*Il barbiere di siviglia*] and Semiramide [both operas by Rossini] with unshaken confidence in their freshness and adequacy, perhaps adding, as a concession to the public demand for novelty, a promise of Ponchielli's La Gioconda.

But now an unlooked-for thing has happened. Italian opera has been born again. The extirpation of the Rossinian dynasty, which neither Mozart nor Wagner could effect, since what they offered in its place was too far above the heads of both the public and the artists, is now being accomplished with ease by Mascagni, Leoncavallo, Puccini, and Verdi. Nobody has ever greeted a performance of Tristan und Isolde by such a remark as "We shall never be able to go back to L'Elisir d'Amore [Donizetti's] after this," or declare that Lucrezia [title character, *Lucrezia Borgia*—opera by Donizetti] was impossible after Brynhild [Brünnhilde from Wagner's *Ring*]. The things were too far apart to affect oneanother: as well might it be supposed that Ibsen's plays could be accepted as a substitute for popular melodrama, or Shakespear wean people from the circus. It is only by an advance in melodrama itself or in circuses themselves that the melodrama or circus of today can become unpresentable to the audiences of ten years hence.

The same thing is true of Italian opera. The improvement of higher forms of art, or the introduction of new forms at a different level, cannot affect it at all; and that is why Tristan has no more killed L'Elisir than Brahms's symphonies have killed Jullien's British Army Quadrilles. But the moment you hear Pagliacci [opera by Leoncavallo], you feel that it is all up with L'Elisir. It is true that Leoncavallo has shewn as yet nothing comparable to the melodic inspiration of Donizetti;

but the advance in serious workmanship, in elaboration of detail, in variety of interest, and in capital expenditure on the orchestra and the stage, is enormous. There is more work in the composition of Cavalleria than in La Favorita, Lucrezia, and Lucia put together, though I cannot think—perhaps this is only my own old-fashionedness—that any part of it will live as long or move the world as much as the best half-dozen numbers in those three obsolete masterpieces.

And when you come to Puccini, the composer of the latest Manon Lescaut, then indeed the ground is so transformed that you could almost think yourself in a new country. In Cavalleria and Pagliacci I can find nothing but Donizettian opera rationalized, condensed, filled in, and thoroughly brought up to date; but in Manon Lescaut the domain of Italian opera is enlarged by an annexation of German territory. The first act, which is as gay and effective and romantic as the opening of any version of Manon need be, is also unmistakably symphonic in its treatment. There is genuine symphonic modification, development, and occasionally combination of the thematic material, all in a dramatic way, but also in a musically homogeneous way, so that the act is really a single movement with episodes instead of being a succession of separate numbers, linked together, to conform to the modern fashion, by substituting interrupted cadences for full closes and parading a Leitmotif occasionally.

Further, the experiments in harmony and syncopation, reminding one often of the intellectual curiosities which abound in Schumann's less popular pianoforte works, shew a strong technical interest which is, in Italian music, a most refreshing symptom of mental vigor, even when it is not strictly to the real artistic point. The less studied harmonies are of the most modern and stimulating kind. When one thinks of the old school, in which a dominant seventh, or at most a minor ninth, was the extreme of permissible discord, only to be tolerated in the harsher inversions when there was a murder or a ghost on hand, one gets a rousing sense of getting along from hearing young Italy beginning its most light-hearted melodies to the chord of the thirteenth on the tonic.

Puccini is particularly fond of this chord; and it may be taken as a general technical criticism of the young Italian school that its free use of tonic discords, and its reckless prodigality of orchestral resources, give its music a robustness and variety that reduce the limited tonic and dominant harmonic technique of Donizetti and Bellini, by contrast, to mere Christy minstrelsy. No doubt this very poverty of the older masters made them so utterly dependent on the invention of tunes that they invented them better than the new men, who, with a good drama to work on, can turn out vigorous, imposing, and even enthralling operas without a bar that is their own in the sense in which *Casta Diva* is Bellini's own; but Puccini, at least, shews no signs of atrophy of the melodic faculty: he breaks out into catching melodies quite in the vein of Verdi: for example, *Tra voi, belle,* in the first act of Manon, has all the charm of the tunes beloved by the old operatic guard.

On that and other accounts, Puccini looks to me more like the heir of Verdi than any of his rivals. He has arranged his own libretto from Prévost d'Exiles' novel; and though the miserable end of poor Manon has compelled him to fall back on a rather conventional operatic death scene in which the *prima donna* at Covent Garden failed to make anyone believe, his third act, with the roll-call of the female convicts and the embarkation, is admirably contrived and carried out: he has served himself in this as well as Scribe ever served Meyerbeer, or Boïto Verdi.

If now it is considered that this opening week at Covent Garden began with Manon, and ended with Falstaff; Cavalleria and Pagliacci coming in between, with nothing older than Faust and Carmen to fill up except the immortal Orfeo, it will be understood how I find myself with the startling new idea that Italian opera has a future as well as a past, and that perhaps Sir Augustus Harris, in keeping a house open for it, has not been acting altogether as an enemy of the human race, as I used sometimes to declare in my agony when, in a moment of relenting towards that dreary past, he would let loose some stout matron to disport herself once more as Favorita, or spend untold gold in indulging Jean de Reszke with a revival of that concentrated bore and outrage, [Meyerbeer's] Le Prophète, when I wanted to see the prince of tenors and procrastinators as Siegfried or Tristan.

Falstaff drew an enormous house on Saturday, and was received with an enthusiasm which was quite unforced up to the end of the clothes-basket scene. After that the opera suffered for a while from the play outlasting the freshness of the subject, a fate that invariably overtakes The Merry Wives of Windsor, except when the actor who plays Falstaff has an extraordinary power of inventing humorous and varied character traits.

The first scene of the third act was undeniably a little dull. The merry wives cackled wearisomely; Pessina's comic stock was exhausted, so that he could do nothing but repeat the business of the earlier scenes; and Mrs Quickly, who had been charming for the first ten minutes in the novel character of the youthful and charming Signorina Ravogli, gave the final blow to the dramatic interest of the scene by not being her detestable old self.

Fortunately, the excitement revived in the forest scene at the end, which is full of life and charm. It ends with a sort of musical practical joke in the shape of a fugue which is everything that a fugue ought not to be, and which, failing more rehearsal than it is worth, has to be execrably sung in order to get the parts picked up. It was listened to with deep reverence, as if Verdi, in his old age, had clasped hands with Sebastian Bach. Always excepting the first scene of the third act, the opera went like wildfire.

Boïto's libretto is excellent as far as it is a condensation of Shakespear, except that he has not appreciated the great stage effectiveness of Falstaff's description to Ford of his misadventure in the basket, with its climaxes, dear to old Shakespearean actors, of "Think of that, Master Brook." His alterations, notably the screen business in the basket scene, make some fun; but they also make the scene in Ford's house quite outrageously impossible. As far as acting is concerned, the weight of the whole opera lies in the scene between Ford and Falstaff at the Garter Inn; and here Pessina played with considerable humor and vigor, though without any particular subtlety.

Pini-Corsi's [Italian baritone, 1859–1918] acting was better than operatic acting generally is; but it hardly satisfied those of us who have seen anything like an adequate impersonation of Ford on the English stage. The women were rather unintelligently and monotonously merry; and on the whole the success was, past all question, a success of the musical setting, which is immensely vivacious and interesting. The medieval scenery is attractive, especially the garden and the room in Ford's house. The interior of the inn is not sunny enough: modern painting, with its repudiation of the studio light, and its insistence on work in the open air, has made the traditional stage interior look old-fashioned in this respect.

The company at Covent Garden is a very strong one. The representations of Cavalleria and Pagliacci derive an altogether exceptional dramatic force from the acting of De Lucia and Ancona in parts which are in constant danger of being handed over to a second-rate tenor and baritone. Beduschi, who plays Des Grieux in Manon with success, is another tenor of the Gayarré school, without the goat bleat and *tremolo* of its extreme disciples. He is a capable actor, small in figure, with a face which will probably be described as dark and ugly by a good many people, nevertheless by no means an unprepossessing face. Cossira [1854–1923], a tenor of heavier build than Beduschi, made some effect by his passion and sincerity in the love scene in the second act of Carmen. Albers [Johan Hendrik Albers, Dutch, 1866–1926], a baritone, made his first appearances as Valentin in Faust and the Toreador in Carmen. His treatment of Bizet's daintily written scene between Jose and Escamillo before the fight in the third act gave me an extremely unfavorable impression of the delicacy of his musical sense; but the rougher part of his work was presentably done. Bonnard, a French *tenorino*, made a satisfactory Philémon in Philémon et Baucis, in which, however, the honors went to Plancon for a splendid appearance as Jupiter.

Philémon brought back Mlle Simonnet [French soprano, born 1865], whose voice is somewhat thicker and richer, especially in the middle, than when she charmed us first in Bruneau's Le Rêve. I am not sure that the same remark does not apply, in a slight degree, to Mlle Simonnet's figure, though she was certainly as trim and youthful as could be desired as Micaela in Carmen. She also played Marguerite in Faust, of which I saw only the last act and a half. Her Micaela was not good: she slipped through the music in a pointless way, apparently finding the part trivial and uninteresting, and certainly making it so. Her Marguerite—what I saw of it—was clever and pretty, but prosaic. It was only as Baucis that she fully justified the admiration excited by her first performances in this country, though none of her three appearances passed without a burst of applause for some happily sung passage. The leading parts in the two new operas were taken by Olga Olghina, a clever Russian lady with chiseled features and a somewhat courtly fastidiousness of manner, just a little too ladylike for Manon and a little too mundane for Anne Page, but able to make a distinct mark in both by her acting in the embarkation scene of the one opera and her singing in the forest scene of the other. Mlle Pauline Joran [American soprano, 1870–1954] played Siebel and Lola in Cavalleria, the latter cleverly. Of Bauermeister [Matilde, 1849–1926] the invaluable, the inevitable, I need not speak; and of Signorine Zilli and Kitzu I shall perhaps speak later on, when my impressions of them are more definite. Of the two great dramatic artists of the company, Giulia Ravogli [mezzo, 1850] struck me as suffering from underwork; and as to the incomparable Calvé, at least a week must elapse before I can trust myself to speak of her Carmen and her Santuzza, or, indeed, of herself, with a decent pretence of critical coolness.

The Amsterdam Choir, after a brief spell at St Martin's Hall, is singing this week at Queen's Hall. The expectations I expressed last week have been far surpassed. The choir now consists of twentytwo singers, each of them a singer in a thousand. In England we should set the whole thousand bawling together, and then brag all over Europe about our supremacy in choral music.

Mr Daniel de Lange eliminates the worst nine hundred and ninetynine from each thousand, and produces with the remainder a choir the *fortissimo* of which would drown the biggest of our feebly monstrous choral societies, and the *pianissimo* of which almost embraces perfect silence. I wish I had space to do justice to the extraordinary excellence of their execution and the surpassing interest and beauty of the music, sacred and secular, of Josquin, Orlando, Sweelinck, and the rest of the heros of the old Netherlandish school.

20. La Navarraise

The World, 27 June 1894

On Wednesday last week, at about half-past ten at night or thereabout, the inhabitants of Covent Garden and the neighborhood were startled by a most tremendous cannonade. It was the beginning of La Navarraise [opera by Massenet]; and it did heavy execution among the ladies and gentlemen who cultivate their nerves on tea and alcohol. As one who has relieved the serious work of musical criticism by the amusement of dramatic authorship, I can testify to the great difficulty of getting artillery and musketry fire of really good tone for stage purposes; and I can compliment Sir Augustus Harris unreservedly on the thundering amplitude of sound and vigorous attack of his almost smokeless explosives.

They gave the piece a magnificent send-off: Calvé [Emma, 1858–1942] had no need to shake a ladder behind the scenes, according to the old receipt, in order "to strike twelve at once"; for before the curtain had been up thirty seconds, during which little more than half a ton of gunpowder can have been consumed, she was a living volcano, wild with anxiety, to be presently mad with joy, ecstatic with love, desperate with disappointment, and so on in ever culminating transitions through mortification, despair, fury, terror, and finally—the mainspring breaking at the worst of the strain—silly maniacal laughter. The opera, which lasts less than an hour, went like lightning; and when the curtain came down there was something like a riot both on the stage and off. All sorts of ridiculous incidents crowded upon oneanother. Plançon, fetching bouquets for Calvé, turned to present them to her with stately courtesy, and found himself bowing elaborately to the curtain, which had just descended behind him and cut him off from the main body of the stage army. When it went up—and stayed up, there being no prospect of the applause stopping—it became evident that Massenet [1842–1912] was bashfully concealed in the wing. Calvé rushed off to fetch him, but returned empty-handed, breathless, and conveying to the audience by speaking gestures that the composer had wrestled with her victoriously. Then the stalls, forgetting the decorum proper to indispensable evening dress, positively yelled for Massenet. Calvé made another attempt, and again returned defeated. The tumult thereupon redoubled; and she, resolving in her desperation to have somebody out, made a fresh plunge, and came up with Flon of Brussels, the conductor. But the house would not be satisfied with Flon; and finally Sir Augustus himself had to appear. As he stepped forward to the footlights a deep hush fell on the assembled multitude. He looked for a moment at some person behind the scenes; and immediately I was reminded of Captain Cuttle's last appeal to Bunsby [in *Dombey and Son*] when that unfortunate mariner was allowing himself to be married to Mrs Macstinger for mere want of resolution enough to run away. Everyone remembers the formula "Jack Bunsby, will you once?" "Jack Bunsby, will you twice?" and so on. If Sir Augustus had actually uttered the words "Jules Massenet, will you once?" the situation could not have been more patent. But, like the fated Bunsby, Jules Massenet wouldnt once; and Sir Augustus, looking the audience in the face with that steadfastness to which the mere truth can never nerve a mortal man, explained that M. Massenet had left the theatre to smoke a cigaret, and that the gratifying news of the success of his work should be communicated to him, by telegraph, or otherwise, as soon as possible. I immediately withdrew, feeling that I could no longer lend the moral sanction of my presence to the proceedings; and for all I know, the audience may be there calling for Jules still.

As to the work itself, there is hardly anything to be said in face of the frankness with which Massenet has modeled it on Cavalleria. He has not composed an opera: he has made up a prescription; and his justification is that it has been perfectly efficacious. The drama is simple and powerful, the events actually represented being credible and touching, and the assumptions, explanations, and pretexts on which they are brought about so simple and convenient that nobody minds their being impossible. Alvarez [1861–1933], in the tenor part, seconded Calvé with almost brutal force and vividness, dividing the honors with her in the final scene: that is to say, making a remarkable success as an actor.

But no triumph of the genius of an individual artist has half the significance in operatic history of the fact that in La Navarraise we had the management at last in full artistic activity. La Navarraise has not been shoveled on to the stage: it has been really *produced*. It was no mere matter of extravagance in gunpowder: the whole staging of the piece was excellent. The scenery was not ordered from the painter and exhibited anyhow: it was lighted, placed, and considered in the exits and entrances of the troops in such a manner as to secure the utmost illusion and make the audience imagine much more than it was possible to make them actually see. The change from night to morning during the intermezzo, with the mountain summit brightening in the sun while the town below was still in darkness, and the stealing down of the light, were capitally represented.

The couple of bells sounding the F sharp and G an octave below the bass stave (which means that they were huge and expensive pieces of bell-founding) must have been cast expressly for the occasion. In short, when Sir Augustus came on the stage at the end, he was, as manager, in his place as an artist who had taken a leading and highly successful part in the performance.

But in criticism there is no such thing as gratitude. I have got, in La Navarraise, what I have been clamoring for all these years; and now I want more. The newly born operas are splendid; but when are the old operas going to be born over again? I have spoken of shoveling operas on to the stage, and trusting to the genius of the principal artists to pull them through; and I know quite well that, with such a repertory as the London one, shoveling is forced on the management by the mere limits of time, space, and skilled labor. But even shoveling can be carefully or carelessly done; and what I have said in praise of the way in which La Navarraise has been handled would carry no weight if I did not couple it with a most vehement protest against the way in which [Wagner's] Die Walküre was shoveled on at Drury Lane on Tuesday last week, when the German opera season opened.

Take the second act, for example, which is supposed to take place in a mountain gorge. Now I am not going to be unreasonable. I do not ask for a new scene. I do not object to the mountains being provided with flights of stairs and galleries exactly like the hall of an old manor house; for however seldom these freaks of natural architecture may be met with by the chamois, they are undoubtedly convenient for opera singers who have to bound up four thousand feet or so and cross from one range to another whilst the orchestra is playing a dozen bars. Neither do I complain of the venerable smuggler's cave which provides a useful entrance on the ground floor of the valley. To bring these things into some remote harmony with nature would involve a revolution; and you cannot, let it be fairly admitted, make revolutions at Drury Lane and produce La Navarraise at Covent Garden on successive evenings.

But there are some things that you can do, or at least blow up the responsible official for not doing; and one of them is lighting the stage properly. When a rock in the foreground, supposed to be illuminated by the sun overhead, throws a strong black shadow *upwards* on a rock behind which is higher than itself; and when this system of black shadows is carried out through the whole scene, destroying all effects of distance, and making the stage look like a mere store room for dingy canvases, then you can go round and speak burning words to the person whose business it was to have seen that there were sufficient lights placed on the floor between each set of rocks to overcome the shadow from the footlights and to make the back of the stage look five miles away from the front.

The fact is, the music of Die Walküre so enthrals the imagination of both Sir Augustus and most of the audience that they are unconscious of things that would instantly leap to their apprehension in Faust or Carmen. I am under no such spell, the music being as familiar to me as God save the Queen, and the work as capable of boring me as any oldfashioned opera when it is not finely executed.

There is another reform in the staging of these Nibelung dramas upon which I must appeal to the leading artists. Why is it that Brynhild always looks ridiculous and ugly, no matter how attractive the artist impersonating her may be? And why, on the night in question, did Fraulein Klafsky [Hungarian soprano, 1855–1896], in bounding up the mountain staircase, trip, tumble, and have a narrow escape of adding to the year's list of Alpine casualties? Simply because she would go mountaineering, according to German etiquet, in a trailing white skirt. Imagine a helmeted, breastplated, spear-armed warmaiden dashing through battles and scaling crags in a skirt in which no sensible woman would walk down Regent-street! I do not suggest gaiters and a tailor-made skirt, nor yet bicycling knickerbockers, though either would be better than the present Valkyrie fashion; but I do urge the claims of a tunic.

Surely the antique Diana is more beautiful and more decent than the late Hablot Browne's picture of Mrs Leo Hunter as Minerva in a gown, which is exactly the model followed by the Valkyries. The modern lyric drama owes to the German nation three leading features. First, the works of Wagner. Second, tenors who never sing in tune. Third, *prima donnas* who dress badly. I plead earnestly with Sir Augustus for a strenuous resistance to the two last, combined with a hearty welcome to the first. It must never be forgotten that on De Reszke nights, when Covent Garden is at its best, there are moments when Bayreuth is left positively nowhere in point of vocal beauty and dramatic grace; and in bringing the other moments—which are certainly rather numerous—up to a corresponding level, it cannot be too patriotically believed that we have nothing to learn from the Germans, tolerant as they are of uglinesses and stupidities, that we cannot teach ourselves much better for our own purposes. The performance of Die Walküre improved as it went on. The first act was bad—very bad. Sieglinde was a cipher. Alvary [German tenor, 1856–1898] began by singing out of the key. Later on he found the key, and merely sang out of tune. He posed with remarkable grace and dramatic eloquence: I can imagine no finer Siegmund from the point of view of a deaf man; but he may take my word for it—the word of a critic who has highly appreciated some of his performances—that he will have to get much nearer the mark in point of pitch, and assimilate his vocal phrasing much more to his admirable pantomime in point of grace, if he intends to hold his own within two minutes' walk of Jean de Reszke.

The white-armed Klafsky herself, in spite of her dramatic passion, which produced all its old effect in the more tempestuous passages, often betrayed the influence of a low standard of accuracy in intonation and distinction in phrasing. In the more violent passages she sang in tune or out of tune just as it came; and throughout the performance her "in tune" only meant commonly—seldom or never exquisitely—in tune. The only one of the principals who was free from the touch of provincialism given by this sort of laxness was Mr Bispham [American, 1857–1921].

Wiegand was a rather inert Wotan, grumbling, crusty, and distinctly lazy; but he woke up at the end and finished well. He made a few inessential alterations here and there to avoid the highest notes; but happily he did not, like Theodore Reichmann, for whom the part lies too low, ruin the second act by cutting out the first half of the narrative to Brynhild. This, one of the finest passages in the drama, was powerfully supported by Klafsky, who, having nothing to do but listen, did so with a dramatic intensity that helped Wiegand out very materially.

Sieglinde, a part which requires an artist of the first rank, did not have one on this occasion, to the great detriment of the first act. Fricka was more fortunate in the hands of Olitska, who played very well, and could easily have sustained the interest of the pages which were cut. Herr Lohse, the conductor, was energetic; but he failed to get really fine work out of the band, partly, perhaps, because the men were overworked with the Richter concerts and the Handel Festival, and partly, I venture to guess, because they were sulky about the low pitch.

One circumstance struck me as curious in connexion with the stress laid on the fact that Drury Lane is "the National Theatre." One at least of the Valkyries was an English lady, Mrs Lee. But the playbill of the National Theatre drew the line at "Mrs." In Klafsky's case it wavered between Frau and Fräulein; Pauline Joran was Miss one day and Mlle the next; "Mr" was tolerated in the case of Mr Bispham; but Mrs Lee was always Madame Lee. May I suggest in a friendly way that it is time to drop this old-fashioned nonsense?

21. German Opera at Drury Lane

The World, 18 July 1894

The production of [Weber's] Der Freischütz and [Beethoven's] Fidelio at the German Opera momentarily transferred the centre of operatic interest, for me at least, from Covent Garden to Drury Lane. It was amusing to find these two masterpieces arousing quite a patronizing interest as old-fashioned curiosities, somewhat dowdy perhaps, but still deserving of indulgence for the sake of tradition. As to the Freischütz, hardly anyone could remember its last performance in London; and I was astonished when the questions addressed to me on this point made me conscious that although the work is as familiar to me as the most familiar of Shakespear's plays, and counts, indeed, as a permanent factor in my consciousness, I could only clearly recollect two actual representations of it, one in Munich, and the other in my native town, which is not in England. I will not swear that I have not seen it oftener; for I have long since given free play to my inestimable gift of forgetting, and have lost count of the performances I have witnessed almost as completely as I have lost count of my headaches, but still, even in my case, it is somewhat significant that I should be unable to recall a representation of Der Freischütz in London. Such a doubt as to the abysmally inferior Carmen would be a ridiculous affectation.

Perhaps, therefore, the first question to answer is "How has Der Freischütz worn?" To which I am happy to be able to reply that its freshness and charm delighted everyone as much as its unaffected sincerity of sentiment impressed them, I will not, of course, pretend that the hermit strikes the popular imagination as he did in the days when hermits habitually trod the stage, and were deferred to, at sight of their brown gowns, rope girdles, and white beards, by all the civil and military authorities, exactly as if they were modern French deputies exhibiting their scarves to the police in émeutes.

And it would be vain to conceal the fact that the terrors of the Wolf's Gulch and the casting of the magic bullets were received with audible chuckling, although Sir Augustus Harris had made a supreme effort to ensure the unearthliness of the incantation by making the stage a sort of museum of all the effects of magic and devilry known in the modern theatre. He had illuminated steam clouds from Bayreuth, and fiery rain from the Lyceum Faust; he had red fire, glowing hell-mouth caverns, apparitions, skeletons, vampire bats, explosions, conflagrations, besides the traditional wheels, the skulls, the owl, and the charmed circle.

And yet nobody could help laughing, least of all, I should imagine, Sir Augustus himself. The owl alone would have sufficed to set me off, because, though its eyes were not red like those of previous stage owls, and it was therefore not so irresistibly suggestive of a railway signal as I had expected, one of its eyes was much larger than the other, so that it seemed to contemplate the house derisively through a single eyeglass. This quaint monocle notwithstanding, the scene produced some effect until the other phenomena supervened. If they had been omitted—if the apparitions had been left to our imaginations and to Weber's music, the effect would have been enormously heightened. Owls, bats, ravens, and skeletons have no supernatural associations for our rising generations: the only function an owl or a bat can now fulfil in such a scene is to heighten that sense of night in a forest which is one of Nature's most wonderful effects.

But this change in public susceptibility makes it necessary to take much greater pains with stage illusions than formerly. When the bat was a mere bogy to terrify an audience of grown-up children, it was, no doubt, sufficient to dangle something like a stuffed bustard with huge moth's wings at the end of a string from the flies to make the pit's flesh creep. Nowadays, unless a manager can devize some sort of aërial top that will imitate the peculiar flitting of the real flittermouse he must forgo bats altogether.

To appeal to our extinct sense of the supernatural by means that outrage our heightened sense of the natural is to court ridicule. Pasteboard pies and paper flowers are being banished from the stage by the growth of that power of accurate observation which is commonly called cynicism by those who have not got it; and impossible bats and owls must be banished with them. Der Freischütz may be depended on to suggest plenty of phantasmagoria without help from out-of-date stage machinists and property masters.

Except during the absurdities of the Wolf's Gulch, the performance appeared to me to be an exceptionally successful one. The orchestra has improved greatly since the first week; and though Lohse has one trick which I greatly dislike—that of hurrying at every *crescendo*—he is equal to his weighty duties as Wagner and Beethoven conductor. His handling of Fidelio was at many points admirable. Beethoven had not any bats or skeletons to contend with; but he had what was quite as bad in its way: to wit, an execrable chorus of prisoners who, on catching sight of the sentinels, would break in on the German text with mistuned howls of "Silenzio, silenzio." In both operas there were moments when the singing was beyond all apology.

Alvary's Florestan, vocally considered, was an atrocious performance; and Klafsky did not finish the aria in the first act without perceptible effort. Weber's music was, of course, far more singable; and even Alvary, saving a few intervals the corruption of which must, I suppose, be put up with from him as part of his mannerism, sang fairly in tune according to his German scale, which, let me point out, not for the first time, is not precisely the southern scale dear to our ears.

But Wiegand, as Caspar, dropped all pretence of singing before he came to the *coda* of the Revenge song. He simply shouted the words hoarsely through the orchestration, and left the audience to infer that Weber meant it to be done that way—a notion of which I beg somewhat indignantly to disabuse them. Yet in spite of all this and more, these three artists, Klafsky, Alvary, and Wiegand, with Mr Bispham and Rodemund [German tenor, 1856–1918] to help them, made Fidelio and Der Freischütz live again. Their sincerity, their affectionate intimacy with the works, their complete absorption in their parts, enable them to achieve most interesting and satisfactory performances, and to elicit demonstrations of respect and enthusiasm from the audience, which, nevertheless, if it has any ears, must know perfectly well that the singing has been at best second-rate, and at worst quite outside the category of music.

Klafsky is the best German leading soprano we have accepted here since Titiens; and though Klafsky has in her favor the enormous superiority of the era of Brynhild and Isolde to the era of Semiramide and Lucrezia, Titiens would certainly have been greatly disconcerted, if not actually terrified, had she, at Klafsky's age, been overtaken by as many vocal disasters in the course of an opera as Klafsky seems to take as a matter of course. It is a great mistake to assume, as these German artists evidently do, that their rough, violent, and inaccurate singing does not matter.

A very striking proof of this was forthcoming at the last concert at the Albert Hall, where Patti continued her new departure into Wagnerland by singing Elisabeth's prayer from Tannhäuser. Now, if I express some scepticism as to whether Patti cares a snap of her fingers for Elisabeth or Wagner, I may, after all these years of *Una voce* and *Bel raggio*, very well be pardoned. But it is beyond all doubt that Patti cares most intensely for the beauty of her own voice and the perfection of her singing. What is the result? She attacks the prayer with the single aim of making it sound as beautiful as possible; and this being precisely what Wagner's own musical aim was, she goes straight to the right phrasing, the right vocal touch, and the right turn of every musical figure, thus making her German rivals not only appear in comparison clumsy as singers, but actually obtuse as to Wagner's meaning.

At the first performance of Tristan at Drury Lane this season Klafsky, by sheer dramatic power, was really great in the death song which is the climax of the opera; but she did not sing it half as well as Nordica, who carries much lighter guns as a dramatic artist, has sung it here; and what is more, she completely perverted the music by making it express the most poignant grief for the loss of Tristan—the very sort of stage commonplace to which Isolde's sacred joy in the death towards which the whole work is an aspiration, ought to be the most complete rebuke.

If the song were beautifully sung, it simply could not take the wrong expression; and if Patti were to return to the stage and play Isolde, though she might very possibly stop the drama half a dozen times in each act to acknowledge applause and work in an *encore*—though she might introduce Home, Sweet Home, in the ship scene, and The Last Rose in the garden scene—though nobody would be in the least surprised to see her jump up out of her trance in the last act to run to the footlights for a basket of flowers, yet the public might learn a good deal about Isolde from her which they will never learn from any of the illustrious band of German Wagner heroines who are queens at Bayreuth, but who cannot sing a *gruppetto* for all that.

In offering these disparagements to the German artists, I am not for a moment forgetting that to them we owe the fact that we have any lyric stage left at all. When I turn from Klafsky playing Leonore, Agathe, Brynhild, and Isolde at Drury Lane, to Melba trying to revive Lucia at Covent Garden, or even to Calvé playing Carmen and scoring cheap triumphs with trashy one-act melodramas; and when I go on the same night from witnessing the discordant but heroic struggles of Alvary with Florestan to see Jean de Reszke gravely airing his latest achievement—nothing less than getting up the tenor part in Mr Bemberg's inanely pretty Elaine (Mr Bemberg [Argentinian/German composer, 1859–1931] being, as I am told, and can well believe, a rich young gentleman much better worth obliging than Beethoven or Wagner)—when I see all this, remembering what I do of the miserable decay and extinction of the old operatic *regime* under the sway of the two-hundred-a-night *prima donnas*, I am in no danger of losing sight of the fact that when singers sing so well that it no longer matters what they sing, they keep the theatre stagnant with all their might, the stagnation, of course, presently producing putrescence; whilst, on the other hand, the ambition of lyric artists who could not by mere charm of vocalization raise the receipts at any concert or theatre bureau by £5 makes strongly for dramatic activity and for the reinforcement of the attractions of the individual artist by those of the masterpieces of musical composition.

It is because Alvary is a much less attractive singer than Jean de Reszke that he has to summon Wagner to his aid, and play Siegfried or Tristan with infinite pains while de Reszke is giving his thousandth impersonation of such comparatively cheap and easy characters as Gounod's Faust or Romeo. This is not altogether creditable to Monsieur Jean: it makes him appear too little the chivalrous hero and devoted artist, and too much "the economic man" (sometimes supposed to be a figment of Adam Smith's, but actually one of the most real of ancient and modern types of humanity). I have appealed so often and so utterly in vain to de Reszke in these columns to do for the sake of art what Alvary does because he must, that I do not propose to waste any more ink on the matter.

To the Germans I would point out that their apparent devotion to the poetic and dramatic side of their art can claim no credit as long as it is forced upon them by the fact that they sing so badly that nobody would listen to them for their own sakes alone. The standard of beauty of execution in vocal music has fallen so low on their stage that we find an artist like Rodemund going through the music of Mime without taking the trouble to sing a single note in tune, and thereby losing all the elfin charm and doting pathos which Lieban's fine musical instinct enabled him to get from it. Yet Rodemund can distinguish the pitch of a note accurately enough, as he shewed in Beethoven's music and Weber's. In Wagner's he evidently believes it does not matter.

What the Germans have to learn from us is that it does matter. Wagner meant his music to be sung with the most exquisite sensitiveness in point of quality of tone and precision of pitch, exactly as Mozart did. In a day or two I shall be within the walls of the temple at Bayreuth, laying in a stock of observations for the further enforcement of this moral; for I am really tired of going to the theatre to hear the best music associated with the worst singing, and the best singing with the worst music.

Part V: Richard Wagner

From almost the beginning of his career Shaw promoted Wagner as the new form of opera, which Shaw referred to by the term "music drama," as the culmination of nineteenth century operatic music. He covered every performance of Wagner's operas in London theatres, and travelled several times to Bayreuth once Wagner's theatre had been built—having stated that he refused to travel to anywhere else (including Milan) for opera. Frequently, as with other forms of opera, Shaw criticized the singing and the staging, as well as the conducting (even criticizing Wagner himself). Shaw saw his political views reflected in Wagner's Ring cycle, and ended his promotion of Wagner with his book The Perfect Wagnerite, *which expresses his political interpretation, and which went through no fewer than four editions during his lifetime.*

1. The Wagner Festival

The Hornet, 6 June 1877

On the 29th of last month the last concert of the Wagner Festival took place at the Albert Hall. It is not, however, our intention to criticize any of the concerts in particular, but simply to make a few remarks about the festival generally. Herr Wagner, as a conductor, must be very unsatisfactory to an orchestra unused to his peculiarities. He does not, as has been stated, lack vigor, but his beat is nervous and abrupt; the player's intuition is of no avail to warn him when it will come; and the *tempo* is capriciously hurried or retarded without any apparent reason. Herr Richter, whose assumption of the *bâton* was hailed by the band on each occasion with a relief rather unbecomingly expressed, is an excellent conductor, his beat being most intelligible in its method, and withal sufficiently spirited. The orchestra acquitted themselves imperfectly as a rule, the inner parts dragging sometimes so much as to destroy the effect, more especially in such brisk contrapuntal movements as occur in Die Meistersinger.

The vocalists were of exceptional excellence. Frau Materna [1844–1918] justified her great reputation, not only as to the brilliancy of her tone and her great powers of endurance, but in the equally important matter of expressive delivery and distinct articulation. Frau von Sadler Grün's [1836–1917] voice is of that rare quality which has some indefinable sympathy with melancholy. Her rendering of Brangane's ominous warning in the Tristan and Isolde conveyed the spirit of the verse to perfection, and her performance of Senta's music in Der Fliegende Holländer has fixed for us a high standard for future reference. No less remarkable was her singing as the woodbird in Siegfried. Owing to a severe cold, the mellow and powerful voice of Herr Unger [1837–1887] was heard at a disadvantage. Herr Karl Hill [1831–1893] made good his claim as a singer of the first rank by his expressive and refined singing of the parts of Vanderdecken and King Marke. At each concert Herr Wagner was received with tempestuous applause. On the 19th May he was presented with an address, and a laurel wreath was placed on his brow, which latter distinction was probably more gratifying to his feelings than favorable to the dignity of his appearance. After the last concert he made a brief speech to the orchestra, expressing a satisfaction at their performance which we hope was sincere. Addresses were also presented to Herren Richter [conductor] and Wilhelmj [violinist, and sponsor of the Festival].

2. Wagner at Covent Garden Theatre

The Hornet, 27 June 1877

On the 16th inst. the popularity which Wagner's Flying Dutchman [earned] in the hands of Mr Carl Rosa [1842–1899] last year was followed up by its production at Covent Garden, with Mlle Albani and M. Maurel [1848–1923] in the principal parts. Some weeks ago we departed from the usual cautious reserve of critics as far as to predict a failure for the orchestral portion of the opera. Signor Vianesi's band has obligingly borne out our statement, but not without a faint effort to redeem its reputation. The strings and reeds were a little better than usual, whilst the brass exercised an unwonted self-denial in the matter of noise, and so added indecision and feebleness to their customary defects of coarse tone and absence of phrasing. The rendering of the picturesque and forcible overture was quite colorless; and throughout the opera the bold phrases which constantly recur were so meanly interpreted that those who had formed their expectations of the work from the spirited representation at the Lyceum must have been sadly disappointed by its new aspect under the *baton* of Signor Vianesi [1837–1908].

The scenic arrangements were elaborate, but not always appropriate. The phantom ship was represented by a substantial structure which moved with the deliberation of a canal barge, and in the last act came to pieces, or rather folded itself up with a gravity that tacitly rebuked all inclination to excitement. The violence of the waves sometimes lifted them entirely from their bed, and revealed strange submarine monsters disporting themselves in perpendicular jumps below. The billows in the opening storm were represented by an ingenious application of the principle of the corkscrew to a sheet of green canvas. The atmospheric effects were the most successful.

From Mlle Albani, as the acknowledged exponent of Wagner in this country, an interesting impersonation of Senta was expected. She was, as she always is, extremely conscientious, and the music displayed the clear beauty of her upper notes to great advantage. But Mlle Albani has not attained to that highest art which lies in the concealment of art, and consequently her acting lacked spontaneity, and had a melodramatic tinge wholly repugnant to the pure simplicity of the ideal Senta. Nevertheless, her performance may still claim a high degree of merit for its earnestness and the care with which it had evidently been studied. M. Maurel, as the Dutchman, looked very well, and sang very well. It is the more to be regretted that he should mistake fervid affectation for true acting, and so neutralize his great natural gifts. His demeanor suggested an inartistic self-consciousness, and in one or two situations he verged dangerously on the ridiculous. Signor Bagagiolo's fine voice carried him through the least intelligent impersonation of Daland we have ever witnessed. Signor Carpi was a tolerable Erik. Signor Rosario was an unsatisfactory pilot, and made nothing of the charming song in the first act. The small part of Mary was undertaken by Mlle Ghiotti. The choruses were executed without any regard to light and shade, and suffered accordingly, more especially the spinning song.

The performance generally shews that Mr Gye has good material at his command if it could only be put to any good account. Its misuse is more to be deplored in the present case because it is not so much the reputation of Covent Garden which is at stake as the popularity already too long withheld from the works of Wagner.

3. A Butchered Lohengrin

The Star, 31 May 1889

It is a sign of the shallow musical culture of the classes that they come late for Lohengrin merely because it begins at eight instead of half-past. A set that will not sacrifice its cheese and ice pudding to hear the Lohengrin prelude—the first work of Wagner's that really conquered the world and changed the face of music for us—may be a smart set for dancing; it is the reverse at music. When the *élite* of the *beau monde* did come they found that Mr McGuckin [1852–1913] had sprained his ankle badly, and had refused all proposals to go through his part in a Bath chair. His place was accordingly taken by Signor A. d'Andrade [1859–1921], who phrased his narrative in the last act very nicely. Miss Nordica [1857–1914] turned Elsa of Brabant into Elsa of Bond-street, by appearing in a corset. She produces her voice so skillfully that its want of color, and her inability to fill up with expressive action the long periods left by Wagner for that purpose, were the more to be regretted. Madame Fürsch-Madi [1847–1894], who has been subject to Italian opera for many years, got severe attacks of spasms and staggers at the emotional crises of her part. Her music, however, was not ill sung. Signor F. d'Andrade rather distinguished himself as Telramond; but on the whole, the principal singers lacked weight, breadth of style, richness of voice, and sincerity of expression needed for Lohengrin. Signor Mancinelli's Italian temperament [conductor, 1848–1921] came repeatedly into conflict with the German temperament of the composer. Where the music should have risen to its noblest and broadest sweep he hurried on in the impetuous, self-assertive, emphatic Southern way that is less compatible than any other manner on earth with the grand calm of the ideal Germany. He perpetrates, too, that abominable butcherly cut in the prelude to the second act, which is an odious inheritance from the bad old times. I confess that I cannot speak amiably of performances at which I am subjected to wanton outrages of this sort. There are reasons for the other cuts: bad reasons, but ones which must be let pass under the circumstances. But this particular cut is without excuse. Under its exasperating influence I proceeded to complain that the choristers shouted instead of singing. This is an improvement on the old choristers, who could not even shout; but shouting should not be the goal of even an operatic choir's ambition, and I do not see why, if Mr Mansfield [actor-manager, 1857–1907] has trumpets on the stage in Richard III., the Royal Italian Opera should be unable to get anything better than four vile cornets. And I wish those ladies of the chorus whom Mr Harris has provided with train-bearers and splendid dresses, would learn to walk in the true *grande dame* manner, and not make the bridal procession ridiculous by their bearing. And I should have liked more precision and delicacy from the orchestra. And, generally speaking, I do not think they can do Lohengrin worth a cent at Covent Garden; and that is the long and short of it. This is the sort of temper you get a critic into when you carry your eternal Cut! Cut! Cut! A bar too far.

4. Bassetto at Bayreuth

The Star, 1 August 1889

Imagine yourself in a state of high indignation at having paid
a pound for admission to a theatre, and finding yourself in
a dim freestone-colored auditorium, reminding you strongly
of a lecture theatre by the steepness of the bank of seats and
the absence of a gallery. But wheras most lecture theatres are
fan-shaped or circular, with a rostrum at the pivot or centre,
this one is wedge-shaped, with a shabby striped curtain cutting off the thin end of the wedge, the difference being that
the parallel benches are straight instead of curved. Partition
walls jut out at right angles to the wall of the building at intervals along the side, and break off short just in time to avoid
getting between the people in the end seats and the stage.
These walls, which do not quite reach the ceiling, are sur-
mounted by branches of lamps in round globes, which shed a
dun-colored light over the dun-colored house. You come prepared by countless photographs and engravings for the shape
of the place; but this prevailing dun tone, and the prevailing absence of cushion, curtain, fringe, gilding, or any gay
theatrical garniture, with the steepness of the bank of seats
(no pictures give you an adequate idea of this), make you inclined to think that the manager might really have touched
up the place a little for you. But you have nothing else to
complain of; for your hinged seat, though of uncushioned
cane, is comfortably wide and broad, and your view of the
striped curtain perfect. The highly esteemed ladies are requested by public notice obligingly their hats to remove, and
those who have innocent little bonnets, which would not ob-
struct a child's view, carefully remove them. The ladies with
the Eiffel hats, regarding them as objects of public interest
not second to any work of Wagner's, steadfastly disregard the
notice; and Germany, with all its martinets, dare not enforce

discipline. You open your libretto, your score, your synopsis of *leitmotifs*, or other idiotic device for distracting your attention from the performance; and immediately the lights go out and leave you in what for the moment seems all but total darkness. There is a clatter of cane seats turned down; a great rustle, as of wind through a forest, caused by 1300 skirts and coat tails coming into contact with the cane; followed by an angry hushing and hissing from overstrained Wagnerians who resent every noise by adding to it with an irritability much more trying to healthy nerves than the occasional inevitable dropping of a stick or opera-glass. Then the prelude is heard; and you at once recognize that you are in the most perfect theatre in the world for comfort, effect, and concentration of attention. You inwardly exclaim that you are hearing the prelude played for the first time as it ought to be played. And here, leaving you to enjoy yourself as a member of the analytical public, I strike in with the remark that the perfection is not in the performance, which does not touch the excellence of one which Richter conducted at the Albert Hall, but in the conditions of the performance. And I may say here, once for all, that the undiscriminating praise that is lavished on the Bayreuth representations is due to the effect of these conditions before the curtain and not behind it. The much boasted staging is marred by obsolete contrivances which would astonish us at the Lyceum as much as a return to candle-lighting or half price at nine o'clock. Mr Mansfield playing Richard III. in the dress of Garrick, or Mr Irving Hamlet in that of Kemble [each representative nineteenth- and eighteenth-century actors], would seem modern and original compared with the unspeakable ballroom costume which Madame Materna dons to fascinate Parsifal in the second act. The magic flower garden would be simply the most horribly vulgar and foolish transformation scene ever allowed to escape from a provincial pantomime, were it not recommended to mercy by a certain enormous *naïveté*

and a pleasantly childish love of magnified red blossoms and
trailing creepers. As to the canvas set piece and Gower-St.
sofa visibly pulled on to the stage with Madame Materna se-
ductively reposing on it, the steam from a copper under the
boards which filled the house with a smell of laundry and
melted axillary gutta-percha linings, the indescribable impossibility of the wigs and beards, the characterless historical-
school draperies of the knights, the obvious wire connexion
of the electric light which glowed in the ruby bowl of the
Holy Grail, and the senseless violation of Wagner's directions by allowing Gurnemanz and Parsifal to walk off the
stage whilst the panoramic change of scene was taking place
in the first act (obviously the absence of the two men who
are supposed to be traversing the landscape reduces the exhibition to the alternative absurdities of the trees taking a
walk or the auditorium turning round): all these faults shew
the danger of allowing to any theatre, however imposing its
associations, the ruinous privilege of exemption from vig-
ilant and implacable criticism. The performance of Parsifal
on Sunday last suffered additionally from Herr Grüning ex-
ecuting a hornpipe on the appearance of Klingsor with the
sacred spear; but this was introduced not as an act of whim-
sical defiance, but under pressure of the desperate necessity
of disentangling Parsifal's ankle from the snapped string on
which the spear was presently to have flown at him.

Now if you, my Wagnerian friends, wonder how I can scoff
thus at so impressive a celebration, I reply that Wagner is
dead, and that the evil of deliberately making the Bayreuth
Festival Playhouse a temple of dead traditions, instead of an
arena for live impulses, has begun already. It is because I,
too, am an enthusiastic Wagnerite that the Bayreuth management cannot deceive me by dressing itself in the skin of the
dead lion. The life has not quite gone out of the thing yet:
there are moments when the spirit of the master inspires the
puppets, and the whole scene glows into real life. From the

beginning of the Good Friday music in the last act, after the scene where the woman washes Parsifal's feet and dries them with her hair—the moment at which Parsifal's true character of Redeemer becomes unmistakably obvious to the crassest Philistine globetrotter present—the sacred fire descended, and the close of the representation was deeply impressive. Before that, a point had been brought out strongly here and there by individual artists; but nothing more. I shall return to the subject and deal more particularly with the two casts later on, when I see the work again on Thursday. For the present I need only warn readers that my censure of some of the scenic arrangements must not be allowed to obscure the fact that the Grail scene is unsurpassed as a stage picture; that the first scene, though conventional, is finely painted; and that the Spanish landscape, from which the magic garden suddenly withers (this is a capital effect), and the Good Friday landscape in the last act, are fine pieces of stage scenery.

5. Siegfried at Covent Garden

The World, 15 June 1892

Last Wednesday I was told that Siegfried was to be produced that evening at Covent Garden. I was incredulous, and asked my informant whether he did not mean Carmen, with Miss Zélie de Lussan [1869–1941] in the title part. He said he thought not. I suggested Faust, Les Huguenots, even Die Meistersinger; but he stuck to his story: Siegfried, he said, was really and truly in the bills, and the house was sold out. Still doubting, I went to the boxoffice, where they confirmed the intelligence, except that they had just one stall left. I took it, and went away wondering and only half convinced. But when I reached the theatre in the evening a little late, fully expecting to find notices on the seats to the effect that Siegfried was unavoidably postponed, in consequence of the sudden indisposition of the dragon, and Philémon and Cavalleria substituted, I found the lights out and the belated stall-holders wandering like ghosts through the gloom in search of their numbers, helped only by the glimmer from the huge orchestra and some faint daylight from the ventilators.

The darkness was audible as well as visible; for there was no mistaking that cavernous music, with the tubas lowing like Plutonian bullocks, Mime's hammer rapping weirdly, and the drums muttering the subterranean thunder of Nibelheim. And before I left the house—to be exact, it was at half-past twelve next morning—I actually saw Rosa Sucher [1849–1927] and Sir Augustus Harris hand in hand before the curtain, looking as if Covent Garden had been the birthplace of her reputation, and as if he had never heard [Donizetti's] La Favorita in his life. Perhaps it was all a dream; but it seemed real to me, and does so still. Assuming that I was awake, I may claim that at least one of those curtain calls was not for the manager at all, but for me and for those colleagues of mine who so strongly urged Sir Augustus Harris to try this experiment in the golden years when money was plenty and there was no Dissolution impending, even at the cost of depriving London of the opportunity of witnessing the debut of Signor Rawner as Manrico.

The performance was vigorous, complete, earnest—in short, all that was needed to make Siegfried enormously interesting to operatic starvelings like the Covent Garden frequenters. The German orchestra is rough; but the men know the work, and are under perfect and willing discipline. In readiness and certainty of execution they are fully equal, if not superior, to the ordinary Covent Garden orchestra. But I cannot say as much for them in the matter of purity and individuality of tone. After making every allowance for the difference between the German orchestral tradition, which is partly popular, and the English, which is purely classic, as well as for the effect, peculiar to the Nibelungen tetralogy, of the rugged and massive ground bass which pervades so much of the score, I still cannot accept this imported orchestra as being up to the standard of tone quality we have been accustomed to expect in London.

In that vast mass of brass, it seemed to me that instead of three distinct and finely contrasted families of thoroughbred trombones, horns, and tubas, we had a huge tribe of mongrels, differing chiefly in size. I felt that some ancestor of the trombones had been guilty of a *mésalliance* with a bombardon; that each cornet, though itself already an admittedly half-bred trumpet, was further disgracing itself by a leaning towards the flügel horn; and that the mother of the horns must have run away with a whole military band. Something of the same doubt hangs over the lineage of the woodwind, the bass clarinet alone being above suspicion. Even in the strings, the cellos and tenors lack distinction, though here the thicker and heavier tone is partly due to the lower pitch, which is in every other respect a prodigious relief. I think it will not be disputed that the Covent Garden orchestra, if it had half the opportunities of the German one, could handle the score of Siegfried not only with much greater distinction of tone and consequent variety of effect, but also with a more delicate and finished execution of the phrases which make up the mosaic of leading-motives, and with a wider range of gradation from *pianissimo* to *fortissimo* than Herr Mahler's band achieved, excellent in many respects as its performance certainly was. This is no mere conjecture: we have already heard the Siegfried blacksmith music and forest music played by our own orchestras in concert selections better than it was played on Wednesday last.

And that is why I still complain that Sir Augustus Harris is no more establishing the Wagnerian music-drama in London than Mr Kiralfy [creator of musical spectacles, 1848–1932] is establishing the gondola. When he organized the performance of Die Meistersinger by his own company and his own orchestra, he achieved his great feat as an *impresario*. This time he has only sent for a German *impresario* and a German company to help him out of the difficulty; and for that I grudge him the smallest exaltation, as I could have done as much myself if I had the requisite commercial credit.

The impression created by the performance was extraordinary, the gallery cheering wildly at the end of each act. Everybody was delighted with the change from the tailormade operatic tenor in velvet and tights to the wild young hero who forges his own weapons and tans his own coat and buskins. We all breathed that vast orchestral atmosphere of fire, air, earth, and water, with unbounded relief and invigoration; and I doubt if half a dozen people in the house were troubled with the critical reflections which occurred to me whenever the orchestra took a particularly rough spin over exquisitely delicate ground, as in the scene between Wotan and Erda. It is not to be doubted that all the women found Brynhild an improvement on Carmen and Co.

I say nothing of the great drama of world-forces which the Nibelung story symbolizes, because I must not pretend that the Covent Garden performance was judged on that ground; but considering how very large a proportion of the audience was still seated when the curtain came down at half-past twelve, I think it is fair to assume that the people to whom Wotan is nothing but an unmitigated bore were in a minority. At the same time, Herr Grengg [1853–1914], with his imposing presence, powerful voice, and perpetual *fortissimo*, did very little to break that ponderous monotony which is the besetting sin of the German Wotan. Lorent, who was on the stage for a few minutes as Alberich, was also earnest, but pointless and characterless. Fortunately Mime (Herr Lieban) saved the situation by his unflagging vivacity. It would be unreasonable to ask for a cleverer representation than his of the crafty, timid, covetous, and, one must admit, unmercifully bullied old dwarf. His singing shewed remarkable artistic ingenuity—exactly the quality which Mime's music requires. There are two great points in the part: first, that awful nightmare which comes upon Mime after the question-and-answer scene in the first act, when he curses the shimmering light and falls into a growing terror which is just reaching an intolerable climax when it vanishes as if by magic at the voice of Siegfried in the wood outside; and, second, his attempt to poison Siegfried after the fight with the worm, when he involuntarily talks murder instead of the flattery he intends. Both of these passages were driven home forcibly by Lieban [1857–1940], especially the poison scene, where the effect depends more on the actor and less on the orchestra than in the other. Alvary, though he has something of that air of rather fancying himself in his part which distinguishes some of the most popular impersonations of [the actor-manager, 1846–1904] Mr Wilson Barrett (whom Alvary rather resembles personally), attained a very considerable level of excellence as Siegfried, especially in the forest scene, the remembrance of which will, I think, prove more lasting than that of the first and last acts when we have seen a few rival Siegfrieds and grown a little more critical. Fräulein Traubmann [1866–1951], as the bird, was energetic, purposeful, human, and, in short, everything that a bird ought not to be. For so nice a stage illusion we need wilder and far more spontaneous woodnotes than hers.

As I have already intimated, Fräulein Heink [1861–1936], as Erda, had her scene rather roughly handled both by the orchestra and by Wotan; but she nevertheless succeeded in rescuing something of its ineffable charm by her expressive delivery and her rich contralto tones. As to Rosa Sucher [1849–1927], she was as prompt, as powerful, as vigorous, as perfect in her drill, as solid and gleaming in her tone as ever. Her efficiency, brilliancy, and strength have a charm that is rather military than feminine; and consequently they will fail to rouse the voluptuous enthusiasm of our devotees of that splendid and invariably repentant female, the Womanly Woman; but as Brynhild was no Magdalen, Frau Sucher can hardly be blamed for not making her one. Finally, I have to chronicle several curtain calls for the energetic conductor, Herr Mahler. He knows the score thoroughly, and sets the tempi with excellent judgment. That being so, I hope he will yet succeed in getting a finer quality of execution from his band.

The scenery is of the usual German type, majestic, but intensely prosaic. The dragon, whose vocal utterances were managed jointly by Herr Wiegand and a speaking-trumpet, was a little like Carpaccio's dragon at San Giorgio Schiavone, a little like the Temple Bar griffin, and a little like a camel about the ears, although the general foundation appeared to be an old and mangy donkey. As usual, people are complaining of the dragon as a mistake on Wagner's part, as if he were the man to have omitted a vital scene in his drama merely because our stage machinists are such duffers as to be unable, with all their resources, to make as good a dragon as I could improvize with two old umbrellas, a mackintosh, a clotheshorse, and a couple of towels. Surely it is within the scope of modern engineering to make a thing that will give its tail one smart swing round, and then rear up.

The stage effects throughout were punctual and conscientious (always excepting the flagrant exhibition of Brynhild in the last act as the Sleeping Beauty instead of as an armed figure whose sex remains a mystery until Siegfried removes the helmet and cuts away the coat of mail); but they were not very imaginative. The stithy was lighted like a Board School; and the fires of Loge and the apparition of Erda might have been ordered from the gas company, for all the pictorial art they displayed. Sir Augustus Harris need not look to Bayreuth for a lead in this direction. Where Bayreuth surpasses us is not in picturesque stage composition, but in the seriousness, punctuality, and thoroughness with which it looks after the stage business, which is mostly left to take care of itself at Covent Garden.

I am compelled by want of space to postpone until next week my notice of Mr de Lara's Light of Asia, which was successfully produced on Saturday evening. If it is repeated in the meantime, Mr de Lara [singer as well as composer, 1858–1935] will do well to withdraw the fourth act, unless the establishment can do something better in the way of staging it. It almost eclipses the absurdities of the Tannhäuser *mise en scène* at present.

6. Wagner's Theories

The World, 17 January 1894

It is not often that one comes across a reasonable book about music, much less an entertaining one. Still, I confess to having held out with satisfaction to the end of M. Georges Noufflard's Richard Wagner d'après lui-même (Paris, Fischbacher, 2 vols., at 3.50 fr. apiece). Noufflard is so exceedingly French a Frenchman that he writes a preface to explain that though he admires Wagner, still Alsace and Lorraine must be given back; and when he records an experiment of his hero's in teetotalism, he naïvely adds "What is still more surprising is that this unnatural regime, instead of making Wagner ill, operated exactly as he had expected." More Parisian than this an author can hardly be; and yet Noufflard always understands the Prussian composer's position, and generally agrees with him, though, being racially out of sympathy with him, he never entirely comprehends him. He is remarkably free from the stock vulgarities of French operatic culture: for instance, he washes his hands of Meyerbeer most fastidiously; and he puts Gluck, the hero of French musical classicism, most accurately in his true place.

And here let me give a piece of advice to readers of books about Wagner. Whenever you come to a statement that Wagner was an operatic reformer, and that in this capacity he was merely following in the footsteps of Gluck, who had anticipated some of his most important proposals, you may put your book in the wastepaper basket, as far as Wagner is concerned, with absolute confidence. Gluck was an opera composer who said to his contemporaries "Gentlemen, let us compose our operas more rationally. An opera is not a stage concert, as most of you seem to think. Let us give up our habit of sacrificing our commonsense to the vanity of our singers, and let us compose and orchestrate our airs, our duets, our *recitatives*, and our sinfonias in such a way that they shall always be appropriate to the dramatic situation given to us by the librettist." And having given this excellent advice, he proceeded to shew how it could be followed. How well he did this we can judge, in spite of our scandalous ignorance of Gluck, from Orfeo, with which Giulia Ravogli [born 1866] has made us familiar lately.

When Wagner came on the scene, exactly a hundred years later, he found that the reform movement begun by Gluck had been carried to the utmost limits of possibility by Spontini, who told him flatly that after La Vestale, &c., there was nothing operatic left to be done. Wagner quite agreed with him, and never had the smallest intention of beginning the reform of opera over again at the very moment when it had just been finished. On the contrary, he took the fully reformed opera, with all its improvements, and asked the XIX century to look calmly at it and say whether all this patchwork of stage effects on a purely musical form had really done anything for it but expose the absurd unreality of its pretence to be a form of drama, and whether, in fact, Rossini had not shewn sound commonsense in virtually throwing over that pretence and, like Gluck's Italian contemporaries, treating an opera as a stage concert. The XIX century took a long time to make up its mind on the question, which it was at first perfectly incapable of understanding. Verdi and Gounod kept on trying to get beyond Spontini on operatic lines, without the least success, except on the purely musical side; and Gounod never gave up the attempt, though Verdi did. Meanwhile, however, Wagner, to shew what he meant, abandoned operatic composition altogether, and took to writing dramatic poems, and using all the resources of orchestral harmony and vocal tone to give them the utmost reality and intensity of expression, thereby producing the new art form which he called "music-drama," which is no more "reformed opera" than a cathedral is a reformed stone quarry. The whole secret of the amazing futility of the first attempts at Wagner criticism is the mistaking of this new form for an improved pattern of the old one. Once you conceive Wagner as the patentee of certain novel features in operas and librettos, you can demolish him point by point with impeccable logic, and without the least misgiving that you are publicly making a ludicrous exhibition of yourself.

The process is fatally easy, and consists mainly in shewing that the pretended novelties of reformed opera are no novelties at all. The "leading motives," regarded as operatic melodies recurring in connexion with the entry of a certain character, are as old as opera itself; the instrumentation, regarded merely as instrumentation, is no better than Mozart's and much more expensive; wheras of those features that really tax the invention of the operatic composer, the airs, the duos, the quartets, the *cabalettas* to display the virtuosity of the trained Italian singer, the dances, the marches, the choruses, and so on, there is a deadly dearth, their place being taken by—of all things—an interminably dull recitative.

The plain conclusion follows that Wagner was a barren rascal whose whole reputation rested on a shop-ballad, O star of eve, and a march which he accidentally squeezed out when composing his interminable Tannhauser. And so you go on, wading with fatuous self-satisfaction deeper and deeper into a morass of elaborately reasoned and highly conscientious error. You need fear nothing of this sort from Noufﬁard. He knows perfectly well the difference between music-drama and opera; and the result is that he not only does not tumble into blind hero worship of Wagner, but is able to criticize him—a thing the blunderers never could do. Some of his criticisms: for example, his observation that in Wagner's earlier work the melody is by no means so original as Weber's, are indisputable—indeed he might have said Meyerbeer or anybody else; for Wagner's melody was never original at all in that sense, any more than Giotto's figures are picturesque or Shakespear's lines elegant.

But I entirely—though quite respectfully—dissent from Noufflard's suggestion that in composing Tristan Wagner turned his back on the theoretic basis of Siegfried, and returned to "absolute music." It is true, as Noufflard points out, that in Tristan, and even in Der Ring itself, Wagner sometimes got so rapt from the objective drama that he got away from the words too, and in Tristan came to writing music without coherent words at all. But wordless music is not absolute music. Absolute music is the purely decorative sound pattern: tone-poetry is the musical expression of poetic feeling. When Tristan gives musical expression to an excess of feeling for which he can find no coherent words, he is no more uttering absolute music than the shepherd who carries on the drama at one of its most deeply felt passages by playing on his pipe.

Wagner regarded all Beethoven's important instrumental works as tone-poems; and he himself, though he wrote so much for the orchestra alone in the course of his music-dramas, never wrote, or could write, a note of absolute music. The fact is, there is a great deal of feeling, highly poetic and highly dramatic, which cannot be expressed by mere words—because words are the counters of thinking, not of feeling—but which can be supremely expressed by music. The poet tries to make words serve his purpose by arranging them musically, but is hampered by the certainty of becoming absurd if he does not make his musically arranged words mean something to the intellect as well as to the feeling. For example, the unfortunate Shakespear could not make Juliet say:

O Romeo, Romeo, Romeo, Romeo, Romeo;

and so on for twenty lines. He had to make her, in an extremity of unnaturalness, begin to argue the case in a sort of amatory legal fashion, thus:

O Romeo, Romeo, wherefore art thou Romeo?
Deny thy father and refuse thy name,
Or, if thou wilt not, &c. &c. &c.

It is verbally decorative; but it is not love. And again:

Parting is such sweet sorrow
That I shall say goodnight till it be morrow;

which is a most ingenious conceit, but one which a woman would no more utter at such a moment than she would prove the rope ladder to be the shortest way out because any two sides of a triangle are together greater than the third.

Now these difficulties do not exist for the tone-poet. He can make Isolde say nothing but "Tristan, Tristan, Tristan, Tristan, Tristan," and Tristan nothing but "Isolde, Isolde, Isolde, Isolde, Isolde," to their hearts' content without creating the smallest demand for more definite explanations; and as for the number of times a tenor and soprano can repeat "Addio, addio, addio," there is no limit to it. There is a great deal of this reduction of speech to mere ejaculation in Wagner; and it is a reduction directly pointed to in those very pages of Opera and Drama which seem to make the words all-important by putting the poem in the first place as the seed of the whole music-drama, and yet make a clean sweep of nine-tenths of the dictionary by insisting that it is only the language of feeling that craves for musical expression, or even is susceptible of it.

Nay, you may not only reduce the words to pure ejaculation, you may substitute mere *roulade* vocalization, or even balderdash, for them, provided the music sustains the feeling which is the real subject of the drama, as has been proved by many pages of genuinely dramatic music, both in opera and elsewhere, which either have no words at all, or else belie them. It is only when a thought interpenetrated with intense feeling has to be expressed, as in the Ode to Joy in the Ninth Symphony, that coherent words must come with the music. You have such words in Tristan; you have also ejaculations void of thought, though full of feeling; and you have plenty of instrumental music with no words at all. But you have no "absolute" music, and no "opera."

Nothing in the world convinces you more of the fact that a dramatic poem cannot possibly take the form of an opera libretto than listening to Tristan and comparing it with, say, Gounod's Romeo and Juliet. I submit, then, to Noufflard (whose two volumes I none the less cordially recommend to all amateurs who can appreciate a thinker) that the contradictions into which Wagner has fallen in this matter are merely such verbal ones as are inevitable from the imperfection of language as an instrument for conveying ideas; and that the progress from Der Fliegende Holländer to Parsifal takes a perfectly straight line ahead in theory as well as in artistic execution.

The above observations on the perfect consistency of Wagner's theories with the dramatic validity of music without words must not be taken as an endorsement of the Wagner selections given at the London Symphony Concert last Thursday. Not that it was a bad concert: on the contrary, it brought Mr Henschel's enterprise back again to the first-rate standard which it attained last spring, and from which it fell off a little on the resumption of business towards the end of last year. The performance of Schubert's unfinished symphony was admirable, not so much for its technical execution—though that left nothing to be reasonably desired—as for the significant interpretation of several passages which are generally passed over as part of the mere routine of the symphonic form. If all our conductors could "read music" in this fashion we should not hear so much of the tedium of classical music, which certainly is the very dullest infliction in the world when it is served out mechanically from the band parts under the *baton* of a gentleman to whom conducting a symphony presents itself as a feat exactly analogous to driving eighty trained and perfectly willing horses round a circus ring. But my enjoyment of the symphony did not soften me towards the "arrangements" from Wagner. They may be very well for promenade concerts and provincial tours; but in London there is no reason why we should accept such makeshifts. The procession of the gods into Valhalla with the gods left out does not satisfy me. You may give me the Rhine daughters or not, as you please; but you are not entitled to tantalize me with a ridiculous squeaking oboe imitation of them; and if you are not prepared to build the rainbow-bridge for me with the full complement of harps, then leave the gulf unspanned, and do not make the scene ridiculous by a little thread of a bridge that would not support a sparrow, much less a procession of thunderers. The fact is, these arrangements, except as regards certain string effects, are paltry and misleading. They are allowable when nothing better is attainable; but in a capital city, where plenty of singers, wind players, and harpists are available, as well as halls big enough to cover their cost, the Nibelungen music ought to be performed as Wagner scored it, and not as "arranged" to suit everybody's purse by Messrs Zumpe, Humperdinck & Co. By this time it ought to be possible to repeat the 1877 experiment of an Albert Hall recital of The Ring with a fair chance of success.

The part of the concert which most excited the audience was the appearance of M. César Thomson, a violinist bearing a certain resemblance to the Chandos portrait of Shakespear, with perhaps—I think I may say so without offence to an artist who evidently cultivates the Paganini tradition of unearthliness—a dash of the Wandering Jew. His tone is remarkably sensitive, and not less so on the fourth string than on the chanterelle; whilst his skill extends to the most morbid impossibilities of trick fiddling. His metrical sense is by no means acute: it is difficult to keep the orchestra with him, as Mr Henschel found in Goldmark's concerto, which the band stumbled through in a state which I can only describe as one of utter botheration.

As to his rank as an artist, I altogether decline to give an opinion on the strength of Paganini's contemptible variations on Non più mesta, to which I listened with the haughtiest indignation, though they of course produced the usual hysterical effect on those connoisseurs of the marvelous to whom great violinists are only sideshows in a world of fat ladies and children with two heads. As to the concerto by Goldmark [Austrian composer, 1830–1915], most unwisely substituted at the last moment for that of Brahms, it contained no music good enough to test the higher qualities of the player. It will be remembered chiefly for a gratuitous explosion of scholarship in the shape of an irresistibly ludicrous fugato on the theme of Wagner's Kaisermarsch, and a cadenza so difficult that its execution gave the artist the air of a conjurer, and so disagreeable that it gave me a pain the scientific name of which I cannot at this moment recall. M. César Thomson [Belgian violinist and composer, 1857–1931], however, will be listened to with considerable interest as soon as he has taken the measure of London sufficiently to choose his program properly. He may take my word for it that a first-rate violinist no more dreams of playing Paganini's variations on Rossini at St James's Hall than Paderewski does of dropping Beethoven and Chopin out of his repertory, and replacing them by Thalberg and Gottschalk.

Part VI: Oratorios and Religious Music

For Shaw, Handel's Messiah *is the high point against which all other religious music is measured, as the first item signifies, although when he reviews performances of this oratorio Shaw continually criticizes the singers and the conductor. Choral events such as these were the major things in London at the time. But this selection demonstrates his extremely critical view of oratorio composers, apart from Handel, particularly his own contemporaries from the nineteenth century, and it is somewhat typical that he chooses to either compare them to Gilbert and Sullivan, or to put together a review of two comic operettas with his review of the religious music.*

1. The Redemption at the Crystal Palace

The Dramatic Review, 8 May 1886

Why should the Handel Festival occur only once in every three years? Would it pay to make it biennial, annual, half-yearly, quarterly, weekly? Cannot something be made out of our gold-laden visitors from the colonies this year by a festival or two? An experiment in the direction of answering these questions was made last Saturday at the Crystal Palace, when M. Gounod's Redemption was performed at the Crystal Palace by the Handel orchestra, with three thousand singers in the choir, and four hundred players in the orchestra. Additional solemnity was given to the occasion by the prohibition of the sale of intoxicating liquor at the refreshment bars during the performance (so I was assured by a neighbor on his return from a short and unsuccessful absence); and nothing was allowed to distract the attention of the audience from the oratorio except a large signboard with the inscription "OYSTERS," which was conspicuous on the left of the orchestra. The audience behaved much like a church congregation, stolid, unintelligent, and silent, except once, when Madame Albani [Canadian-born soprano, 1847–1930] took her place on the orchestra after the first part, and again when one of her highest notes excited the representatives of that large and influential section of the public which regards a vocalist as an interesting variety of locomotive with a powerful whistle.

M. Gounod is almost as hard to dispraise as the President of the Royal Academy. Both produce works so graceful, so harmonious, so smooth, so delicate, so refined, and so handsomely sentimental, that it is difficult to convey, without appearing ungracious or insensible, the exact measure of disparagement needed to prevent the reader from concluding that M. Gounod is another Handel, or Sir Frederick Leighton

[Pre-Raphaelite painter, 1830–1869] another Raphael. And indeed M. Gounod does not express his ideas worse than Handel; but then he has fewer ideas to express. No one has ever been bored by an adequate performance of the Messiah. Even a Good Friday tumble through it at the Albert Hall—ordinarily the worst thing of its kind in the whole cosmos—inspires rage and longing for justice to Handel rather than weariness. But the best conceivable performance of the Redemption would not hold an audience to the last note if the half-past five train back to town from Sydenham were at stake, much less make them impatient for a repetition of the oratorio, which is, in truth, an extremely tedious work, not because any particular number is dull or repulsive, but because its beautifies are repeated *ad nauseam*. We all remember how, at the awakening of Margaret in the prison scene of Faust, we were delighted by the harmonic transitions from phrase to phrase by minor ninths resolving on stirring inversions of the common chord of a new tone (technically unskilled readers will kindly excuse this jargon), as her voice rose semitone by semitone to the final cadence. It was a charming device; and M. Gounod used it again and again in his other operas. But when he gives us a long oratorio, consisting from the most part of these phrases on successive degrees of the chromatic scale, not only do we get thoroughly tired of them, but the pious among us feel scandalized at hearing the central figure in the tragedy of the atonement delivering himself exactly in the lovesick manner of Romeo, Faust, and Cinq Mars. No one expected M. Gounod to succeed in making the Redeemer differ from Romeo as Sarastro [character in *Die Zauberflöte* by Mozart], for example, differs from Don Giovanni; but he might at least have made him as impressive as Friar Laurence. Instead, he has limited himself to making the Prince of Peace a gentleman; and one cannot help adding that he could have done no less for the Prince of Darkness.

And such a smooth-spoken gentleman! There is a plague of smoothness over the whole work. The fact that M. Gounod has put too much sugar in it for the palate of a British Protestant might be condoned if the music were not so very horizontal. There is nearly always a pedal flowing along, and the other parts are slipping chromatically down to merge in it. Mr Compton Reade [author and parson: 1834–1909] used to be fond of calling Handel the great Dagon [national deity of the ancient Philistines] of music. But when, at the end of the second part of the trilogy, the celestial choir demands Who is the King of Glory? words cannot express the longing that arises to have done with M. Gounod's sweetly grandiose periods, and to hear great Dagon answer concerning The Lord strong and mighty; the Lord mighty in battle. And again, in the chorus of mockers at the crucifixion, Ah, thou dost declare, though the composer's dramatic instinct does make a faint struggle against his love of suave harmony, the lamenting listener's memory reverts enviously to the sinister turbulence of great Dagon's sardonic He trusted in God that He would deliver Him. If Mr Compton Reade, or anyone else, still doubts that M. Gounod is to Handel as a Parisian duel is to Armageddon, let him seek greater wisdom at the next Crystal Palace performance of the Redemption or Mors et Vita. Depend upon it, he will be forced either to change his opinion, or to accuse Handel of an extraordinary lack of variety in rhythm and harmonic treatment, and an essentially frivolous sentimental piety in dealing with a subject which, to a genuinely religious Christian composer, must be the most tremendous in universal history.

The execution of the work on Saturday last was as fine as one has any right to expect under mundane conditions. No doubt a choir of angels would sing M. Gounod's ethereal strains better than a massive detachment from the ranks of the British *bourgeoisie*; but no reasonable exception can be taken to the steady middle-class manner and solid middle-class tone of the Festival choristers. The basses seemed to me to be weak; but that may have been due to our relative positions. Some of the orchestral effects were enhanced by the vast space. Thus, at the beginning of the second part, the chords of the violins pulsating above the veiled melody of the horns, answered by the clear and brilliant notes of the trumpets in the gallery, transported us all into cloudland. Later, in an orchestral interlude full of mystery, entitled The Apostles in Prayer, the perpetual tonic pedal ceased to be tiresome, and almost excused M. Gounod for being unable to tear himself away from the few devices which he used so exquisitely. Of Madame Albani, Miss Marriott [soprano, born 1859], Madame Patey, Mr Lloyd [tenor, 1845–1927], Mr King, and Mr Santley, nothing need be said, except to congratulate them on the easiest Festival engagement that ever fell to the lot of six such vocalists.

2. Parry's Judith

The Star, 18 December 1888;
"By 'The Star's' Own Captious Critic"

London has now had two opportunities of tasting Mr Hubert Parry's Judith, the oratorio which he composed for this year's Birmingham festival. It was performed on the 6th of this month at St James's Hall, and again on Saturday last at the Crystal Palace, with Dr Mackenzie [1847–1935] in the seat of Mr Manns (gone to Scotland), and the Palace choir replaced by that of Novello's oratorio concerts. The truth about the oratorio is one of those matters which a critic is sorely tempted to mince. Mr Parry [1848–1918] is a gentleman of culture and independent means, pursuing his beloved art with a devotion and disinterestedness which is not possible to musicians who have to live by their profession. He is guiltless of potboilers and catchpennies, and both in his compositions and in his excellent literary essays on music he has proved the constant elevation of his musical ideal. Never was there a musician easier and pleasanter to praise, painfuller and more ungracious to disparage. But—! Yes, there is a serious but in the case on the present occasion; and its significance is that when a man takes it upon himself to write an oratorio—perhaps the most gratuitous exploit open to a XIX century Englishman—he must take the consequences.

Judith, then, consists of a sort of musical fabric that any gentleman of Mr Parry's general culture, with a turn for music and the requisite technical training, can turn out to any extent needful for the purposes of a Festival Committee. There is not a rhythm in it, not a progression, not a modulation that brings a breath of freshness with it. The pretentious choruses are made up of phrases mechanically repeated on ascending degrees of the scale, or of hackneyed scraps of *fugato* and pedal point. The unpretentious choruses, smooth and sometimes pretty hymnings about nothing in particular, would pass muster in a mild cantata: in an oratorio they are flavorless. It is impossible to work up any interest in emasculated Handel and watered Mendelssohn, even with all the modern adulterations. The instrumentation is conventional to the sleepiest degree: trombone solemnities, sentimentalities for solo horn with *tremolo* accompaniment, nervous excitement fiddled *in excelsis*, drum points as invented by Beethoven, and the rest of the worn-out novelties of modern scoring.

Of the music assigned to the principal singers, that of Judith is the hardest to judge, as Miss Anna Williams [soprano, 1706–1893] labored through its difficulties without eloquence or appropriate expression, and hardly ever got quite safely and reassuringly into tune. Madame Patey as Meshullemeth discoursed in lugubrious dramatic recitative about desolate courts and profaned altars. She was repaid for her thankless exertions by one popular number in the form of a ballad

which consisted of the first line of The Minstrel Boy [Irish pa-
triotic song by Thomas Moore], followed by the second line
of Tom Bowling [sea song by Charles Dibdin], connected by
an "augmentation" of a passage from the *finale* of the second
act of Lucrezia Borgia, with an ingenious blend of The Girl I
Left Behind Me [Irish folksong, late eighteenth century] and
We Be Three Poor Mariners [1609]. It will be understood,
of course, that the intervals—except in the Lucrezia Borgia
case—are altered, and that the source of Mr Parry's unconscious inspiration is betrayed by the accent and measure only.
Manasseh, a paltry creature who sings Sunday music for the
drawing room whilst his two sons are cremated alive before
his eyes, was impersonated by Mr Barton McGuckin [Irish
tenor, 1852–1913], who roused a bored audience by his delivery
of a Handelian song, which has the fault of not being by Handel, but is otherwise an agreeable composition, and a great
relief to the music which precedes it. Indeed matters generally grow livelier towards the end.

The Israelites become comparatively bright and vigorous
when Judith cuts Holofernes' head off. The ballad is grate-
fully remembered; the enchanting singing of Manasseh's son
is dwelt upon; the Handelian song is quoted as a fine thing;
and so Judith passes muster for the time.

One of the painful features of oratorio performances in
this country is the indifference of most English singers to
the artistic treatment of their own language. Hardly any of
them shew the results of such training as that by which Italian singers used to be kept at *do, re, mi, fa* until they acquired
a certain virtuosity in the sounding of the vowel and the articulation of the consonant. On Saturday afternoon it was
not pleasant to hear Mr Barton McGuckin singing line after
line as if he were vocalizing for the sake of practice on the
very disagreeable vowel *aw*. By a singer who knows this department of his business, such a word, for example, as "command" is a prized opportunity. Mr Barton McGuckin pro-

nounced it "co-mawnnd" and spoiled it. It is somewhat unlucky that artists who are aware of the full importance of
pronunciation, and whose cultivated sense of hearing keeps
them acutely conscious of distinctions to which the ordinary
singer seems deaf, are also for the most part persons with
a strong mannerism, which makes it unsafe to recommend
them as models for imitation. Advise a student to pronounce
as [nineteenth-century actors] Mr Irving does, as Mr Sims
Reeves does, as Mrs Weldon does, or as Madame Antoinette
Sterling [soprano, 1850–1904] does, and the chances are that
that student will simply graft on to his own cockney diphthongs and muddled consonants an absurd burlesque of Mr
Irving's resonant nose, of Mr Sims Reeve's lackadaisical way
of letting the unaccented syllables die away, of Mrs Weldon's
inflexible delivery and shut teeth, or of Madame Sterling's
peculiar cadence and Scottish-American accent.

The importance of this question of English as she is sung is
emphasized just now by the advertisement which announces
Mr Leslie's [composer and conductor, 1822–1896] very laud-
able and farsighted plan of making the new Lyric Theatre an
English opera house. English opera suggests at once the Carl
Rosa style of entertainment. Now, with all due honor to Mr
Carl Rosa's enterprise and perseverance, the performances of
his company have never, even at their best, achieved a satisfactory degree of distinction and refinement. But what is
peculiar to its representation is the slovenliness in uttering
the national language. In an institution which ought to be
a school of pure English this is disgraceful, the more so as
the defect is, of course, not really the result of social and educational disadvantages, but only of indifference caused by
colloquial habit, and by want of artistic sensibility and vigi-
lance.

The Gilbert-Sullivan form of opera caused a remarkable
improvement in this respect by making the success of the
whole enterprise depend on the pointed and intelligible de-

livery of the words. It is an encouraging sign, too, that in the success of Dorothy a very important share has been borne by Mr Hayden Coffin [baritone, 1862–1935], an American, who is a much more accomplished master of his language than many older and more famous baritones of English birth. If Mr Leslie is well advised he will test the artists whom he engages for his new theatre no less carefully as speakers than as singers.

The other day a small but select audience assembled in one of Messrs Broadwood's rooms to hear Miss Florence May play a pianoforte concerto by Brahms. An orchestra being out of the question, Mr Otto Goldschmidt [composer and conductor, 1829–1907] and Mr Kemp played an arrangement of the band parts on two pianofortes. Brahm's music is at bottom only a prodigiously elaborated compound of incoherent reminiscences, and it is quite possible for a young lady with one of those wonderful "techniques," which are freely manufactured at Leipzig and other places, to struggle with his music for an hour at a stretch without giving such an insight to her higher powers as half a dozen bars of sonata by Mozart. All that can be said confidently of Miss May is that her technique is undeniable. The ensemble of the three Broadwood grands was not so dreadful as might have been expected, and the pretty *finale* pleased everybody.

(The above hasty (not to say silly) description of Brahm's music will, I hope, be a warning to critics who know too much. In every composer's work there are passages that are part of the common stock of music of the time; and when a new genius arises, and his idiom is still unfamiliar and therefore even disagreeable, it is easy for a critic who knows that stock to recognize its contributions to the new work and fail to take in the original complexion put upon it. Beethoven denounced Weber's Euryanthe overture as a string of diminished sevenths. I had not yet got hold of the idiosyncratic Brahms. I apologize. (1936))

3. Miss Smyth's Decorative Instinct

The World, 25 January 1893

To Miss E. M. Smyth [1858–1944], the composer of the Mass performed for the first time at the Albert Hall last Wednesday, I owe at least one hearty acknowledgment. Her Mass was not a Requiem. True, it was carefully announced as "a Solemn Mass"; but when it came to the point it was not so very solemn: in fact, the Gloria, which was taken out of its proper place and sung at the end by way of a finish, began exactly like the opening choruses which are now de rigueur in comic operas. Indeed, the whole work, though externally highly decorous, has an underlying profanity that makes the audience's work easy.

If you take an average mundane young lady, and ask her what service to religion she most enjoys rendering, she will probably, if she is a reasonably truthful person, instance the decoration of a church at Christmas. And, beyond question, a girl of taste in that direction will often set forth in a very attractive and becoming way texts of the deepest and most moving significance, which, nevertheless, mean no more to her than the Chinese alphabet. Now I will not go so far as to say that Miss Smyth's musical decoration of the Mass is an exactly analogous case; for there are several passages in which her sense of what is pretty and becoming deepens into sentimental fervor, just as it also slips back occasionally into a very unmistakable reminiscence of the enjoyment of the ballroom; but I must at least declare that the decorative instinct is decidedly in front of the religious instinct all through, and that the religion is not of the widest and most satisfying sort.

There are great passages in the Mass, such as "I look for the life of the world to come," which stir all men who have any faith or hope left in them, whether the life they look for is to be lived in London streets and squares, or in another world, and which stand out in adequate modern settings of religious services from among the outworn, dead matter with which creeds inevitably become clogged in the course of centuries. Every critic who goes to hear a setting of words written hundreds of years ago knows that some of them will have lost their sincerity, if not their very meaning, to the composer of today; and at such points he looks for a display of pure musicianship to fill the void; whilst he waits with intense interest and hope for the live bits.

Miss Smyth, however, makes no distinctions. She writes undiscriminatingly, with the faith of a child and the orthodoxy of a lady. She has not even those strong preferences which appear in the early religious works of Mozart and Raphael. Consequently, her Mass belongs to the light literature of Church music, though it is not frivolous and vulgar, as so much Church music unfortunately is. It repeatedly spurts ahead in the briskest fashion; so that one or two of the drum flourishes reminded me, not of anything so vulgar as the Salvation Army, but of a crack cavalry band.

There is, too, an oddly pagan but entirely pleasant association in Miss Smyth's mind of the heavenly with the pastoral: the curious trillings and pipings, with violin *obbligato*, which came into the Creed at the descent from heaven; the *Et vitam venturi*, on the model of the trio of the Ninth Symphony; and the multitudinous warblings, as of all the finches of the grove, at the end of the Gloria, conveyed to me just such an imagination of the plains of heaven as was painted by John Martin [Romantic artist, 1789–1854]. Much of the orchestral decoration is very pretty, and shews a genuine feeling for the instruments. The passage in the Hosanna for the long trumpet which Mr Morrow mastered for the use of the Bach Choir, fairly brought down the house.

I have often tried to induce composers to avail themselves of this instrument; and now that Miss Smyth has set the example, with immediate results in the way of applause both for herself and the player, I do not see what there is to prevent a triumphant renovation of the treble section of the brass, especially now that Mr Wyatt's application of the double slide to the trumpet has at last made the slide-trumpet as practicable as the incurably vulgar but hitherto unavoidable cornet. Miss Smyth's powers of expression do not go beyond what the orchestra can do for her. None of the vocal solos in the Mass have that peculiar variety and eloquence which are distinctively human: the contralto solo, in which the voice is treated merely as a pretty organ-stop, and the setting of the Agnus Dei for the tenor, which is frank violin music, conclusively prove her limitations, which, let us hope, are only due to want of experience of what can be done with really expressive singers.

The work, as a whole, is fragmentary, with too many pretentious *fugato* beginnings which presently come to nothing, and with some appallingly commonplace preparatory passages before the sections of the continuous numbers; but it is very far from being utterly tedious and mechanical like Dvořák's Requiem [composed 1890], or heavy, sententious, and mock-profound like—well, no matter. Above all, it is interesting as the beginning of what I have so often prophesied—the conquest of popular music by woman. Whenever I hear the dictum "Women cannot compose" uttered by some male musician whose whole endowment, intellectual and artistic, might be generously estimated as equivalent to that of the little finger of [popular authors of fiction] Miss Braddon or Miss Broughton, I always chuckle and say to myself "Wait a bit, my lad, until they find out how much easier it is than literature, and how little the public shares your objection to hidden consecutives, descending leading notes, ascending sevenths, false relations, and all the other items in your *index expurgatorius!*"

What musician that has ever read a novel of Ouida's [Maria Louise de la Ramée, 1839–1908] has not exclaimed sometimes

"If she would only lay on this sort of thing with an orchestra, how concerts would begin to pay!" Since women have suc-ceeded conspicuously in Victor Hugo's profession, I cannot see why they should not succeed equally in Liszt's if they turned their attention to it.

The night before the Mass I went to a comic opera at the Shaftesbury; and the night after it I went to another at the Lyric. Miss Smyth could have written up both of them with considerable advantage to the finales. They resemble onean-other in shewing the composer to much greater advantage than the librettist. The book of La Rosière [1769 opera by Charles Simon Favart] is by Mr Monkhouse [baritone, 1854–1901], who has never shewn himself such a thorough actor as in the invention of this opera book. Such a hotch-potch of points, situations, *contretemps*, and Monkhousisms, unattached, unprovoked, uncaused, unrelated, and conse-quently unmeaning and unsuccessful, was never emptied out of any actor's budget. The utmost that can be said for it is that there are some passages which would be funny if the author himself were on the stage to take them in hand. Un-fortunately, they do not suit the style of Messrs Robertson and Barrington Foote [tenor, 1876–1899]. The one advantage of Mr Monkhouse's dramatic method is that the opportunity for improvisation offered to the actors is only limited by the need for finishing in time for the last trains, since the charac-ters and circumstances are nebulous enough to admit of any possible remark falling from the persons on the stage with-out incongruity. The who, the what, the when, the where, and the how of the play remain undecided to the last; and Mr Elton took full advantage of this on the night of my visit, when his colleagues were obviously wondering half the time what he was going to say next. He certainly did manage to dance and droll an impossible part into toleration, and even into popularity. But what saved the piece was the music, the czardas in the second act (a hint taken, possibly, from the

vogue of Liszt's Hungarian Rhapsodies in the concert room),
and, I hope, the scenery—I can only hope it, because it is not
easy to guess how far audiences appreciate the fact that the
finest art presented to them on the stage is often to be found,
not in the music, or the singing, or the acting, but in the
painting of the back-cloth. Such a scene as Mr Hann's Outside the Village [who also designed sets for *The Importance
of Being Ernest*, 1895] is not only charming in itself, but criti-
cally interesting in a high degree to those who remember how
Telbin [set designer, 1815–1873] would have handled the same
subject; and yet it passes unnoticed, whilst yards of criticism
are written every week about Bond-street exhibitions of wa-
tercolor sketches which are the merest trumpery compared
to it or to Mr Hemsley's [well-known set designer, died 1918]
scene in the first act. For my part, I am bound to say that these
two scenes gave me greater pleasure than any other part of La
Rosière and since they have no chance of being "collected"
and passed down to future generations, with an occasional
airing at Christie's or the Winter Exhibition at the Academy,
there is all the more reason why I should make my acknowledgments on the spot.

The music of La Rosière presents no new developments;
but it is more generous and vigorous than the French work
to which we are accustomed, the treatment of the orchestra
in particular being as broad as the work will bear, and so
escaping the reproach of timorous elegance and mean face-
tiousness which many recent comic opera scores have incurred. The orchestra, conducted by Mr Barter Johns, is remarkably good. Miss Marie Halton [American lyric soprano,
born 1871 as Mary Edith Prendergast] acts somewhat in the
manner of Mrs Bancroft [actress and manager, 1839–1921], and
sings somewhat in the manner of Miss St John [burlesque
actress and music hall singer, 1855–1912], though, of course,
chiefly in her own manner, which is vivacious and effective
enough to keep her part from obeying the laws of Nature

by falling flat. Miss Violet Cameron [actress and singer, 1862–1919] and Miss Lucille Saunders [contralto and actress, 1867–1919] add to the interest of the cast, if not of the opera.

The Magic Opal, at the Lyric, is a copious example of that excessive fluency in composition of which Señor Albéniz [Spanish composer, 1860–1909] has already given us sufficient proofs. His music is pretty, shapely, unstinted, lively, good-natured, and far too romantic and refined for the stuff which Mr Arthur Law [playwright, scene designer and librettist for the Savoy Opera and musicals, 1844–1913] has given him to set. But Albéniz has the faults as well as the qualities of his happy and uncritical disposition; and the grace and spirit of his strains are of rather too obvious a kind to make a very deep impression. And he does not write well for the singers. It is not that the phrases are unvocal, or that the notes lie badly for the voice, but that he does not set the words from the comedian's point of view, his double disability as a pianist and a foreigner handicapping him in this department. The favorite performers of the company are not well fitted with parts. Poor Miss Aida Jenoure [Mrs Howard Cochran: actress, active 1884–1929], whose forte is dancing, pantomime, and sprightly comedy with some brains in it, is a mere walking *prima donna* doomed to execute a florid vocal waltz. She could not sing it the least bit; but she dodged her way through it with a pluck and cleverness which earned her an *encore.* Mr Monkhouse [comic actor, 1854–1901], of whom it has been apparent any time these two years that he is potentially much more than a mere buffoon, has to buffoon away all the evening for want of anything better to do with his part. Mr Fred Kaye, too, is wasted. The only success of the first night was made by a Miss May Yohé [American musical theatre actress, 1866–1938], who, though she spoke the American language, actually had *not* ordered her florist to deliver half his stock to her across the footlights. She is personally attractive; her face, figure, and movements are lively and expressive; and her voice is extraordinarily telling: it sounds like a deep contralto; but the low notes beneath the stave, which are powerful in a normally trained contralto, are weak; and she has practically no high notes. But the middle of the voice, which she uses apparently by forcing her chest register, is penetrating and effective. In giving this account of her method I am describing what an ordinary singer would have to do to imitate her (with inevitably ruinous consequences), rather than what she does herself, as to which I am not quite assured. Probably she has one of those abnormal larynxes, examples of which may be found in Sir Morell Mackenzie's [physician, 1837–1892] list of the singers whose registering he examined. Mr Wallace Brownlow [comic opera singer, 1861–1919] was restless and off his balance, which is exactly what an artist ought not to be. Miss Susie Vaughan [Susan Candelin: burlesque dancer with her sister Kate Vaughan, born 1853] helped matters considerably as an amiable Azucena, her mock ballet with Mr Monkhouse being one of the funniest things in the piece. I must apologize to Mlle Candida for having missed her dance through running away for half an hour to the London Symphony Concert, where Mr Henschel [baritone and composer, director of the London Symphony: 1850–1934], with an ingratitude that took me quite aback, celebrated my entrance by striking up Brahms in F.

4. The Most Utter Failure Ever Achieved

The World, 3 May 1893

For some time past I have been carefully dodging Dr Hubert Parry's Job. I had presentiments about it from the first. I foresaw that all the other critics would cleverly imply that they thought it the greatest oratorio of ancient or modern times—that Handel is rebuked, Mendelssohn eclipsed, and the rest nowhere. And I was right: they did. The future historian of music, studying the English papers of 1892–3, will learn that these years produced two entire and perfect chrysolites, Job and Falstaff, especially Job. I was so afraid of being unable to concur unreservedly in the verdict that I lay low and stopped my ears. The first step was to avoid the Gloucester Festival. That gave me no trouble: nothing is easier than not to go to Gloucester.

I am, to tell the truth, not very fond of Festivals. It is not that the oratorios bore me, or even the new works "composed expressly," the word "expressly" here indicating the extra-special dulness supposed to be proper to such solemn occasions. These things are the inevitable hardships of my profession: I face them as the soldier faces fire, feeling that it is the heroic endurance of them that raises criticism from a mere trade to a profession or calling. But a man is expected to have the courage of his own profession only. The soldier must face cold steel; but he may without derogation be afraid of ghosts. The doctor who braves fever may blench from shipwreck; and the clergyman who wars daily against the Prince of Darkness is permitted to quit a field in which he unexpectedly meets a mad bull. The musical critic is ready at duty's call to stand up fearlessly to oratorios, miscellaneous concerts, requiems, and comic operas; but it is no part of his bargain to put up with the stewards at a provincial festival. It is not that these gentlemen intend to be uncivil, or are by nature more evilly dispositioned than their fellow creatures; but they have no manners, no *savoir vivre*: they are unsocially afraid of the public, snobbishly afraid of being mistaken for professional attendants, unaccustomed to their work (which requires either experience or tact and self-possession), and inflated with a sense of their importance instead of sobered by a sense of their responsibility.

Consequently they are fussy, suspicious, rude or nervous, as the case may be, constantly referring helplessly to the one or two of their number who have their wits about them, and not unfrequently blundering unintentionally to within a per-ilous distance of the point at which the more choleric and muscular sort of visitor will threaten violence and execute profanity, and the more subtly malicious will patronizingly offer the blunderer a tip. By good luck, I have never myself been outraged by a festival steward; but the mere flavor of ir-responsible and incompetent officialism poisons the artistic atmosphere for me.

It brings before me the appalling centralization of English intellectual and artistic life, and therefore of social grace, with the consequent boorification of the provinces. It will never be merrie England until every man who goes down from Lon-don to a festival or other provincial function will frankly say to his host "My friend: your house is uncommonly comfort-able, and your grub of the best. You are hospitable; and you gratify my vanity by treating me, who am a Nobody at home, as a Somebody from London. You are not bad company when you go out into the fields to kill something. But owing to the fact that you have been brought up in a town where the the-atre, the picture gallery, and the orchestra count for nothing, and the exchanges count for everything, you are, saving your presence, a hopelessly dull dog; and your son is growing up as dull a dog as you." Not a polite speech, maybe; but you can-not make revolutions with rosewater; and what is wanted in English provincial life is nothing short of a revolution.

Such being my sentiments, it will be understood that I forewent Gloucester and Job last autumn without regret. I have explained the matter at some length, not because I have not said all the above before, but solely to put off for awhile the moment when I must at last say what I think of Dr Parry's masterpiece. For I unluckily went last Wednesday to the con-cert of the Middlesex Choral Union, where the first thing that happened was the appearance of Dr Parry amid the burst of affectionate applause which always greets him. That made me uneasy; and I was not reassured when he mounted the conductor's rostrum, and led the band into a prelude which struck me as being a serious set of footnotes to the bridal march from [Wagner's] Lohengrin. Presently up got Mr Bantock Pierpoint [baritone, 1854–1933], and sang, without a word of warning, There was a man in the land of Uz whose name was Job. Then I knew I was in for it; and now I must do my duty.

I take Job to be, on the whole, the most utter failure ever achieved by a thoroughly respectworthy musician. There is not one bar in it that comes within fifty thousand miles of the tamest line in the poem. This is the naked, unexaggerated truth. Is anybody surprised at it? Here, on the one hand, is an ancient poem which has lived from civilization to civilization, and has been translated into an English version of haunting beauty and nobility of style, offering to the musician a subject which would have taxed to the utmost the highest powers of Bach, Handel, Mozart, Beethoven, or Wagner. Here on the other is, not Bach nor Handel nor Mozart nor Beethoven nor Wagner, not even Mendelssohn or Schumann, but Dr Parry, an enthusiastic and popular professor, fortyfive years old, and therefore of ascertained powers.

Now, will any reasonable person pretend that it lies within the limits of those powers to let us hear the morning stars singing together and the sons of God shouting for joy? True, it is impossible to say what a man can do until he tries. I may before the end of this year write a tragedy on the subject of King Lear that will efface Shakespear's; but if I do it will be a surprise, not perhaps to myself, but to the public. It is certain that if I took the work in hand I should be able to turn out five acts about King Lear that would be, at least, grammatical, superficially coherent, and arranged in lines that would scan. And I doubt not at all that some friendly and ingenuous critic would say of it "Lear is, from beginning to end, a remarkable work, and one which nobody but an English author could have written. Every page bears the stamp of G. B. S.'s genius; and no higher praise can be awarded to it than to say that it is fully worthy of his reputation." What critic would need to be so unfriendly as to face the plain question "Has the author been able for his subject?"

I might easily shirk that question in the case of Job: there are no end of nice little things I could point out about the workmanship shewn in the score, its fine feeling, its scrupulous moderation, its entire freedom from any base element of art or character, and so on through a whole epitaph of pleasant and perfectly true irrelevancies. I might even say that Dr Parry's setting of Job placed him infinitely above the gentleman [Fred Gilbert, 1892] who set to music The Man that broke the Bank. But would that alter the fact that Dr Parry has left his subject practically untouched, whilst his music hall rival has most exhaustively succeeded in covering his? It is the great glory of Job that he shamed the devil. Let me imitate him by telling the truth about the work as it appeared to me. Of course I may be wrong: even I am not infallible, at least not always.

And it must be remembered that I am violently prejudiced against the professorial school of which Dr Parry is a distinguished member [President, Royal School of Music]. I always said, and say still, that his much-admired oratorio Judith has absolutely no merit whatever. I allowed a certain vigor and geniality in his L'Allegro ed il Penseroso, and a certain youthful inspiration in his Prometheus. But even these admissions I regarded as concessions to the academic faction which he leans to; and I was so afraid of being further disarmed that I lived in fear of meeting him and making his acquaintance; for I had noticed that the critics to whom this happens become hopelessly corrupt, and say anything to please him without the least regard to public duty. Let Job then have the benefit of whatever suspicion may be cast on my verdict by my prepossessions against the composer's school.

The first conspicuous failure in the work is Satan, who, after a feeble attempt to give himself an infernal air by getting the bassoon to announce him with a few frog-like croaks, gives up the pretence, and, though a tenor and a fiend, models himself on Mendelssohn's St Paul. He has no tact as an orator. For example, when he says "Put forth thine hand now and touch all that he hath, and he will curse thee to thy face," there is not a shade of skepticism or irony in him; and he ineptly tries to drive his point home by a melodramatic shriek on the word "curse." When one thinks—I will not say of Loki or Klingsor, but of Verdi's Iago [*Otello*, 1887] and Boïto's Mefistofele [1868], and even of Gounod's stage devil, it is impossible to accept this pale shadow of an excitable curate as one of the poles of the great world magnet.

As to Job, there is no sort of grit in him: he is abject from first to last, and is only genuinely touching when he longs to lie still and be quiet where the wicked cease from troubling and the weary are at rest. That is the one tolerable moment in the work; and Job passes from it to relapse into dulness, not to rise into greater strength of spirit. He is much distracted by fragments of themes from the best composers coming into his head from time to time, and sometimes cutting off the thread of his discourse altogether. When he talks of mountains being removed, he flourishes on the flute in an absurdly inadequate manner; and his challenge to God, Shew me wherefore Thou contendest with me, is too poor to be described.

Not until he has given in completely, and is saying his last word, does it suddenly occur to him to make a hit; and then, in announcing that he repents in dust and ashes, he explodes in the most unlooked-for way on the final word "ashes," which produces the effect of a sneeze. The expostulation of God with Job is given to the chorus: the voice that sometimes speaks through the mouths of babes and sucklings here speaks through the mouths of Brixton and

Bayswater, and the effect is precisely what might have been expected. It is hard to come down thus from the "heil'gen Hallen" ["In diesen heiligen Hallen" from *Die Zauberflöte* by Mozart] of Sarastro to the suburbs.

There is one stroke of humor in the work. When Job says, The Lord gave, and the Lord taketh away: blessed be the name of the Lord, a long and rueful interval after the words "taketh away" elapses before poor Job can resign himself to utter the last clause. That is the sole trace of real dramatic treatment in this dreary ramble of Dr Parry's through the wastes of artistic error. It is the old academic story—an attempt to bedizen a dramatic poem with scraps of sonata music.

Dr Parry reads, The walls are broken down: destroyed are the pleasant places; and it sounds beautifully to him. So it associates itself with something else that sounds beautifully—Mendelssohn's violin concerto, as it happens in this case—and straightway he rambles off into a rhythm suggested by the first movement of the concerto, and produces a tedious combination which has none of the charm or propriety of either poem or concerto. For the sake of relief he drags in by the ears a piece of martial tumult—See! upon the distant plain, a white cloud of dust, the ravagers come—compounded from the same academic prescription as the business of the dragon's teeth coming up armed men in Mackenzie's Jason [1882]; and the two pieces of music are consequently indistinguishable in my memory—in fact, I do not remember a note of either of them.

I have no wish to linger over a barbarous task. In time I may forgive Dr Parry, especially if he will write a few more essays on the great composers, and confine himself to the composition of "absolute music," with not more than three pedal points to the page. But at this moment I feel sore. He might have let Job alone, and let me alone; for, patient as we both are, there are limits to human endurance. I hope he will burn the score, and throw Judith in when the blaze begins to flag.

As to the performance, it did not greatly matter. On the whole, it was somewhat tame, even relatively to the music. Mr Piercy's [tenor, 1855–1900] treatment of the high notes in his part offended all my notions of artistic singing. Mr Newman [impresario and bass, 1858–1926] did what he could with the part of Job; and his performance was entirely creditable to him. Mr Bantock Pierpoint, as the Narrator, gave more pleasure than any of his colleagues. Miss Palliser [American soprano, born 1872] was the shepherd boy. The chorus was not very vigorous or majestic; but it made the most of itself.

Part VII: Family

Shaw uses members of his family—in particular his surrogate father, Vandeleur Lee, and his sister Lucy Shaw, a singer of operetta on the London stage—as references in his music reviews. However he also focused on them in two reviews. These are separated out from the opera section to highlight Shaw's commitment; and it is noticeable that his highly negative review of the pastoral comic opera, Dorothy, in which his sister starred, does not mention her by name although he praises her artistic ability.

1. Amateur Opera at Londonderry House

The Court Journal, 8 July 1882
Unsigned

The fine banqueting hall of Londonderry House, Park Lane, was crowded on Saturday evening by a fashionable audience assembled to witness an amateur operatic performance in aid of the fund for the relief of distressed Irish ladies. The room was brilliantly lighted, and the historical portraits of illustrious members of the Stewart-Vane-Tempest families were seen to advantage. Conspicuous were the portraits of the eminent statesman Viscount Castlereagh, who represented this country at the Congress at Vienna, which followed the Revolutionary and Napoleonic wars; and of Baron Stewart (third Marquis), the gallant Peninsular general. The room also contains some fine statuary presented to Charles William (third Marquis), by the Emperor Nicholas of Russia in 1837, and busts of [English Prime Ministers] Pitt and Castlereagh.

The performance, which was efficiently conducted by Mr Vandeleur Lee [who requested that Shaw review his piece, and persuaded the *Journal* to publish it], began at nine o'clock, and terminated just before midnight. We append the program.

The amateurs, in selecting such familiar operas as Faust and Il Trovatore, set themselves a difficult task, which, upon the whole, they satisfactorily fulfilled. All present must have heard the familiar strains from the most popular works of Gounod and Verdi repeatedly; and it was hardly judicious, therefore, to invite a comparison with the most consummate vocalists of the present and the past. However, we can speak well of Mrs Herbert Chatteris's performance, which, vocally and dramatically, was of the highest order. Mrs Inez Bell also filled her part in an adequate manner. Miss Gordon Archibald obtained a recall after singing Siebel's air *Le parlate d'amor*. Mr Barnes Newton, as Manrico, gained credit by his delivery of *Ah! che la morte*, and earned a share of the applause which greeted Mrs Inez Bell's rendering of the popular duet *Si la stanchezza*. The remaining characters were assumed by Captain Holled Smith (the Count di Luna) and Messrs Hirchfield and Maitland.

The amateurs were quite at home in comic opera, and a most enjoyable representation of Gilbert and Sullivan's Trial by Jury took place. The piece, it will be remembered, is founded upon an alleged breach of promise of marriage, and Captain Barrington Foote, R.A., was the representative of the gay deceiver.

> "It was wrong of him to do so,
> For the girl had bought her trousseau."

With yellow hair parted in the middle, an eyeglass, light garments, and vacant look, he sang and played admirably. Captain Liddell, R.A., was a most facetious judge. The offer of his breast for the bride to recline upon, and the brilliant inspiration to marry the fascinating plaintiff himself, the jury acquiescing with the words, "For he's a judge, and a good judge too," caused, as usual, much hilarity. Captain Barrington Foote's song, Lovesick boy, and Captain Liddell's ditty, How I became a judge, were humorously rendered, and the concerted music especially was very good, reflecting great credit on the pretty bevy of bridesmaids and the jury. Captain FitzGeorge, R.N., was the plaintiff's counsel, and Viscount Fielding was a droll usher of the court. Mrs Godfrey Pearse looked very pretty in bridal attire, and she played and sang with charming effect.

The difficult task of conducting this enterprising body of amateurs was discharged by Mr Vandeleur Lee, who, with the sympathetic cooperation of an orchestra of remarkable excellence, skilfully led the vocalists through the dangers of Italian opera, and dexterously rescued them from the consequences of their errors, which, it should be added, were surprisingly few.

The performers were subsequently entertained at supper by the Marchioness of Londonderry, to whose interest and hospitality the Amateur Opera Committee are largely indebted for a financial success which will, we are informed, enable Mr Herbert Chatteris, the honorary treasurer, to place at the disposal of the fund for the relief of distressed Irish ladies a substantial sum. The costumes, fittings, stage scenery, and decorations for the operas were supplied by Messrs L. and H. Nathan, 17, Coventry-street.

2. The 789th Performance of Dorothy

The Star, 13 September 1889

Last Saturday evening, feeling the worse for want of change and country air, I happened to voyage in the company of Mr William Archer [drama critic, 1856–1924] as far as Greenwich. Hardly had we inhaled the refreshing ozone of that place for ninety seconds when, suddenly finding ourselves opposite a palatial theatre, gorgeous with a million gaslights, we felt that it was idiotic to have been to Wagner's Theatre at Bayreuth and yet be utterly ignorant concerning Morton's Theatre at Greenwich. So we rushed into the struggling crowd at the doors, only to be informed that the theatre was full. Stalls full; dress circles full; pit, standing room only. As Archer, in self-defence, habitually sleeps during performances and is subject to nightmare when he sleeps standing, the pit was out of the question. Was there room anywhere, we asked. Yes, in a private box or in the gallery. Which was the cheaper? The gallery, decidedly. So up we went to the gallery, where we found two precarious perches vacant at the side. It was rather like trying to see Trafalgar Square from the knifeboard of an omnibus halfway up St Martin's Lane; but by hanging on to a stanchion, and occasionally standing with one foot on the seat and the other on the backs of the people in the front row, we succeeded in seeing as much of the entertainment as we could stand.

The first thing we did was to purchase a bill, which informed us that we were in for "the entirely original pastoral comedy-opera in three acts, by B. C. Stephenson [librettist for numerous London musicals of the time] and Alfred Cellier [composer, 1844–1891], entitled Dorothy, which has been played to crowded houses at the Lyric Theatre, London, 950 and (still playing) in the provinces 788 times." This playbill, I should add, was thoughtfully decorated with a view of the theatre shewing all the exits, for use in the event of the performance proving unbearable. From it we further learnt that we should be regaled by an augmented and powerful orchestra; that the company was "Leslie's No. 1"; that C. J. Francis believes he is now the only HATTER in the county of Kent who exists on the profits arising solely from the sale of HATS and CAPS; and so on. Need I add that Archer and I sat bursting with expectation until the overture began.

I cannot truthfully say that the augmented and powerful orchestra proved quite so augmented or so powerful as the composer could have wished; but let that pass: I disdain the cheap sort of breaking a daddy-long-legs on a wheel (butterfly is out of the question, it was such a dingy band). My object is rather to call attention to the condition to which 788 nights of Dorothying have reduced the unfortunate wanderers known as "Leslie's No. 1." I submit to Mr Leslie [accountant who purchased the production] that in his own interest he should take better care of No. 1. Here are several young persons doomed to spend the flower of their years in mechanically repeating the silliest libretto in modern theatrical literature, set to music which, pretty as it is, must pall somewhat on the seven hundred and eighty-eighth performance.

As might have been expected, a settled weariness of life, an utter perfunctoriness, an unfathomable inanity pervaded the very souls of "No. 1." The tenor [Charles Butterfield, husband of Shaw's sister Lucy], originally, I have no doubt, a fine young man, but now cherubically adipose, was evidently counting the days until death should release him from the part of Wilder. He has a pleasant speaking voice; and his affability and forbearance were highly creditable to him under the circumstances; but Nature rebelled in him against the loathed strains of a seven hundred-times repeated *rôle*. He omitted the song in the first act, and sang Though Born a Man of High Degree as if with the last rally of an energy decayed and a willing spirit crushed. The G at the end was a vocal earthquake. And yet methought he was not displeased when the inhabitants of Greenwich, coming fresh to the slaughter, encored him.

The baritone had been affected the other way: he was thin and worn; and his clothes had lost their lustre. He sang Queen of My Heart twice in a hardened manner, as one who was prepared to sing it a thousand times in a thousand quarter hours for a sufficient wager. The comic part, being simply that of a circus clown transferred to the lyric stage, is better suited for infinite repetition; and the gentleman who undertook it addressed a comic lady called Priscilla as Sarsaparilla during his interludes between the *haute-école* acts of the *prima donna* and tenor, with a delight in the rare aroma of the joke, and in the roars of laughter it elicited, which will probably never pall. But anything that he himself escaped in the way of tedium was added tenfold to his unlucky colleagues, who sat out his buffooneries with an expression of deadly malignity. I trust the gentleman may die in his bed; but he would be unwise to build too much on doing so. There is a point at which tedium becomes homicidal mania.

The ladies fared best. The female of the human species has not yet developed a conscience: she will apparently spend her life in artistic self-murder by induced Dorothitis without a pang of remorse, provided she be praised and paid regularly. Dorothy herself [played by Shaw's sister, Lucy], a beauteous young lady of distinguished mien, with an immense variety of accents ranging from the finest Tunbridge Wells English (for genteel comedy) to the broadest Irish (for repartee and low comedy), sang without the slightest effort and without the slightest point, and was all the more desperately vapid because she suggested artistic gifts wasting in complacent abeyance. Lydia's voice, a hollow and spectral contralto, alone betrayed the desolating effect of perpetual Dorothy: her figure retains a pleasing plumpness akin to that of the tenor; and her spirits were wonderful, all things considered. The chorus, too, seemed happy; but that was obviously because they did not know any better. The pack of hounds darted in at the end of the second act evidently full of the mad hope of finding something new going on; and their depression, when they discovered it was Dorothy again, was pitiable. The S.P.C.A. should interfere. If there is no law to protect men and women from Dorothy, there is at least one that can be strained to protect dogs.

I did not wait for the third act. My companion had several times all but fallen into the pit from sleep and heaviness of spirit combined; and I felt as if I were playing Geoffrey Wilder for the millionth night. As we moped homeward in the moonlight we brooded over what we had seen. Even now I cannot think with composure of the fact that they are playing Dorothy tonight again—will play it tomorrow—next year—next decade—next century. I do not know what the average lifetime of a member of "No. 1" may be; but I do not think it can exceed five years from the date of joining; so there is no question here of old men and old women playing it with white hair beneath their wigs and deep furrows underlying their makeup. Doubtless they do not die on the stage: they first become mad and are removed to an asylum, where they incessantly sing, One, two three: one, two, three: one, two, three: one, two, be wi-eyes in, ti-I'm oh, Ph-ill is, mine, &c., until the King of Terrors (who ought to marry Dorothy) mercifully seals their tortured ears for ever.

I have always denounced the old-fashioned stock company, and laughed to scorn the theorists who fancy that they saw in them a training school for actors; but I never bargained for such a thing as this 789th performance of Dorothy. No: it is a criminal waste of young lives and young talents; and though it may for a time make more money for Mr Leslie, yet in the end it leaves him with a worn-out opera and a parcel of untrained novices on his hands when he might have a repertory of at least half a dozen works and a company of fairly skilled artists able to play them at a day's notice. We exclaim at the dock directors' disregard of laborers' bodies; but what shall we say of the managers' disregard of artists' souls. Ti, rum ti ty, rum ti ty, rum ti ty, rum m m: tiddy tum tiddy tum tiddity, tum! Heavens! what hum I? Be wi-eyes in—Malediction!

Part VIII: Instrumental Concerts

Unless he is discussing a specific conductor, like Hans Richter, or a particular composer and pianist, like Edvard Grieg, in his longer pieces Shaw generally deals with several instrumental concerts in a single review. In some cases he appends short reviews of concerts to his reviews of opera performances, which are almost always longer than his reviews of instrumental music; and he seems to favour concerts in which a vocal piece is included.

1. Mozart and Haydn with Strings

6 December 1876

At the Popular Concert on the 25th ult., Mozart's string quartet, No. 2 in D minor, was performed. This work, with its *andante* which seems to forecast the sweetness and depth of the Zauberflote, its *finale* with variations, and its gay minuet and trio, is generally heard at least once during each season, and is always welcome. On this occasion, the minuet was encored. On the following Monday, the same master was represented by his quartet in D major, No. 7, and the Strinasacchi sonata for pianoforte and violin [written by Mozart for a female violinist, Regina Strinasacchi, 1761–1839]. The quartet, composed about a year later than the wellknown Jupiter symphony, displays in common with it that clear form and contrasted variety of effect, in the command of which Mozart has never been equaled. It was executed by Madame Norman-Neruda [Moravian violinist, 1838–1911, married Sir Charles Hallé, 1888], MM. Kies [pianist], Zerbini [viola], and Piatti [Italian cellist, 1822–1931], with vigor and sonority of tone, but with some want of refinement in the delicate *forte pianos* of the minuet. The Strinasacchi sonata, written hurriedly at the request of a friend, is one of the composer's less important works, and, with those who were fortunate enough to hear Madame Neruda's performance of Beethoven's Kreutzer Sonata, with Mr Hallé at the previous concert, it must have suffered by the inevitable comparison. The pianoforte part was in the able hands of Miss Zimmermann, who also played Mendelssohn's Fantasia, Op. 28, with her accustomed skill, the presto finale being taken at a dazzling speed.

Judging by the high standard taught us by the artists themselves, they scarcely did justice to Haydn's quartet, No. 6, of Op. 17. The gigue-like *presto* was satisfactorily rendered; but in the following movements the concert of the instruments was less perfect, and the F in alt, sustained by the first violin in the *largo*, was hardly up to the pitch. Miss Butterworth was the vocalist on Saturday; and on Monday Signor Gustave Garcia [Italian baritone, 1837–1925] sang Handel's Tyrannic Love and Schubert's Appeal in an exaggerated style, which obtained for the latter an ill-deserved encore.

2. Herr Richter and His Blue Ribbon

The Dramatic Review, 8 February 1885

Herr Richter's popularity as an orchestral conductor began, not in the auditorium, but in the orchestra. It dates from his first visit here in 1877 to conduct the Wagner festivals at the Albert Hall. At these concerts there was a large and somewhat clumsy band of about 170 players, not well accustomed to the music, and not at all accustomed to the composer, who had contracted to heighten the sensation by conducting a portion of each concert. It is not easy to make an English orchestra nervous, but Wagner's tense neuralgic glare at the players as they waited for the beat with their bows poised above the strings was hard upon the sympathetic men, whilst the intolerable length of the pause exasperated the tougher spirits. When all were effectually disconcerted, the composer's *bâton* was suddenly jerked upwards, as if by a sharp twinge of gout in his elbow; and, after a moment of confusion, a scrambling start was made. During the performance Wagner's glare never relaxed: he never looked pleased. When he wanted more emphasis he stamped; when the division into bars was merely conventional he disdained counting, and looked daggers—spoke them too, sometimes—at innocent instrumentalists who were enjoying the last few bars of their rest without any suspicion that the impatient composer had just discounted half a stave or so and was angrily waiting for them. When he laid down the *bâton* it was with the air of a man who hoped he might never be condemned to listen to such a performance again. Then Herr Richter [1843–1916] stepped into the conductor's desk; and the orchestra, tapping their desks noisily with their bows, revenged themselves by an ebullition of delight and deep relief, which scandalized Wagner's personal admirers, but which set the fashion of applauding the new conductor, whose broad, calm style was doubly reassuring after that of Wagner. He, meanwhile, sat humbly among the harps until he could no longer bear to listen quietly to his own music, when he would rise, get into the way of the players, seek flight by no thoroughfares and return discomfited, to escape at last into the stalls and prowl from chair to chair like a man lost and friendless. As it is difficult to remain in the room with the greatest living composer without watching his movements, even at the risk of missing some of his music—which, after all, you will have other chances of hearing—you perhaps paid less attention to Herr Richter than he deserved.

After the Wagner festival nothing remarkable in the way of conducting occurred in London until the following year (1878), when, at a series of concerts given by Madame Viard-Louis, Mr Weist Hill [choral composer, 1828–1891] achieved some extraordinary successes, which the London public would probably have recognized in the course of, say, ten years or so, had Madame Viard-Louis [pianist, 1831–1903] been able to prosecute her undertaking at a loss for so long. But this was impossible; and next year Herr Richter came again to conduct "Festival Concerts," so called because the managers knew that his reputation as conductor of the Bayreuth Festival was likely to attract the public far more than his artistic ability. In 1880, however, his position was secure; and since then we have had "Richter Concerts" annually. These concerts had many pleasant peculiarities, which their good example soon rendered less peculiar. The conductor seemed to be familiar with the music, and did not conduct at sight from a score from which he hardly ventured to raise his eyes lest he should lose his place. He did not pose and gesticulate like a savage at a war dance, nor did he, like an overbred man of St James's, scorn to appear more impressionable than a regimental bandmaster. He seemed to think about his business rather than about himself, and, in rare snatches, when the band had fallen into perfect swing, about the music rather than about his business. In these ecstatic moments his extended arms would pulsate almost imperceptibly; and poetic admirers would compare him to a benignant bird balancing itself in a cloud of blond sunshine (the blond sunshine being diffused from his fair Saxon locks). A point missed would bring him quickly to earth, alert, yet still gracious; but a point overdone—nothing short of monumental stolidity could endure his eye then. For the rest, he could indicate the subdivisions of a bar when it was helpful to do so; and he declined to follow the fashion, set by acrobats of the pianoforte, of playing all allegros against time, on the principle that fastest is cleverest.

The public felt the gain in dignity, and respected Herr Richter for it, probably without knowing why. Then he let slip the secret that the scores of Wagner were not to be taken too literally. "How" exclaimed the average violinist in anger and despair "is a man to be expected to play this reiterated motive, or this complicated figuration, in demisemiquavers at the rate of sixteen in a second? What can he do but go a-swishing up and down as best he can?" "What, indeed?" replied Herr Richter encouragingly. "That is precisely what is intended by the composer." So the relieved violinists went swishing up and down, and the public heard the hissing of Loki's fires in it and were delighted; whilst those who had scores and were able to read them said "Oh! thats how it's done, is it?" and perhaps winked. And Herr Richter flourished, as he deserved; so that even when his band is positively bad, as it was once or twice at the German Opera last year, or weary and demoralized, as it cannot but become towards the end of a long concert in the stuffiness of St James's Hall, his credit shields them from the censure of the few who know, and from the suspicion of the many who dont. He has now been engaged to conduct the Birmingham Festival, and Sir Arthur Sullivan [1842–1900], who appreciates him better than the general public, whose admiration of a musical celebrity is always half superstitious, thinks that a post of such honor should have been given to a native conductor. He has suggested Mr Cowen [composer and conductor, 1852–1935], Mr Villiers Stanford [Irish composer and conductor, 1852–1924], and Mr Barnby [composer and conductor, 1838–1896] as competent substitutes. But Mr Villiers Stanford is an Irishman; Mr Cowen is a Jew; and Mr Barnby, though an industrious and enterprising musician, accustomed to deal with large choirs, has been more successful with new works like Verdi's Requiem or [Wagner's] Parsifal than with our stock oratorios, which somehow have a stale sound under his direction which Herr Richter has not yet succeeded in imparting to any performance entrusted to his care. Besides, Mr Barnby's reputation is local. If he were selected, dozens of other local celebrities, who doubtless consider themselves equally efficient, would raise the cry of favoritism, if not of downright jobbery. To select the only popular conductor who enjoys a European reputation was the least invidious course open to the Festival Committee; and it is difficult to imagine any alternative which would not have caused more general dissatisfaction both to the profession and to the public.

It is certainly true that Herr Richter, years before he had even chosen the profession in which he is so eminent, succumbed to those "temptations to belong to other nations" which the hero of Pinafore withstood. He is not an Englishman, and he does not even intend to become one: a course quite open to him, as Sir Arthur pointed out when reminded of the supremacy of the late Sir Michael Costa [Italian-born conductor, 1808–1884]. Costa was an Englishman by domicile; and Sir Arthur himself, who was born a little westward of these shores, and who is of a darker and southerlier strain than the Saxon Richter, can claim no more. Since, however, we use a musical scale which is not specially English, but European and American also, we must go east of the Ural mountains or south of the Mediterranean to find a real "musical foreigner." Still, there is something in the remark of Sir Arthur Sullivan that "a German who cannot speak English appears oddly selected to conduct English choruses." It is less to the point that Herr Richter is not, as Costa was, conductor of the Sacred Harmonic Society and of the Italian opera, that being clearly so much the worse for the Italian opera, whilst the Sacred Harmonic, by appointing Mr Charles Hallé [conductor and pianist, 1819–1895] as successor to Costa, set the Birmingham committee the example of appointing a foreigner. And if the conductorship of a series of concerts of established reputation justified the position allowed to Costa, the Viennese conductor is qualified in that respect by the Richter concerts, which are not second in popularity or musical importance to any in London. Indeed, the increased alertness of our older institutions dates from the year in which Herr Richter gave them something tolerable to compete with. I have a particularly deadly-lively recollection of the seasons which immediately preceded his invasion; and I do not think he came a day too soon, nor have I ever met a musician who did. The objection that he is not a master of the English tongue, though invalid against a conductor of orchestral concerts or of German opera, deserves to be weighed when an English oratorio is to be performed. Orchestras only need to be sworn at; and a German is consequently at an advantage with them, as English profanity, except in America, has not gone beyond a limited technology of perdition, extremely monotonous in the recurrent irritation set up by an unsat-

isfactory rehearsal. But choristers must have their pronunciation corrected by somebody if we are ever to escape from
that hearty British "Thah wooaht Ee-li-jar," with which our
choirs are accustomed to denounce Mr Santley [baritone,
1834–1922] for troubling Israel's peace. Herr Richter clearly
cannot do this with authority. If anyone else will undertake
to polish the elocution of the Birmingham choir in the course
of a few rehearsals, he has a fair claim—other things being
equal—as against the foreigner. Pending the production of
his testimonials, we seem to bear with the foreigner very
cheerfully.

3. Crystal Palace Variety

The Star, 10 December 1888
Unsigned

Mr August Manns evidently made up his mind last week that
nobody should reproach him again with want of variety in
the Saturday program. Mozart, Schubert, Berlioz, Mr Hamish
MacCunn [Scottish Romantic composer, 1868–1916], and Sir
Arthur Sullivan were represented by some of their most characteristic work. The concert began with the overture to the
Yeomen of the Guard, by way of signalizing the replacement
in Gilbert-Sullivan opera of *pot-pourri* prelude by orthodox
overture. Then the orchestra got to serious business in the
G minor symphony. The performance of the first and last
movements only shewed that Mozart can utterly baffle a band
for which Beethoven, Berlioz, and Wagner have no terrors.
It is useless to try to make the G minor symphony "go" by
driving a too heavy body of strings through it with all the
splendor and impetuosity of an Edinburgh express. That has
been tried over and over again in London, with the result that
Mozart's reputation positively declined steadily until Hans
Richter conducted the E flat symphony here. Wagner has

told us how, when he first began to frequent concerts, he was astonished to find that conductors always contrived to make Mozart's music sound vapid. Vapid is hardly the word for any performance conducted by Mr Manns; but on Saturday, except in the slow movement and minuet, his energy was unavailing. It was magnificent; but it was not Mozart. When M. Marsick [Belgian violinist, 1847–1924] began Wieniawski's [Polish composer, 1835–1880] concerto in D minor, it at first seemed that a disappointment was in store. Wieniawski's work, which is much more truly violin music than the Beethoven and Mendelssohn concertos, requires above all a violinist who can play with perfect spontaneity, and even with abandonment. M. Marsick was constrained and mechanical, and his instrument, not at all in the vein, whined comfortlessly. Not until the movement was half over did his spirits improve. In the *andante* he completely recovered himself, and the final *allegro* was a triumph for him. A handsome recall at the end put him on the best of terms with the audience, who subsequently applauded him enthusiastically for a very pretty *Dans Slavacque*, which he played exquisitely. The vocal pieces were sung by Miss Antoinette Trebelli [also known as Mme Dolores, born 1864], who imitates, with the facility of a child, what she has heard other people doing around her all her life; but who certainly displays as yet no individuality, style, purpose, or even earnest respect for her work. For the sake of the distinguished artist whose name she bears, Miss Trebelli has been allowed a very favorable start. But she will lose that start if she allows herself to be spoilt by the foolish people who recalled her for an immature trifling with *Non mi dir* [aria from Mozart's *Don Giovanni*], an aria which only very intelligent, refined, and sympathetic singers should attempt. Miss Trebelli not only attempted it without these qualifications, but actually tampered with the concluding bars by way of improvement upon Mozart. Mr Hamish MacCunn's happy thought of setting Lord Ullin's Daughter

[poem by Thomas Campbell 1777–1844] in the freest and easiest way for chorus and orchestra was as successful as ever.
Pearsall would have laughed at the cheapness of the success;
but Pearsall would have been wrong; the *naïveté* with which
Mr MacCunn [Scottish composer, 1868–1916] has gone to
work in the simplest fashion is his great merit. The concert
ended with Berlioz's first overture, Les Francs-Juges, one of
the most striking examples of his curious gift of brains and
brimstone. A few old-fashioned bars of Rossinian tum-tum
in it sounded odd beside the poignantly expressive section in
C minor, the effect of which will not readily be forgotten by
those who heard it for the first time.

4. The Grieg Concert

The Star, 21 March 1889
Unsigned

The Grieg [Norwegian composer, 1843–1907] concert yesterday afternoon at St James's Hall is an event which the musical
world of London may look back upon with considerable pleasure and satisfaction. The Norwegian composer and his wife
will also, no doubt, carry back with them the pleasantest rec-
ollections of their enthusiastic reception at the hands of a
highly appreciative St James's Hall audience. It is, indeed, a
rare occurrence to be present at a concert the program of
which not only consists wholly of one composer's works, but
which is performed by the composer himself and his wife.
The concert opened with his Holberg Suite, or "Suite in old
style," as it was called on the program. This suite was composed on the occasion of the Holberg Jubilee in 1884, when
the Danes and Norwegians celebrated in great style the 200th
anniversary of the birth of Ludvig Holberg [Danish/Norwe-
gian author, 1684–1754], the father of the literature of those
countries, and who, by the bye, is a townsman of Mr Greig.

The composer has succeeded in reproducing with much fidelity the spirit of those "good old times," and it is almost unnecessary to say that he rendered his own composition in his elegant and attractive manner. The suite has already been performed at one of the Popular Concerts this season, but it was yesterday again received with hearty applause.

Mrs Grieg [Nina Hagerup, 1845–1935] sang Ragna and Hope, both characteristic of those "melodies of the heart" which have made her husband famous. The more we hear Mrs Grieg the more we are convinced that no one else can sing these songs so feelingly, and do such justice to them, as she. What would not most composers give for such wives, such better halves, to interpret their songs! Mr and Mrs Grieg next played a piano duet, Norwegian Dances (Op. 35). Here again the wife proved herself a valuable partner, and both she and her husband were enthusiastically applauded. In this composition Mr Grieg shews how ingeniously and artistically he contrives to weave the national melodies of his country into his composition.

The event of the day was, however, no doubt, the performance of his Sonata in C minor (Op. 45) for piano and violin. It was an excellent idea to secure the services of the brilliant violinist, Mr Johannes Wolff [1869–1947], for the violin part in this very spirited composition. It is some time since we heard a violinist who displayed so much fire and power of execution. There were moments when we were forcibly reminded of the style of Grieg's great countryman, the late Ole Bull [composer and violinist, 1810–1880]. No virtuoso on the violin can desire a better accompanist than Mr Grieg. Both Mr Grieg and Mr Wolff were rapturously applauded, and had to appear three times in response to the calls of the delighted audience.

Mrs Grieg sang three more songs, With a Water-lily, Margaret's Cradle Song, and The Rosebud. Forced to sing an *encore* she gave Björnson's well-known song *Dagen er oppe* (Day is breaking) in her most spirited and effective style. In conclusion Mr Grieg played three of his piano pieces, Berceuse, a most original and elegant composition, Humoreske, and the well-known Bridal Procession. The last is, undoubtedly, one of Grieg's most characteristic pieces for the piano, but it is necessary to hear the composition played by the composer himself the better to understand its peculiar character.

5. Circenses

The World, 24 December 1890

The musical season is turning out badly for orchestral concert givers. Mr Henschel [baritone and conductor, 1850–1934], who began by declaring that he would trust the public, and venture without a guarantee, has now sorrowfully announced that he is beaten, and cannot complete his series of symphony concerts unless more stalls are subscribed for. And Sir Charles Hallé was abandoned at his first two concerts in a way really discreditable to London amateurism. Hereupon Mr Arthur Symons [well-known poet of the time], in the Pall Mall Gazette, endeavors to sting London into doing its musical duty by declaring that we can no longer pretend to be a musical nation. As to that, it cannot be said that symphony concerts have ever been much of a national matter: so long as St James's Hall suffices for our needs in that department, it is hardly worth discussing its fullness or emptiness from the national point of view. But for the few of us who require good music as part of our weekly subsistence, the cutting off of our opportunities by no less than two concert series out of a total of four is not to be borne without remonstrance. No doubt the weather has been partly to blame: thick boots and a warm coat buttoned up to the neighborhood of the chin are indispensable in St James's Hall just now for people who wish to enjoy their music without a castanet accompaniment from their own teeth; and as the ordinary patron of the stalls is condemned by custom to garnish himself with indoor fireside wear, he naturally shirks his concerts unless the attraction is exceptionally strong. Still, I do not see why the subscriptions should not be forthcoming, whether the subscribers attend or not. Many very rich people in London seem to me to suppose that they have nothing but their own private whims to consult in the disposition of their incomes. I demur to this, and contend that they are as much bound to support orchestral concerts by their subscriptions as they are to support hospitals. That they may dislike music and never go to a concert when they can help it is clearly no more to the point than that they dislike being ill, and would not go to a hospital on any terms. If concerts of high-class music are vitally necessary, as I believe they are, and if they cannot be kept on foot without the support of the rich, why, the rich must do their duty.

As a plebeian, I demand *circenses*, if not *panem*, to that extent. And it cannot be urged that there is at present any difficulty in finding worthy enterprises to support. Hallé has long been above suspicion in this respect; and though Henschel is comparatively a beginner, the value of his concerts is already beyond question. And it must be remembered in estimating the general effect of their labors that they have only asked the public for a shilling where Richter has demanded half-a-crown, whilst the scale of their performances is equally expensive.

The Bach Choir gave a concert on the 16th. I was not present. There are some sacrifices which should not be demanded twice from any man; and one of them is listening to Brahms's Requiem. On some future evening, perhaps, when the weather is balmy, and I can be accommodated with a comfortable armchair, an interesting book, and all the evening papers, I may venture; but last week I should have required a requiem for myself if I had attempted such a feat of endurance. I am sorry to have to play the "disgruntled" critic over a composition so learnedly contrapuntal, not to say so fugacious; but I really cannot stand Brahms as a serious composer. It is nothing short of a European misfortune that such prodigious musical powers should have nothing better in the way of ideas to express than incoherent commonplace. However, that is what is always happening in music: the world is full of great musicians who are no composers, and great composers who are no musicians.

In his youth, Brahms [1833–1897] when writing songs or serenades, or trifles of one kind or another, seemed a giant at play; and he still does small things well. I listened to his cleverly harmonized gypsy songs at the last Monday Popular Concert of the year with respectful satisfaction, though I shall not attempt to deny that fifteen minutes of them would have been better than twentyfive. This last remark, by the bye, shews that I am full of malice against "holy John," as Wagner called Brahms, even when he does what I have admitted his fitness for. Consequently my criticism, though it relieves my mind, is not likely to be of much value. Let me therefore drop the subject, and recall the attention of the Bach Choir to a composer of whom I entertain a very different opinion, to wit, John Sebastian Bach [1685–1760] himself. It is the special business of this society to hammer away at Bach's works until it at last masters them to the point of being able to sing them as Bach meant them to be sung. For instance, there is the great Mass in B minor. The choir has given several public performances of that; but all have been timid, mechanical, and intolerably slow. And when the elderly German conductor who got up the first performances was succeeded by a young and talented Irishman, the Mass became duller and slower than ever. The public did not take to the work as performed in this manner. It satisfied its curiosity, received an impression of vast magnitude, yawned, and felt no great impatience for a repetition of the experience. If the society thinks that this was the fault of Bach, it is most unspeakably mistaken.

Nothing can be more ruinous to the spirited action of the individual parts in Bach's music, or to the sublime march of his polyphony, than the dragging, tentative, unintelligent, half-bewildered operations of a choir still in the stage of feeling its way from interval to interval and counting one, two, three, four, for dear life. Yet the Bach Choir never got far beyond this stage with the B minor Mass. Even at the great bicentenary performance at the Albert Hall no attempt was made to attain the proper speed; and the work, as far as it came to light at all, loomed dimly and hugely through a gloomy, comfortless atmosphere of stolid awkwardness and anxiety. The effect the slow movements would make if executed with delicacy of touch and depth of expression, and of the quick ones if taken in the true Bach major mood, energetic, spontaneous, vivid, jubilant, was left to the imagination of the audience; and I fear that for the most part they rather declined to take it on trust. All this can be remedied by the Bach choristers if they stick at it, and are led with sufficient faith and courage. There is more reason than ever for persevering with their task at present; for Bach belongs, not to the past, but to the future—perhaps the near future. When he wrote such works as *Wachet auf!*, for example, we were no more ready for them than the children for whom we are now buying Christmas gift-books of fairy tales are to receive volumes of Goethe and Ibsen. Acis and Galatea [Handel, 1781] and Alexander's Feast [ode by Dryden, 1697, set to music by Handel, 1736], the ever-charming child literature of music, were what we were fit for then.

But now we are growing up we require passion, romance, picturesqueness, and a few easy bits of psychology. We are actually able to relish Faust [Gounod, 1859] and Carmen [Bizet, 1875]. And beyond Faust there is Tristan and Isolde [Wagner, 1865], which is at last music for grown men. Mr

Augustus Harris [actor, manager of Drury Lane Theatre, 1852–1896] has never heard of it, as it is only thirty years old; but as he goes about a good deal, I cannot doubt that in the course of the next ten years or so he will not only have it mentioned to him by some ambitious prima donna who aspires to eclipse Frau Sucher [German soprano, 1849–1927], but may even be moved to try whether a performance of it would not be better business than a revival of Favorita [Donizetti, 1840]. Now the reaction of Tristan on *Wachet auf!* will be a notable one. The Bach cantata, which seemed as dry and archaic after Acis and Galatea as Emperor and Galilean would after Cinderella, will, after Tristan, suddenly send forth leaves, blossoms, and perfume from every one of its seemingly dry sticks, which have yet more sap in them than all the groves of the temple of Gounod. Provided, that is—and here I ask the ladies and gentlemen of the Bach Choir to favor me with their best attention for a moment—provided always that there shall be at that time a choir capable of singing *Wachet auf!* as it ought to be sung.

Messrs Richard Gompertz, Haydn Inwards, Emil Kreuz, and Charles Ould, honorably associated as "The Cambridge University Musical Society's String Quartet," have given a couple of concerts at Prince's Hall, at the second of which I enjoyed myself without stint until they began to play Brahms, when I precipitately retired. Mr Edward German's symphony, performed at the last Crystal Palace concert, shews that he is still hampered by that hesitation between two distinct *genres* which spoiled his Richard III. overture. If Mr German [composer, 1832–1936] wishes to follow up his academic training by writing absolute music in symmetrical periods and orderly ingenuity of variation, let him by all means do so. On the other hand, if he prefers to take significant *motifs*, and develop them through all the emotional phases of a definite poem or drama, he cannot do better. But it is useless nowadays to try to combine the two; and since Mr German has not yet made up his mind to discard one or the other, the result is that his symphonic movements proceed for awhile with the smoothness and regularity of a Mendelssohn scholar's exercise, and then, without rhyme or reason, are shattered by a volcanic eruption which sounds like the last page of a very exciting opera *finale*, only to subside the next moment into their original decorum. I can but take a "symphony" of this sort as a bag of samples of what Mr German can do in the operatic style and in the absolute style, handsomely admitting that the quality of the samples is excellent, and that if Mr German's intelligence and originality equal his musicianship, he can no doubt *compose* successfully as soon as he realizes exactly what composition means.

At the last Monday Popular Concert of the year Madame Neruda distinguished herself greatly in the slow movement of the Mozart Quartet (No. 3 in B flat) and in Grieg's Sonata in F. In the quick movements of the quartet poor Mozart was polished off with the usual scant ceremony. Madame Haas [pianist, 1847–1932], who is always happy with Beethoven, played those variations on an original theme (in F), an affection for which is a sure sign of tenderness and depth of feeling in a player. The audience acted wisely in recalling Madame Haas twice, as her only fault is an occasional timidity in expressing herself fully—a timidity which must be caused by doubt as to whether her relations with Beethoven are being understood or appreciated.

Part IX: The Voice

Throughout his career as a music critic, Bernard Shaw reviewed books relating to vocal training, possibly in response to his appreciation of Vandeleur Lee's 1870 path-breaking book on the subject. A selection of these are included here as a way of introducing Shaw's own writings on "The Voice," which as previously indicated were intended to form part of a new edition of Lee's book, although this turned out to be impossible due to Lee's untimely and unexpected death.

It is significant that, in addition to standard sections such as "Qualifications of a Singer" or "Classification of Voices," this unpublished text includes "Physiology of the Vocal Organs" that both highlights Lee's scientific approach and challenges Lee's original theories, as well as "The Common Dread of Classical Music," "Singing in Tune" and "Pronunciation," in addition to "Effort."

1. A Pamphlet on the Voice

Review of Arthur Barraclough's Observations on the Physical Education of the Vocal Organs.
The Hornet, 7 March 1877

This is one of a large number of pamphlets which have been called forth by the success of certain works on the voice, which have recently come into general notice. Mr Barraclough, being, as we presume, a teacher of singing, has made some observations in the exercise of his profession which possess the merit of being quite incontrovertible, and strictly in accordance with the results of scientific research. Such, for instance, is the statement that voice production results from the action of muscles controlled by the will that every period of activity must be followed by a period of repose, and that Nature's laws cannot be violated with impunity. If the public consider these facts sufficiently startling to call for an outlay of a shilling on a pamphlet embodying them, Mr Barraclough's book will probably have a large circulation. If, on the contrary, it should occur to them that the said facts are abundantly promulgated elsewhere, and are, indeed, the property of most intelligent schoolboys, they will lay down the Observations with a passing wonder why they should have been printed at all.

Mr Barraclough's special knowledge of voice production may be estimated by his references to singers as "vocal athletes," to "force of blast" as a condition of vocalization, and to physical exhaustion as a necessary consequence of singing which must be provided for, on the principle of training a prizefighter. He mentions that "the vocal ligaments are brought together," a fact which we would recommend him to test by the laryngoscope before issuing a second edition of his work. And to clergymen who suffer from loss of voice, he recommends daily practice at reading lessons, which would infallibly leave them without any voice at all, their affection not being want of practice, as Mr Barraclough erroneously supposes, but an improper method of production, usually brought about by the endeavor to read with a sombre inflexion not natural to them.

Matter of this kind, eked out to twentytwo pages by some commonplace remarks, and a misquotation of Shakespear, constitutes the Observations on the Physical Education of the Vocal Organs, without throwing the smallest light, even suggestively, on one of the most important musical questions of the age, and, unfortunately, one of the most obscure.

2. A Typical "Popular" Vocalist

The Hornet, 26 September 1877

Amongst artists the struggle for existence resolves itself into a struggle for popularity. Popularity is attained by different persons in different ways. Twice or thrice in a century some gifted being appears, and, by an occult power, gains the idolatry of the public in a night or two, retaining it often for years after the last traces of the original fascination have succumbed to age, misuse, or the intoxication of success. Others enter the arena in humble guise, and toil laboriously in the pursuit of artistic excellence, their love of music sustaining them against the coldness of unscrupulous rivals who resent conscientiousness, and the indifference of the mob to exalted considerations of all kinds. They often have to wait; but, as a rule, the solid weight of genuine art material establishes itself at last, and that unassailably. Nevertheless, the process is a slow one for this age of quick returns and impatient aspirations; and a quicker method of succeeding is usually adopted.

The outward and visible signs of this royal road to popularity are of infinite variety, according to the ingenuity of the traveler. If a female vocalist (and such are the most brilliant professors of the science of claptrap) desire to shine in this way, she must bear in mind that her work begins from the moment her audience first catches sight of her. Let her then smile and trip forth as captivatingly as possible. If she have to make her way through an orchestra, a little judicious embarrassment as she threads the row of fiddlers (who will tap their desks vigorously and so ensure a reception) will often lay the foundation of an enthusiastic *encore* before she utters a note. A prettily whispered conference with the conductor or accompanist will dispose of the suffrages of every youth present of average susceptibility. The fashion in which the sheet of music is held is of much importance, but no positive rule can be laid down respecting it. To dispense with the copy altogether is sometimes advisable as being impressive, but, perhaps, the most irresistible plan is to have a small card or scrap of paper on which the words are scribbled. A timely lapse of memory is useful when the singer has the gift of displaying confusion agreeably.

The purely musical portion of the task is of minor importance. If the song be English, the words must be pointedly delivered at the audience in a confidentially colloquial style. The pathetic parts should be drawled, and those notes made the most of which best display the power of the voice. In justice to all present, each line must be delivered to the right and left of the platform alternately; and the vocalist must bear in mind that it is impossible to smile too often. In Italian music, shakes must be introduced at every suitable or unsuitable opportunity. They must by no means be steadily delivered, as such a mode savors of old-fashioned classicalism, but shot forth in a series of jerks. During the process the pitch may be allowed to fall half a tone, but not more, as it might be difficult to regain the key with sufficient rapidity. Considerations of this kind are, however, immaterial, as very few persons will have the least idea as to whether the singer is in or out of tune. Applause should be promptly improved by reappearance and many obeisances. If an *encore* be doubtful, it should be accepted as a matter of generosity to the public.

From these few and unskilful hints may be gathered the manner in which popularity can be obtained without taste, culture, or voice. Those who adopt it are not necessarily devoid of these attributes, but they pervert rather than improve them. Of their school more than one that we could name is a prominent professor of this theory; and in drawing attention to this *spurious imitation of real art*, we now remind them that, though speaking now in general terms, we may be led on some future occasion to particularize offenders.

3. A Volume on Voice Training

The Pall Mall Gazette, 12 November 1886
Unsigned review of J. P. Sandlands' How to Develop General Vocal Power.

Of this little "Book for Everybody" the author hopefully says "It will be useful to the general public. It will serve to brighten and sharpen articulation, and render conversation more intelligible." And no doubt it will, if its precepts be discreetly followed; for it is not a bad book of its kind, in spite of such funny sentences as "The word horse calls up into the presence-chamber of the mind a certain animal with four legs and without feathers"; or "The student may think out for himself the color he would like to give to the several phrases in Ex. 6. There is no better practice than applying the color of anger"—a recommendation which suggests that at Brigstock, of which Mr Sandlands is vicar, the parishioners are accustomed to energetic and even comminatory sermons. In the same vein are many misleading exhortations to "tease it out," to "strive after power," and the like. The singers and speakers who "strive after power" are those who never get it. They do, as Talma [French actor, 1763–1826] said, "*ce que font tous les jeunes acteurs.*" One is afraid to think of what Rev. Mr Sandlands would say to Talma's calm estimate of "at least twenty years" as the necessary apprenticeship for a man who would move assemblies.

Another of the vicar's questionable bits of advice is to read at the pitch of "F in the bass," and to persevere at it in spite of difficulty. This is, in another form, the old pet precept of second rate teachers to "get it from the chest." What would Charles Mathews [theatre manager and comic actor, 1776–1835] whose voice never aged, and who gave the widest of berths to F in the bass, have said to it? And what would our curates, with their "clergyman's sore throat," brought on by persisting in what Artemus Ward called "a sollum vois," say to it? "F" Mr Sandlands assures us "is the foundation tone; and the student must get it. It is as necessary for good speaking as a good foundation is for building that is meant to be permanent." This means simply that Mr Sandlands has a bass voice; that its normal pitch in speaking is F; and that he therefore concludes that all other men have bass voices with the same normal pitch, or, if they have not, that they ought to be made have them. Imagine the effect of a sepulchral course of lessons in the key of F on [well-known actors of the time] Mr Hare, Mr Grossmith, Mr Penley, Mr Giddens, Mr George Barrett, or Signor Salvini! These so-called "foundation tones" vary with each individual: [François] Delsarte's favorite one was B flat, which was at least less likely to be generally mischievous than F. Then, as to speaking with gutta-percha balls in the mouth (a practice not unknown among schoolboys), we are told that Demosthenes used pebbles; so doubtless there is something to be gained by the exercise, though it is hard to see exactly what.

The stress laid by Mr Sandlands upon the importance of seeing in the mind's eye what one speaks about shews that he possesses the faculty which Mr Galton has named "visualization," and that he supposes every one else to possess it too, which is by no means the case. Besides, speakers are not always engaged in describing material objects. So much for Mr Sandlands' errors, which are those of robust innocence and impatience rather than of pretence and quackery—the usual failings of the voice-trainer. As a set-off against them may be taken his ingenious and useful exercises, of which two specimens may be quoted: "The soldiers steer the boat. The soldier's tear fell on the page." Here the point is of course not the sensibility of the literary soldier, but the difficulty of differentiating "soldiers steer" from "soldier's tear." Again, "Violins and violoncellos vigorously vamped with very versatile voices vociferating various strains very vehemently vexes Valentine's violent valet" is good practice. So is "The zealot Zephaniah rode a zebra zigzag up Zeboim." On the other hand, it is nothing short of a duty to protest against the student saying in "full voice"—or, indeed, in any voice whatever:

Not a drum was heard, not a funeral note.

An excellent feature in the book is the condemnation of the rule that, if the consonants are watched, the vowels will take care of themselves. An Englishman who can pronounce *do, re, mi, fa* decently is a *rara avis*.

4. Specialists in Singing

The World, 16 November 1892

Last season appears to have been a favorable one for specialists in singing, for volumes and pamphlets on voice production have been hurled at me from all sides; and this, I suppose, indicates a wave of interest in the subject. All such treatises used to be practically identical as to their preliminary matter, which invariably dealt with the need for a new departure, so as to get away from the quackery of the ordinary singing-master and rediscover the lost art of Porpora [composer of Baroque operas and teacher of singing, 1686–1768].

Nowadays, the new departure is still advocated; but there is a tendency to leave Porpora out of the question, and to claim for the latest methods a modern scientific basis, consisting mostly of extracts from Huxley [President of the Royal Society, a Darwinian anatomist and natural historian] and Helmholtz [German physician and physicist; Shaw is referring to his discoveries on perception of sound and tone sensation]. With all due respect, however, I beg to remark that there is no sort of sense in attempting to base the art of singing on physiology. You can no more sing on physiological principles than you can fence on anatomical principles, paint on optical principles, or compose on acoustic principles.

Sir Joshua Reynolds [1723–1792] painted none the worse for believing that there were three primary colors, and that the human eye was one of the most exquisite and perfect instruments ever designed for the use of man; nor have his successors painted any the better since Young [David Young (original surname Cameron), 1865–1945] exploded the three primary colors for ever, and Helmholtz [German scientist, 1821–1898] scandalized Europe by informing his pupils that if an optician were to send him an instrument with so many easily avoidable and remediable defects as the human eye, he would feel bound to censure him severely. Again, half a century ago every singing-master firmly believed that there were in the human body three glands—one in the head, immediately behind the frontal sinus; one in the throat; and one in the chest: each secreting a different quality of voice.

Nowadays even an Italian singing-master must, on pain of appearing a gross ignoramus to his pupils, know that all voice is produced by the same organ, the larynx, and that the so-called three voices are "registers" made by varying the adjustment of the vocal cords. This advance in scientific knowledge does not alter the position of those teachers of singing who study their profession *by ear*, or of the painters who paint *by eye*—who are artists, in short. But it has a good effect on the gentlemen whose methods are "scientific." In the days of the three primary colors, there were teachers of painting who held that the right color for a scarf across a blue robe was orange, because blue was a primary color, and the proper contrast to it was a compound of the other primary colors, red and yellow. The Divine Artist had colored the rainbow on these principles; therefore they were natural, scientific, and orthodox.

There are still gentlemen who teach coloring on natural, scientific, orthodox principles; and to them the discovery that the doctrine of the three primary colors will not do, and that Shelley's "million-colored bow" is nearer the truth than Newton's tri-colored one, no doubt has its value, since their daubs are more varied than before, though the artist-colorist remains no wiser than Bellini or Velasquez. In the same way, the scientific vocal methods based on the latest observations of the laryngoscopists are, on the whole, less likely to be dangerous than those based on the theory of the three glands, although the artistic method is just the same as ever it was.

Now, I am hopelessly prejudiced in favor of the artistic method, which is, of course, the genuinely scientific method according to the science of art itself. On behalf of my prejudice I plead two chapters in my experience of "scientific" methods. When the study of the vocal cords first began, it led straight to the theory that the larynx was a simple stringed instrument, and that singing was, physically, a mere question of varying the tension of the vocal cords, and throwing them into vibration by a vigorous current of air. This was duly confirmed by an experiment, of the physiological-laboratory type, by [Johannes] Müller; and then we had the "tension-of-cords-and-force-of-blast" theory of singing, which all the violent and villainous methods prevalent in the middle of the century, to the ruin of innumerable pupil-victims, claimed as their "scientific" foundation, and which every true artist was able to explode to his or her own satisfaction by the simple experiment of listening to its results.

The second chapter concerns composers more than singers. When it was discovered that musical sounds, instead of being simple, are really enriched by a series of "partial tones," and that the most prominent of these "partial tones" correspond to the notes of the commonest chords, all the professors who could not distinguish between science and art jumped at the notion of discovering a scientific method of harmonizing which should quite supersede the barbarous thoroughbass of Handel and Mozart. A stupendous monument of ingenious folly, in the form of a treatise on harmony by Dr [Alfred] Day, was installed at the Royal Academy of Music, where it reigns, for aught I know, to this day; and the unhappy pupils who wanted certificates of their competence to write music could not obtain them without answering absurd challenges to name "the root" of a chord, meaning the sound that would generate the notes of that chord among its series of "partial tones."

Now as, if you only look far enough through your series, you can find every note used in music among those generated by any one note used in it, the professors, though tolerably unanimous as to the root of C, E, G, or C, E, G, B flat, could not agree about the chromatic chords, and even the more extreme diatonic discords. The result was that when you went to get coached for your Mus. Bac. degree, the first thing your coach had to ascertain was where you were going to be examined, as you had to give different answers to the same questions, according to whether they were put by [Professors] Ouseley and Macfarren, or Stainer. (Sir John Stainer [composer of carols and music editor] finally succumbed to an acute attack of commonsense, and invested Day's system with that quality in the only modern treatise on harmony I have ever recommended anyone to open.) Sterndale Bennett [composer, 1816–1875] was a convinced Dayite, and sometimes spoiled passages in his music in order to make the harmony "scientific."

Meanwhile Wagner, working by ear, heedless of Day, was immensely enlarging the harmonic stock-in-trade of the profession. Macfarren kept on proving that the Wagnerian procedure was improper, until at last one could not help admiring the resolute conviction with which the veteran professor, old, blind, and hopelessly in the wrong, would still rise to utter his protest whenever there was an opening for it.

Here, then, we have science, in the two most conspicuous cases of its application to musical art, doing serious mischief in the hands of the teachers who fell back on it to eke out the poverty of their artistic resources. Yet do not suppose that I am an advocate of old-fashioned ignorance. No: I admit that a young teacher of singing, if he cannot handle the laryngoscope, and knows nothing of anatomy or physics, deserves to be mistrusted as an uneducated person, likely to offer fantastic and ambiguous suggestions instead of exact instructions.

But I do declare emphatically that all methods which have come into existence by logical deduction from scientific theory can only be good through the extravagantly improbable accident of a coincidence between the result of two absolutely unrelated processes, one right and the other wrong. Practically, they are certain to be delusive; and this conclusion is not the anti-scientific, but the scientific one. And in all books on the subject which I may happen to review here I shall concern myself solely with the practical instructions offered, and criticize them in the light of my own empirical observation of singing, without the slightest regard to the hooking of them on to physiology or acoustics.

First comes the redoubtable Mr Lunn with a reprint (Forster Groom—a sixpenny pamphlet) of the lecture he delivered last May at Prince's Hall, which I noticed at the time. I disagree with him flatly in his denunciation of the vowel *oo* for practice, and am quite of the opinion of the sensible and practical author of Our Voices, and How to Improve Them, by A Lady (Willcocks—a two-shilling manual), who recommends practice on *oo* in the middle of the voice, and points out that the traditional Italian a is invariably translated here into the English ah, which would have driven the old Italian masters out of their senses.

Mr Lunn's objection is that *oo* sets people "blowing," against which vice his pamphlet gives effective and valuable warning. But if Mr Lunn will teach his pupils to round the back of the throat (the pharynx) as they sing—and this is a trick of the old school which he does not seem to know—he will find that they can "compress the air," as he puts it, just as effectually on *oo* as on Italian *a*; and his well-taught tenor pupil, Mr Arthur, will be able to do in one breath that passage in *Il mio tesoro* which cost him one and a quarter at Prince's Hall. A Lady might learn something from Mr Lunn as to the importance of not wasting the breath (the skilled singer, in rounding the pharynx, has an imaginary sensation of holding the breath back—of *compressing* it at the larynx, though the control really comes from the diaphragm). She says "The voice should be directed forward, always forward, until the vibrating air is felt right on the lips."

This is both fanciful and misleading. The phrase "direction of the voice" means really shaping the cavity of the mouth by the disposition of the lips, tongue, and jaw, the voice being immovable; and the attempt to carry out the precept as to feeling the air on the lips would lead in practice simply to "blowing." Dr J. W. Bernhardt, [choral conductor] the author of Vox Humana (Simpkin, Marshall—a five-shilling book), gives the proper word of command for this particular emergency in the ten quite invaluable paragraphs (94 to 103) in which he urges the necessity of putting no strain on the geniohyoid muscles—in other words, of keeping your chin loose whatever you do. By his emphasis on this point and his knowledge of the importance of the pharynx, he is able to give some excellent advice; but in suggesting the vowel *o* for practice, he forgot that it would be read as ah-oo, ow, aw-oo, &c., by different readers, Mr Irving being the only living Englishman who makes it a pure vowel.

Dr Bernhardt's plan of beginning it with an aspirate and an *n*, thus, *h'n'o*, is a clever trick as far as the *n* is concerned; but the *h* belongs to his notion (also Mr Lunn's) that the air should be compressed by the vocal cords as by a safety valve. He carries this so far as to advocate attacking a note, not merely by the *coup de glotte*, as Mr Lunn does, but by nothing short of an explosion. I quite agree with Maurel, that the *coup de glotte* is objectionable; and I never heard a good singer who attacked notes explosively. I am convinced that both Mr Lunn and Dr Bernhardt have been misled by the imaginary sensation, described above, of pressing back the air with the vocal cords.

Any good singer can touch a note gently, reinforce it to its loudest, and let it diminish again, without the least alteration of the pitch, and consequently without the least alteration of, or pressure downwards of, the glottis, the *crescendo* and *diminuendo* being visibly effected by the diaphragm. The explosive process produces bawling, not singing; and Dr Bernhardt virtually admits this when he says that the ladies who, when asked to sing louder, plead "I really have no more voice," would scream loud enough to awaken the echoes a mile away if any sudden fright came upon them. If one of Dr Bernhardt's pupils were to apply this remark practically, by beginning to scream instead of singing (as many prima donnas do), he would, I have no doubt, pull her up with a remarkably short turn.

But at this point I must pull myself up with equal sharpness, leaving unnoticed many points in these three interesting books, for which I beg Mr Lunn, Dr Bernhardt, and A Lady, to accept my best thanks.

THE VOICE

Singing in Tune
(In Tune, Not In Tune, and Out Of Tune)

It is commonly said of people who sing disagreeably that they sing out of tune. Accidentally the phrase is often appropriate, but there are many persons who sing in tune with surprisingly disagreeable effect, and again there are deservedly popular singers (there is at least one popular singer) who contrive the species of beauty spotted by a certain piquant falseness of intonation which the ear accepts with a disturbed pleasure which is not without charm. The same thing may be remarked of players. In English orchestras, the trombone is rarely tolerable, but it is hardly ever out of tune. On the other hand, I have heard a great violinist, renowned for sweetness of his tone, who delighted his audience, and delighted me, and yet did not play in tune. His object, whether consciously aimed at or not, was to produce a thrilling effect by playing just sharp enough to set up a slight crispation of the auditory nerves. It is useless to condemn such a practice in the face of its success; but I do not recommend students to adopt it if they can help doing so. It is cited here for the instruction of ill-advised persons who, feeling bound to give reasons for their impression of musical performance, consider "which is so dreadfully out of tune" and "which is always so beautifully in tune" to be phrases universally applicable to artists who please or displease them. Again, it is often said of the pianoforte "it is out of tune" as if a pianoforte ever was in tune. All instruments which represent the sounds of your musical system by 12 fixed tones only (as the pianoforte, organ, and harmonium) are purposely mistuned. Their chief use in educating the ear is to accustom it to tolerate inaccurate intervals. When the intervals are so false that the ear cannot tolerate them, the instrument needs to be tuned. When they are tolerable, the instrument is well tuned; but it is not in tune. For conversational purpose the distinction is pedantic, but it is important for the student of singing who might easily be led to refer to his pianoforte as an infallible standard of intonation. This system of mistuning is called equal measurement, a name which has the defect of suggesting equality as in the sense of just temperament, whereas it means that every key departs equally from just untampered intonation. The well tuned pianoforte of the present day would have been repudiated as grossly out of tune by Handel, who never heard equal temperament, the tuning used in his time being the unequal temperament, in which all extreme keys were impracticable, their intervals being sacrificed to the "nodal" keys, which were much more nearly in tune. The impracticable keys were said to be afflicted with wolves. Sebastian Bach, a contemporary of Handel, brought equal temperament in use in Germany because it doubled the number of keys at his disposal. Thus, he published his two sets of fugues and preludes in all the major and minor keys under the apparently quaint title Well Tempered Clavichord. Students will have remarked that keys with more than 3 flat or sharp do not occur in the music of Handel, whereas Bach modulates freely into such keys as b sharp and d flat. The effect of these keys as experimentally known to Handel may be tested by transposing one of his compositions into them, and playing it on the English harp which is still tuned upon the old system. The subject of temperament, though not particularly abstruse, is one which seldom receives any attention from musicians, most of whom, however, are vaguely aware that there is some difficulty in the tuner's mastery. For the benefit of those who, without studying it seriously, desire to be able to speak of it in a manner not absolutely senseless, I will give a brief example of the considerations which necessitate the tempering of key instruments. On referring to the pianoforte it will be found that each octave contains exactly 3 major 3rds. Thus the convenience of this arrangement is beyond praise. Its beauty is brought into question by the fact that 3 true major 3rds fall considerably short of the octave. It follows that all the 3 must be made too sharp, and this is in fact what is done. If only the following notes had to be tuned on such an instrument as the pianoforte the note marked X must fulfil 3 different and, in just intonation, incompatible functions. At (a) it must be a minor 6th above C. At (b) it must be the major above E, the major 3rd of C. At (c) it must be the major 3rd below C, the octave of the first C. One note cannot without violence to the intervals be made to serve these three purposes. Much less can it be as G#, at once a true supertonic in the key of F#, median in B major submedian in E major, leading note in A minor, or as A flat, 6th in C minor, 3rd in F minor, 4th in E flat, 5th in D flat and tonic in A flat. Nevertheless, on the pianoforte one protean note serves for all these intervals, much of which involves relation to other notes too numerous and complicated to be detailed, and serves as badly as might be expected. All better systems, however, involve either a reduction in the number of available keys or the addition of new notes of the keyboard. The sacrifice of keys which all modern composers from Beethoven to Wagner have used freely is out of the question. The addition of new keys presents considerable mechanical difficulty, the magnitude of which may be estimated from the fact that in order to make all the keys effective, the number of notes in each octave would have to be doubled, whilst a system which has been actually put in practice, and which is not distinguishable by the ear from just intonation requires upwards of 50 notes to the octave. Singularly enough, the problem of bringing so large a number of notes under the control of the human hand has been solved by the invention of the keyboard in which octaves of 80 notes are perfectly manageable, and which is nevertheless simpler than the ordinary keyboard of 12 notes, which only a few persons obtain a mastery of, and that at great cost of labour. This invention, the importance of which it would be difficult to overestimate, is due to Mr [Robert] Bosanquet.

The reader, however little the techniques of temperament may interest him, is now probably convinced that the pianoforte is never in tune, and that the less it has to do with the education of the ear, the better. Few singers are as accurate in their intonation as a well tuned pianoforte. A fine singer must be truer than the best pianoforte.

To sing out of tune, with whatever taste of executive ability, is wantonly to disturb the peace which all lovers of art, whether musicians or not, find in silence. It is a grave social offence. Between singing out of tune and singing in tune, however, there is a questionable condition which cannot fairly be described as out of tune (the phrase having come to imply too strong a condemnation) but which is certainly not in tune. The majority of singers, amateur and professional, are in this condition. Persons who play their own accompaniments other than from memory, or who from long practice in choral singing read their way through a song from note to note usually belong to "not in tune" class. Only those with whom the faculty of reading music has become instinctive can attempt to sing at sight for the entertainment of others. The amateur who belongs to the choral association, who gropes through all music in the same pre-occupied fashion, not in tune, not in time, and yet hardly to be fairly stigmatized as out of either, inflicts far more annoyance on a musician than the rash young gentlemen who do not know their notes but are willing to sing Tom Bowling [composed by Charles Dibdin, 1745–1814] by ear after repeated solicitation from their mothers and sisters. The expert reader is the more to be dreaded because of the readiness with which he volunteers for concert music, in which his defects are particularly obnoxious. To sing in tune is to be secure against the possibility of causing pain on any listener, and to possess the only absolutely indispensable qualification of a fine singer.

Pronunciation

Pronunciation, a fine art of cardinal importance to the singer, cannot in this country be taught otherwise than orally. Books are useless because of the exceedingly absurd manner in which the English language is written. In order to represent sounds with mediaeval exactitude, even the phonetic alphabets of Mr Pitman [inventor of shorthand] and others would not suffice, it would be necessary to use the "visible speech" [language for the deaf] of Mr Melville Bell, which, notwithstanding its extraordinary merit and interest, is about as intelligible to the general reader as the characters used by the Chinese. Novelists and humourists like [those] who convey vulgar or provincial pronunciation by facetious variations of the common spelling Artemus Ward [nom de plume for Charles Farrar Ward, 1834–1867] are futile. Any Englishman may convince himself by inviting an Irishman to pronounce the speeches of Sam Weller from the hints afforded by Dickens' spelling [in *Pickwick Papers*], or by attempting to mimic the accent of Caleb Balderston as rendered by [Sir Walter] Scott in the "Bride of Lammermoor" and taking the opinion of a Scotchman on the success of the performance. As much, or rather as little, can be learned on this subject from a pronouncing dictionary as from any treatise on singing. Enough, however, may perhaps be conveyed here to damp the confidence with which many amateurs murdered the most corrupt colloquialisms in their vocal efforts. There are roughly speaking four long vowels in English as commonly spoken; of which only one, ee of bad quality is in the least familiar to us from our textbook of grammar, the remaining four of which are pronounced as diphthongs. This remark, to a Frenchman or Italian the most obvious that could be made on our language, is astonishing to the average Englishman, who may, however, easily convince himself by experiment that *a i o* and *u* are in his mouth something like ayee, awee, or ahee, awoo or before "r" owaw and eeyoo. His stock of long or singable vowels is probably limited to *ah, aw, oo* (as in food) and, as aforesaid, *ee*. The vowel *aw* as substituted for the sound of "*r*" is not used in colloquial English, except when it is followed by a vowel, and even then it is so indistinct that the clear trilled "*r*" has to be specially acquired by actors and singers, to whom it is indispensable. To ballad singers in private circles, who are afraid of appearing affected, some licence may be allowed on this point, but such licence does not justify the prevalence of drawing room deliverance in this fashion.

There is a general tendency to interpolate sounds, sometimes very singular ones, before *i* for instance.

These are not the blunders of uneducated people. They are made, more or less obviously by all Londoners who have not studied pronunciation as an art. Noted actors, who enunciate *a* and *o* as pure vowels are generally ridiculed for their pains by the public, who ignorantly ascribe the unaccustomed sounds to affectation. Persons who habitually... mimic Mr Irving's accurate pronunciation of "slave" and "gold" [do so] with a ludicrous unconsciousness of where the laugh really is.

In studying lyric pronunciation the singer acquires the power of singing the syllables *doh rey me fa* as pure vowels. Thus, the vowels in *doh* must begin as *o* and end as *o*. If it began as *ah* or *aw* and ends as *oo*, which it most probably will at first, it is diphthong. Singers are prone to use the diphthong *o-oo*. Similarly, if the *a* in ray ends as *ee*, it is a diphthong, and the student must persevere until the sound of the French *e* can be sustained as long as the breath lasts, the tip of the tongue never once rising to the front teeth after the articulation of the initial "*r*," which should be distinctly trilled. The *me* should be of clear quality. Many persons, by retracting the tongue against back teeth make this innocent vowel surprisingly disagreeable. The *a* in *fah*, which has been called the mother of vowels, will exercise to the utmost the singer's taste in selecting for each vowel the most beautiful sound it will recognisably bear. Between the bleating Irish *ah* and the gross English *aw* are many gradations from which to choose. The criticism of the Frenchman specially educated to speak his language well is invaluable to the student of vowel sounds, as his native tongue contains many more vowels than English and his tendency is rather to simplify diphthongs than to corrupt vowels. Consonants should be articulated with clearness and without effort and immediately quitted for the ensuing vowel. Consonants should in fact only be sounded at the instant of attacking a note or quitting it. In the following passage [no example cited] an inexperienced singer would probably pronounce the slower word "realized" in the space of one crotchet after which the final d would re-duce him to silence. The vowel—the same as that of *re* in the gamut—should be sustained until there is only time left for the articulation of the *a'd*. In this instance, the consonant, be-ing an explodent cannot be sustained, but most consonants can be sustained as well as vowels, and young ladies some-times give them the preference in this fashion.

Some persons have a habit of adding to each word ending with a consonant an obscure vowel. Thus (representing the obscure vowel by a) such words as tell, head, love, become tella, heada, lova. This way of prolonging words is sometimes practiced intentionally (or apparently so) on the stage. In cer-tain old English songs it is expressly indicated. The two fol-lowing are familiar examples:

Jog on, jog on, the footpath way
And merrily hand the stile a
A merry heart goes all the day
Your sad tires in the mile a

A well there is in the west country
And a clearer ne'er was seen a
There is not a wife in the west country
But has heard of the well of St. Keyne a

The quaintness of the effect here is sufficient warning against its unpremeditated use on all occasions.

It is not always advisable to rouse the conscience of amateur singers on the subject of pronunciation. Perception of a defect usually precedes by a long interval the power of overcoming it with certainty, and those who have not to make themselves intelligible to large audiences, and who speak with refinement or with an agreeable mannerism may generally be allowed to pronounce in their own way. Public singers should be able to sing all the vowels on each note throughout the entire compass of the voice, though it is perhaps too much to expect that they will sacrifice the quality of the note to the duty of conforming exactly to the text. It is not every composer who deserves conscientious interpretation at the hands of artists. A composer has no right to complain of his music being altered when the alteration is virtually a correction. So far as I am aware, Purcell, the greatest of English composers, was also the greatest master of the art of setting the English language to music. The works of Handel and his English imitators are excellent practice for the lyric student who desires to possess the unusual accomplishment of ability to pronounce English. It is, however, an accomplishment on which it is better not to dogmatize. There can be no standard subdivision of England, Scotland, Ireland, the United States and the Colonies. Even when railways, and possibly the introduction of a better system of spelling, have completed their work of amalgamating and destroying dialects, there will still be individual peculiarity to worry the singing master with the perpetual effort to distinguish between what is condemnable and what is merely for the moment unfashionable, individual taste being in this as in all questions of art, the ultimate judge.

As fine pronunciation in singing is incompatible with the least straining of the facial muscles or vocal organs, it is not possible for those who have acquired it to be bad singers.

The Common Dread of Classical Music

People who have no technical knowledge of music are under the impression that all long and dull compositions which they ought to like, and do not, are classical, and that short, pretty, whistleable tunes belong to a sort of music which they should apologize for liking. Their opinion is based on a general experience of trivial music well executed and grand music vilely executed. It may be a relief to such persons to learn that not only is classical music (music written according to academic rule) no more necessarily good music than academic painting is necessarily good painting, but that all compositions which have shown any vitality have been products of the romantic school, denounced by professors as violations of classical traditions until, the professors having died out, and word having progressed, as it always does progress towards greater freedom, these heterodox compositions have come to be accepted by the formalists as standards of classical form and denounced by a fresh generation of rebellious romanticists as antiquated. Of music accepted at the date of its composition as classical, hardly any survives, also every contrapuntist contributes his sonata, his symphony, or at least his overture to the general stock. The labours of these gentlemen are for the most part, wasted. Many of their works display a degree of learning that few of the great composers possessed. Their discords are resolved and prepared according to the best models, all the keys employed are within the proper degrees of relationship, the subjects in each movement are carefully contrasted and are minced up and handled with much contrapuntal ingenuity in the free fantasies, little novelties and licences are introduced to vindicate the composer's incompetence, the laws of form, smarting from Wagnerian contumely, are propitiated by strict observance, and yet all this goes for nothing if the music be not exceptionally beautiful. But if that condition be fulfilled, then, form or no form, the music will live to be the law of future pedants and the delight of future musicians. The truth is and has always been that music is good in proportion to the pleasure with which it is heard, not the difficulty with which it is written.

This is by no means in accordance with the popular impression cited above that the works of a great composer may be lumped together under the name of classical music as something extremely dull and disagreeable, which it is, however, in good taste to affect a relish for. This impression, when not due to incapacity on the part of the listener, is the work of incompetent persons who entertain private society with what they call "a little classical music," much as though a man on the strength of knowing how to read imperfectly should repeat a portion of Hamlet to an unlettered audience as a specimen of Shakespeare's powers. Those who find exhibitions of this class merely dull, are to be envied by musicians, who find them exasperating. If there be anything more dreary than a play of Shakespear's indifferently acted, it is probably a sonata by Beethoven indifferently played. Unfortunately, though the public do not blame Shakespear for the faults of his interpreters, they are quite willing to accept the performance of an ill-advised young lady fresh from school as the perfect realization of the intentions of Beethoven. The truth is that the power to play Beethoven or Bach is fully as rare as the power to act the characters of Shakespear, and as little likely to be picked up as a school accomplishment. At best, drawing room Beethoven, like drawing room Shakespear is usually a bad imitation of some popular performer. It does not seem to have struck society that there can be any other object of learning music than that of performing it for the amusement of others, though no one has yet been found hardy enough to maintain that the sole application of the power of reading poetry is reciting aloud. Probably, when reading was as exceptional an accomplishment as music is now, every person who could read would have been expected to favour the company with choice extracts from popular authors, had it not fortunately at that time been the etiquette to write in Latin.

The bewilderment which commonly overtakes people whose culture is purely literary in their efforts to understand classical music is often the result of the inappropriate mental attitude in which they prepare to receive the charge of musical impressions. There is only one aspect of music known to literature, i.e. the sublime. Therefore a well-read person, when a composition of Beethoven's is to be performed, prepares to hear something sublime. Now Beethoven, in his greatest works, is sometimes jocular, and sometimes boisterous. For example, the first movement of the greatest of his purely instrumental symphonies, the 9th, exhibits simultaneously grandeur, dainty taste, delight in thundering noise and impetuous motion, and capricious humour, an assemblage of qualities inexpressible to the mind hushed in reverent expectation of the sublime. It is true that this expectation is gratified by the beautiful and favourite *Allegretto*, but even here Beethoven no sooner melts his hearers than ridicules their emotion by an abrupt *staccato* passage, and, further on, by an outrageous close in C major, wantonly introduced at the end of an exquisite phrase in A minor. These unseasonable jokes are signally lost on the general listener, who accepts them solemnly as a part of the sublimity which is as yet a little beyond him. The last movement of the 7th symphony, one of the exhilarating orgies of sound into which a superabundance of animal spirits often led the composer, completes the defeat of the hearer, who knows (he has read it in many books) that Beethoven is immense, profound, mysterious, perfect in his grandeur, and rails in his desolation, and he therefore seeks for one or other of these qualities in everything Beethoven did. Not only seeks, but often finds them too, and drafts accounts of them, to the confusion of future generations of readers. It is as though in a church, seeing an archbishop dance a jig in the pulpit, one should find it easier to believe that the irregularity was an unfamiliar portion of the ritual, than that so great a dignitary could be subject, like any common mortal to an irresistible excess of high spirits. Thanks to erroneous preconceptions, we habitually hear well-read and intelligent ladies and gentlemen confessing their inability to appreciate compositions which are the delight of children who have, by dint of taking music innocently as it comes to them, learned what to listen for. The reason why Mozart is so much greater favoured with the reading public than Beethoven (who is in every sense the more popular composer of the two) is that his taste was too severe to permit him to indulge in the musical horseplay which his great successor loved. In listening to Mozart's music, an ignorant audience may lose their sense of its beauty, but never of its dignity and refinement. Mozart's smile was charming, but he never was guilty of the guffaw. Beethoven's mirth, on the contrary, is so obstreperous, that even the most determined sublimity hunter must occasionally have an uneasy suspicion of being laughed at.

The scope of music is so wide, and its powers so various that the vulgar phrase "a taste for music" may imply a marked distaste for much music which is undeniably very fine of its kind. Those who can admire at once the fantastic and yet deliberately wrought compositions of Edgar Poe, the monotonous lusciousness of Swinburne, the egotistic absence of dramatic power combined with wealth of descriptive power in Byron, and the dramatic instinct and subtly interwoven comedy and pathos of Molière, must be allowed to possess a remarkable catholicity of taste, but certainly not more than may be claimed by the would-be amateurs who accept Berlioz, Chopin, Beethoven, and Mozart impartially. The unlettered English peasant might preserve a similarly judicial attitude on hearing a selection of extracts from Cervantes, Goethe and Victor Hugo. This parallel, however, is defective in one very important part. The peasant cannot gain knowledge of Spanish merely from hearing it read aloud no matter how constantly and attentively he may listen. The power to understand music, on the contrary, can be speedily acquired in this way, and indeed cannot be acquired in any other. It is a common mistake to suppose that the science of the contrapuntist or the manipulative dexterity of the pianist are essentials in music. They are merely adjuncts, and have been cultivated to a high degree by persons "born into" the profession, (not born musicians) but not endowed with any special aptitude for it, and are less musicians than many amateurs who have no idea of symbolism by which their favoured airs are committed to paper. A little patience and a determined renunciation of all preconceptions derived from literary descriptions will enable anyone who can whistle "God Save the Queen" to enjoy a Monday popular concert as well as if he were the President of the Royal Academy of Music.

Qualifications of a Singer

The only natural gift indispensable to a singer is the power of recognizing and producing at will sounds having a prescribed pitch relationship to one another—popularly speaking, the power of "picking up a tune." Granted this, a singer will be good or bad in proportion to his or her intelligence in discriminating between good and bad singing. It is a mistake to suppose that those who have the best voices, or the greatest natural aptitude for music, or the most familiarity with it, are necessarily the best singers. They are better than their peers in intelligence and assiduity, but whoever surpasses them in these respects, will, unless labouring under absolutely extraordinary natural disadvantages, eventually take the higher rank. The now obsolete exception dates from the time when singers were merely their masters' mouthpieces, Miss Fotheringays [from Thackeray's *The History of Pendennis*] of the lyric stage, and even then it may be doubted whether there was much sense in it. It must, however, be noted that when remarkable musical aptitude is associated with a very high degree of intelligence, the person so gifted generally becomes a composer rather than an executant. It is perhaps on this account that male performers who are not either musically nor intellectually deficient are so rare. If such beings as inspired idiots and unmusical geniuses exist at all, which the judicious will not readily admit, they will be found among operatic vocalists and eminent pianists respectively.

Fortunately the degree of intelligence needed to turn musical gifts to good account in composition, is so great as to be very rare. The case of Mozart may be taken as an example of this. We are told that the composer of Don Giovanni when a child, could name any note or chord sounded in his hearing. But these feats do not account for Don Giovanni, for there are many schoolgirls who can achieve them. Again, we are assured that he could extemporize on a given theme *ala fugato*. But he was excelled in this accomplishment by a youth named Beckwith, who nevertheless produced no Don Giovanni, nor, as far as the world knows anything else either. The truth is that music was only a medium through which

Mozart preferred to employ the extraordinary powers which enabled him to become the greatest of all artists. His skill at arithmetic, billiards, dancing, and acting, are more significant than the not exceptional sense of absolute pitch on which so much more stress has been laid, for his musical endowments are amply apparent from his compositions, whereas the other elements of his complex personality, containing, as they must, the secret of the difference between him and the other composers, are of far higher interest. For it cannot be maintained that the purely musical side of Mozart was more developed than that of many admittedly his inferiors. Donizetti's genius was phenomenal, he produced and formulated musical ideas with a facility which we have no warrant for believing that Mozart could have surpassed, and yet the distance from The Lady of Lyons [melodrama by Bulwer-Lytton, 1838] and Twelfth Night is not greater than that from Lucretia Borgia to Don Giovanni. Mozart was not only a born musician, but a born dramatist, and his father, intentionally cultivating his musical faculty, accidentally cultivated his dramatic faculty by a course of early travel which gave him a precocious knowledge of men. In the end this dramatic faculty proved to be of such a high order as to enable him not only to transfigure a comedy by Beaumarchais [1732–1799] almost beyond recognition but to select and develop many touching traits of character which Molière only suggested. The character of Donna Elvira in Don Giovanni is a striking example of this. Even when he did not improve on Molière which was seldom possible, he in no wise fell short of him. Compare [Donna Elivira's speech in] Scene 6 of the fourth Act of "Le Festin de Pierre" (*ne soyez point surpris, Dom Juan*) with the corresponding trio "L'ultima prova" in the last act of Don Juan, and judge whether Mozart as the master of pathetic comedy is in any point inferior to Molière, who himself was not inferior to Shakespeare in this department of his art. De Ponte in adapting "Le Festin de Pierre" as an opera libretto robbed it of its dignity. Mozart by his music restored what it had lost with interest, omitting, however, the sophistical philosophy of the hero as incapable of musical treatment, and painting him in as the more popular character of "*l'epouseur du genre humain*". It is this faculty of characterization which stamps Mozart as a dramatist as well as a musician. That the two gifts are quite separate will be felt on referring to Beethoven who, though a great musician, had absolutely no power of characterization and proved it by writing an opera in which every situation and emotion is beautifully described, but not a single character impersonated. In Fidelio there are it is true certain superficial distinctions produced by the rockiness of the music allotted to the old jailer, the savage character of Pizarro's song, and so forth.

The same may be said of Goetz's beautiful opera "The Taming of the Shrew" [1874], where the composer, with as little dramatic powers and as much logic as Beethoven, has attempted to individualize Petrucchio (for instance) by giving him boisterous music because he was a boisterous man. None of these examples display greater merit (if as much) as Offenbach's portraiture of General Boum in "La Grande Duchesse". No such mechanical distinctions exist in Mozart's work. In Don Juan the general character of the music is the same from beginning to end of the opera, yet the music assigned to each person of the drama belongs to them alone, you cannot conceive Don Juan singing *Madamine* or *Notte e gimo* although neither of these songs is, like Leporello, coarse and vulgar. Nor could the music of Zerline be effectively transferred to Elvira, although no definite reason can be assigned for the incongruity, [with] no such obvious differences between the parts as those by which Beethoven and Goetz sought to achieve the same end. This curious power of musical characterization has not been exhibited in any marked degree by any famous composer since Mozart, Meyerbeer always excepted. One this account Mozart and Meyerbeer will hold the stage against Wagner, whose works are of the nature of epic poems. It is perhaps unnecessary to say that in ascribing to Wagner a disability which he shares with Beethoven there is no echo of the vulgar hostility to the greatest of living composers which still shows itself occasionally. It is needless to expatiate on what Mozart might have achieved in literature if he had chosen to adopt it as his profession. His correspondence, though it conforms, adds nothing to the testimony of his operas. His love letters, though written to his wife, are more delightful to connoisseurs in this species of composition than the standard examples by Keats and Mirabeau. In his extravagantly funny vein, he will bear comparison with Dickens without appearing either tame or forced, due allowance being made, of course, for the difference between English and German humour. It should be noted that Mozart was not merely versatile; he also had the most comprehensive knowledge of the arts which his versatility embraced. Absolutely the best lyric comedy and romantic drama known are Le Nozze di Figaro and Don Juan, whilst the Zauberflöte may claim a like prominence in that more subjective sphere of art which appeals to us by its moral significance. These works include every variety of theme from farce to tragedy, and even beyond into the regions of [the sublime] in the treatment of which he stands alone. We have had weird and grotesque ghosts in plenty since his time, but between them and the awful solemnity of the statue in Don Juan there is the same difference as between the popular apparition in the [1852 stage adaptation of Dumas' novel] Corsican Brothers and the ghost in Hamlet. As to the comprehensiveness of his musical powers it is sufficient to say of him what can be said of no other person, that there was no respectable form of his art in which he did not excel. All this he proved by to the world by work done in the fetters imposed on him—not by the schoolmen, from whom he was accustomed to receive the same abuse which the pedants of our day level in his name at Wagner, but by his own taste which was severe to fastidiousness. It is evident that not one abnormally developed faculty, but an extraordinary assemblage of faculties entered into the composite genius of Mozart—the universal Mozart, as his countrymen sometimes call him.

Now occurs the question, what has the universality of Mozart to do with the qualifications of a singer. Simply this, that as a perfect singer is expected to be able to interpret the works of Mozart, he must be as universal in his appreciativeness as Mozart was in his creativeness. He must possess exquisite taste, humour, dignity and character, and he must be an actor capable of doing justice to Molière or Shakespear. Incidentally too, he must be a singer. This lengthy instance of Mozart has been cited only to show that there are no limits to the qualifications of a complete lyric artist, and to justify the meagreness of the assurance with which I shall quit the mastery of the technical part of the subject, i.e. that no pains, musical or unmusical, which the student may take to cultivate his mind and refine his sensibilities will be thrown away when his duty calls him to become the exponent of really great music.

For the simpler kinds of singing, no special qualification is necessary. As everyone with normal faculties can, with more or less trouble, be taught to write a simple letter, so everyone can be taught to sing a simple song. Common as it is to hear people saying—often with a foolish pride in the imaginary disability—"I have no voice. I have not a particle of hearing" etc. those who are really so afflicted are little more frequent than the blind, who cannot be taught to paint, or persons without legs, who cannot be taught to dance. If anyone doubts the application of this to his own case, and will not believe that he has a voice, let him get a competent master to try. He had better not try for himself. One of the gifts which vanish with childhood is a perfectly accurate method of singing. Only one thing in the vocal art is more certain than that a boy, if let alone, will produce his voice properly. That one thing is, that a man on the same conditions will produce his improperly.

Physiology of the Vocal Organs

(Physiological account from "The Voice", with account of the registers from Syler)

If any singer now ask "Of what use is all this physiology to me in my art?" I reply candidly "No use whatever. Nay, more, if you attempt to turn it to account practically by inferring a method of voice production from it, it can hardly fall to do you infinite harm." Singers may take their physiology as a piece of general information connected with a favourite subject, but assuredly not as an essential part of their technical training. Organists who understand organ construction and horn players who have studied acoustics are better informed than their rivals who know nothing of these things, but they are not better players. The same is true of vocalists. A man may become the greatest singer of his age, and yet believe that his vocal is similar to that of a barrel organ, and the world has seen innumerable "queens of song" who certainly had no belief in the subject at all. The golden age of song had passed away before Helmholtz [Prussian physiologist, 1821–1894] published the first rational account of the physics of music, and it may come again long before the problems which have baffled him find their solution.

Entertaining, as I do, a rooted mistrust of all methods and theories which have been arrived at by a process of deductive reasoning upon the facts of physiology, it may surprise those who have not chanced to meet with my previous writings and utterances, and who will probably be in the vast majority among my present readers to learn that these publications were occupied almost exclusively with questions of physiology. In order to explain this apparent inconsistency, I may remark that the theories of professors of science are by no means as important for evil as they are for good, that systems of teaching are based on them, and that these systems, being generally erroneous, have to be combated on their own grounds by professors who make no presence of having any theoretic for their own manner of teaching. When my attention was first directed to the subject, a theory based on the experiments of Müller, an account of which will be found in a standard work on physiology, prevailed which compared the larynx to the string instrument. The effect of this theory at a time when voice culture was apparently a lost art, and when teachers were endeavoring to deduce from science what they could not learn from tradition, was disastrous, since the vocal chords were the strings of a cartilaginous fiddle, singing was evidently a mere matter of tension of chords and force of blast. The natural tendency of young singers to succeed by violence was encouraged, the end aimed at being a muscular strain equivalent to Müller's weights. The disadvantage of this method was that it destroyed the voice, and sometimes killed the vocalist. Feeling no call to perpetuate these results in the name of science, I set myself to correct tradition. Tradition informed me as literal matter of fact, that man possessed three different voices, one in the head, one in the throat, and one in the chest. The voice, it was implied, was a spiritual member, not susceptible of exact definition, but generally akin in its end to the soul. I had no difficulty in seeing that this was a figurative description of the registers of the voice which had been taken literally by thoughtless trustees of the old Italian tradition, and by them handed down as an exact definition. However, as I had observed the existence of the registers before, the discovery of fanciful names for them did not help me materially, and as the theories of the science professors were considerably worse than useless, I had recourse to practical anatomy, which speedily convinced me that the "string theory" was not only musically misleading, but scientifically false. I cannot say that I taught singing any the better for this discovery, but as I had become interested in the question apart from its musical bearing, and as the string theory was fully cited in justification of mischievous methods of teaching, I attempted to show, in the work on the voice published by me in 1870, that there was no direct analogy between the chords of the stringed instrument and the vocal ligaments. So far, however, as this point was concerned, I might have spared my labour, for one of the greatest living physicists, Helmholtz, had already produced his famous work "Die Lehre etc," translated under the title of "Sensations of Tone" by Mr A. J. Ellis in 1875. In this work, Helmholtz ignores the string theory, thereby striking it obsolete at one blow, and classifies the human larynx with reed instruments from which category no subsequent author has attempted to remove it. The classification was not new, and I had expressly rejected it in my own work, in which I described the voice as an instrument of the class known as open flute pipes. At present I do not think I was altogether wrong in my classification, and I do not think that Helmholtz was altogether wrong either. Intermediate classes of instruments between the three (flute, string, and reed) will probably be discriminated, which will spare us from Helmholtz's conclusion that a soprano voice is more closely analogous to the siren than to the flute. However, I do not propose to make any attempt to controvert the opinion of Helmholtz, whose mere assumption would, or at least should, have more authority in the question of physics than that of any musician. It is long since I have had any leisure for experimental investigation, and now that Miller's weights are fully in my mind, and the string analogy finally disposed of, I am content to leave the matter to those whose special business it is to pursue it.

I must not however be understood to imply that teachers of singing are not practically concerned with physiology. My own studies led to results far different to the artistically barren theorizing and counter-theorizing just alluded to. It materially helped me in determining by a strictly inductive process, the method of teaching which I have ever since practiced and advocated. It may be as well to describe the precise extent and end of my studies and of the assistance which I derived from them. First, when tradition and current theory had both failed me, I made myself acquainted with the structure of the vocal apparatus by the direct means of dissection. Its action I studied by watching it and analyzing its movement in myself and others, using the laryngoscope when necessary. After some practice I could, when listening to vocal performances, perceive how the singer [preserves] his voice. I took care to hear as many singers as possible, and when I heard young artists whose voices after a few years expired, were toneless wrecks (and of them I heard many) I noted their method as one to be avoided. When I had the rare good fortune to hear a voice which after 40 years' arduous work still left nothing to be desired, I made a very careful study of the method by which that voice was produced with a view to a like result in the case of my own pupils. Constantly comparing and correcting my observations, I found that on certain conditions a voice would last longer than the disposition to use it, and that the violation of these conditions rendered it impossible to sing, except at the expense of voice, of health, and in some cases even of life. Rational men still spread the belief that singing is dangerous for invalids, and they are so far right that there are many ways of singing (very common ways too) which are dangerous to persons in health. On the other hand, doctors whose conclusions are formed from observation of good singers, recommend delicate patients to sing, and, if patients fall into good hands, the result generally justifies the advice.

I have described the manner in which I studied art thus minutely lest it should be supposed that I profess to deduce a system of teaching directly from physiological principles. Upon any such system I should look with profound distrust, attractive as it would probably be now that every young lady has her fragment of scientific knowledge. I know no other way, and I confess I believe in no other way of discovering a safe method of teaching than that which I have just described as having been taken by myself. And it is an extraordinarily interesting way, though often a very pothering one, beset with apparent contradictions, the taste tripping up the judgment at every other step. Great artists who do not know how to sing are to be heard beside dullards whose voices bid fair to last for ever, because they have been well taught and have not individuality enough to go astray. Causes hidden to the public, such as intemperance produce lamentable fallings off in voices which have been well trained and used with the utmost discretion. Long intervals of rest renovate naturally fine voices which had been misused to verge of destruction. Singers who know the right path, despair of the public taste, and go as far as they dare on the wrong one. These are not all deliberate traitors to art, many of them, from natural vulgarity really prefer coarse and violent singing, and would abandon their masters' precepts altogether but that they fear to lose their voices. Again, mature artists, after years of faultless practice, will unaccountably fall into some bad habit and fall into sudden decay. I may mention as an instance of this, the falling off which was in the splendid powers of Madame [Thérèse] Tietjens [German soprano, 1831–1877] which was observable alas before her lamented death, was not so much to advancing years and ill health as to a habit she had contracted of forcing her chest register far beyond its natural limits. It is a remarkable fact that she was fully aware of the pernicious effect of this habit both on the voice and on the intonation, for she herself expressly and earnestly commented upon it during a conversation which I had with her on the subject in 1874. But in this as in every other art, extremes are rare. The great majority of those who profess it have been drawn, upwards or downwards, to the level of the public taste. Those who were most misled by their masters, have learned something from experience and the necessity of self-preservation. Others, better taught, have either forgotten the refinements on which their teachers insisted or discarded them as too subtle for the public to appreciate (theatrical artists being, as a rule, incurably convinced that those who make the most noise among the audience are those whom they are most concerned to please). This rank and file, some having one defect and some another, whilst many, having no particular method at all, and simply singing on all occasions as best they can, are good and led by turns. (Thus, I have heard a celebrated tenor sing *Celeste Aïda* four times in the opera of Aïda. Two of them could not have been more perfected. The other two could not have been worse). It will be seen that the evidence which the student of voice culture has to collate is by no means easy to digest. Even when the rank and file are put out of court, and the elect remain, there is plenty of contradiction, though perhaps less confusion. Often the faithful and earnest artists are hopelessly wrong in their practice, whilst unscrupulous charlatans, who regard the public as a clever old wily advocate regards a common jury, do not know what fatigue and loss of voice mean. However, artists of the highest class, who unite great patience and industry with intelligence and taste, and who, whether the public appreciates their singing or not cannot bear to sing otherwise than finely, seldom fail to find a safe path for themselves sooner or later. It is true, they get tired of their own excellence and sometimes exhibit amusing aberrations, but they return again to the right way, more convinced of its merits than before.

Classifications of Voices

There are three classes of female voices, soprano, mezzo soprano, and contralto. Male voices are classed, also in three divisions, as basso, baritone, and tenor. The distance from the highest note in a voice to the lowest, is called the range or compass of that voice. Voices are usually classified according to their range in this fashion.

Classifications of this kind are not usually given for the purpose of misleading amateurs, but as they generally have that effect, it is as well to add that voices cannot be satisfactorily classified by their range alone. An untaught singer who can by dint of croaking produce a sound of the pitch of F beneath the bass stave, and who cannot strain at a higher note than the E flat above it need not therefore conclude that he is a basso, since it is equally probable that he is a baritone, and by no means impossible that he is a tenor. Nor would a lady be safe in describing herself as a contralto in respect of her inability to sing up, and a soprano because she cannot sing the notes below the treble stave. Even trained singers, when they have been trained on the common plan of cultivating certain registers of the voice at the expense of the others will give more credit to such classifications which are nevertheless useful to composers of choral music than they deserve. Mozart, in his opera "Die Entführung aus dem Serail" writes for the following ranges:

Soprano   Tenor   Bass

No one will bring against Mozart the charge so frequently made against modern composers, of recklessly abusing the human voice. That he did not consider the compass of his second soprano very wonderful may be inferred from the fact that he, when a boy of 14 heard at Parma a singer [Lucretia Agujari. A transcript of the passage sung by her will be found in most musical dictionaries] who had three octaves from middle C upwards.

After this phenomenal performance the singer for whom he wrote the Queen of the Night in Zauberflöte must have struck him as being a soprano of limited compass. Handel in his early "Acis and Galatea" wrote a song which is too high for the conventional baritone and too low for the conventional basso, the compass being

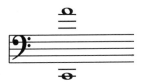

The pitch of these notes in the time of Mozart and Handel was a little more than the notes of the same name on the modern Broadwood concert grand pianoforte and half a semitone lower than at French pitch. Exaggerated notions prevail at the extent to which the pitch has risen since the time of Handel. The most valuable contribution to the history of this subject with which I am acquainted will be found in the communication made by Mr A. J. Ellie [author of a book on *Early English Pronunciation*] to the Society of Arts.

Voices, in short, must be classified according to their quality of tone, and absolutely without reference to their range, though this will generally be found to vary consistently according to the quality. Still, mezzo sopranos and even contraltos may be found possessing a greater range upwards than pure sopranos, and instances may be met with of tenors unable to produce their voices in the *falsetto* register, who class themselves as baritones. The converse of this error is less likely to occur. The not uncommon attempts to manufacture singers of every class into tenors and sopranos are due to the vanity of amateurs, the interest which teachers have in flattering that vanity, and doubtless also in some cases to the fact that exceptionally successful tenors and sopranos are better paid than basses or contraltos.

Roughly speaking it may be said that men and woman who can intone the first series of the chest register powerfully and richly, are basses and contraltos. Men who feel at home in the first series of the *falsetto*, and women who can sing in the head register with perfect clearness of tone. Baritone and mezzosoprano are intermediate voices. Baritones do not possess an effective *falsetto* register, nor have they more than the upper fifth of the first series of the chest register, in the second series of which their main strength lies. The second series of the chest and the whole of the *falsetto* registers are the domain of the mezzo soprano, who competes with the soprano proper in the effectiveness of the head register. It is not possible to convey by verbal description the difference between pure brilliancy of the head notes of the true soprano, and the graver softness of those of the mezzo.

(*Laid aside early in 1882*)

Effort

One of the commonplaces of professors of those executant arts which depend on physical exertion, is "avoid effort". Every professor knows what he means when he says these words, but no pupil understands them, because they do not mean what they are intended to convey. In the Victorian days of the military volunteer organization an instruction book was issued which contained a description of a series of movements by which the amateur soldier was to bring his rifle to be "present". It wound up with "all the above must be performed without the slightest movement". The perplexity of a volunteer endeavouring to comply with this startling condition will be understood by amateur singers who after hearing an impressive and absolutely true account of the loss of health and voice which follow straining of the vocal organs, has been bidden to sing a scale, and to be careful of all things not to use the least effort. As a matter of fact, a man can no more sing without effort than he can row, swim or skate without effort. Nay, singing, to a perfect novice, offers difficulties which do not beat rowing, swimming or skating, for it involves bringing under the control of the will of muscles of whose operation the singer has hitherto been completely unconscious. Few tasks bring such a sense of helplessness and of deserved ridicule as this. If anyone doubt it he can convince himself by a simple and ludicrous experiment. Let him try to wag his ear, as some professional clowns do. He is as fully provided with muscles and motor nerves for the purpose as a donkey. But these muscles, from disuse, have become "involuntary", they have lost the habit of communicating with and responding to his brain. His first efforts to move his ears will result in failure, rendered more absurd by the violent contortions of the nearest moveable muscles—those of the eye. Nevertheless perseverance will develop the power of controlling the movement almost as complete as that enjoyed by a rabbit. The difficulty encountered by a novice in singing is precisely analogous. He is called on for the first time to regulate consciously, the expiration of air from his lungs, keeping his larynx meanwhile in a position which he has previously always associated with inspiration, and simultaneously arranging and maintaining a certain round open condition of the cavity formed by the pharynx and soft palate which is generally known to him, as the actions of eating, breathing and speaking, being unaccompanied by any conscious actions of the organs, are as little use for a training for the performance of conscious direction of any operations. The novice, not knowing what to do, is tempted to do something in the neighbourhood of his pharynx which he has done before, just as the would-be auro-gymnast failing to move his ears, winks. He shouts, screams, roars, cries—produces in short the best imitation of a singer which his existing means enable him to. But the teacher immediately warns him that he must not use force. Force is the essence of shouting. Once effort is forbidden, the singer is paralysed, and he privately feels that his teacher is talking nonsense, and loses faith in him, which is perhaps the very worst discouragement that a beginner can encounter. Let it be understood then, that the efforts depreciated by the teacher of singing are those violent and necessarily (because of the exhaustion that follows them) intermittent ones which render sustained action impossible.

Sources and Further Reading

[*For comprehensive and up-to-date bibliographies and other important research aids for work on Bernard Shaw in electronic and print forms see the Research Aids section on the website of the International Shaw Society: www.shawsociety.org. The selection here focuses on Shaw's musical interests and activities.*]

Biography

Bernard Shaw: an unauthorized biography based on first hand information, with a postscript by Mr Shaw. New York: Book League of America, 1931.

Gibbs, A.M. *Bernard Shaw: a life*. Gainesville: University Press of Florida, 2005.

Holroyd, Michael. *Bernard Shaw*. New York: Random House, 1988–1992.

Letters

Agitations. Letters to the Press 1875–1950. Eds. Dan H. Laurence and James Rambeau. New York: Frederick Ungar, 1985.

Bernard Shaw: Collected Letters. Ed. Dan H. Laurence. 4 vols. New York: Viking Penguin, 1965–88.

Selected Correspondence of Bernard Shaw. Series Editors J. Percy Smith and L. W. Conolly. Toronto: University of Toronto Press, 1995– [ongoing]. *Bernard Shaw Theatrics*, ed. Dan H. Laurence, 1995; *Bernard Shaw and H.G. Wells*, ed. J. Percy Smith, 1995; *Bernard Shaw and Gabriel Pascal*, ed. Bernard F. Dukore, 1996; *Bernard Shaw and Barry Jackson*, ed. L.W. Conolly, 2002; *Bernard Shaw and the Webbs*, eds. Alex C. Michalos and Deborah C. Poff, 2002; *Bernard Shaw and Nancy Astor*, ed. J.P. Wearing, 2005; *Bernard Shaw and His*

Publishers, ed. Michel W. Pharand, 2009; Bernard Shaw and Gilbert Murray, ed. Charles A. Carpenter, 2014.

Context

Brake, L. and Demoor, M. (Ed.). Dictionary of Nineteenth-century Journalism in Great Britain and Ireland. Gent and London: Academia Press, 2009.

Corballis, Richard. 'Bernard Shaw and nineteenth-century music criticism.' IRMT Journal, 23 June 1989 10–15.

Dukore, Bernard F. (Ed.). Bernard Shaw and Gabriel Pascal. Toronto; Buffalo: University of Toronto Press, 1996.

[electronic resource] George Bernard Shaw (1856–1950) Biographies, Criticism, Journal articles, Work overviews. Farmington Hills, MI: Gale, 2003.

Dahlhaus, C. Richard Wagner's Music Dramas (tr. Mary Whittall). Cambridge: Cambridge University Press, 1979.

Redlin, Gebhard. Die Welt der Musik des Bernard Shaw: ein aussergewohnlicher Musikkritiker und seine Zeit. Frankfurt: Lang, 2001.

Weintraub, Stanley. 'The autobiography of Corno di Bassetto.' Shavian 12 iv-v 2013 21–27.

Plays and Prefaces

The Bodley Head Bernard Shaw. Collected Plays with their Prefaces. Under the editorial supervision of Dan H. Laurence. 7 vols. London: Max Reinhardt, the Bodley Head, 1970–74.

Essays

Shaw, Bernard. The Perfect Wagnerite; a Commentary on the Niblung's Ring, New York: Brentano's, 1911 [1909].

Straus, Oscar (music) and Stanislaus Strange (English libretto). The Chocolate Soldier, New York: Remick, 1909.

Criticism

Baake, Friedrich. 'George Bernard Shaw als Musikkritiker.' *Archiv für Musikwissenschaft* 10 (1953): 233–52.

Barber, George S. 'Shaw's contributions to music criticism.' *PMLA* 72 (1957): 1005–17.

Breuer, Hans P. 'Form and feeling: George Bernard Shaw as music critic.' *Journal of Irish Literature* 11 iii (1982): 74–102.

Crompton, Louis. 'Editor's introduction.' in *The great composers: reviews and bombardments by Bernard Shaw* (Berkeley: Univ. of California Pr., 1978) xi-xxvii.

Gahan, Peter. 'Shaw and music: meaning in a basset horn.' *SHAW* 29 (University Park, PA: Penn State University Press, 2009) 145–75 (focuses partly on Corno di Bassetto as music critic and the musical effects in the plays).

Gates, Eugene. 'The music criticism and aesthetics of George Bernard Shaw.' *Journal of Aesthetic Education* 35 (2001): 63–71.

Haywood, Charles. 'George Bernard Shaw on incidental music in the Shakespearean theatre.' *Jahrbuch der Deutschen Shakespeare-Gesellschaft Ost* 105 (1969): 168–82.

Huckvale, David. 'Music and the man: Bernard Shaw and the music collector at Shaw's Corner.' *SHAW* 10 (University Park, PA: Penn State University Press, 1990) 96–112.

Hugo, Leon. *Edwardian Shaw: the writer and his age.* New York, N.Y.: St. Martin's Press, 1999.

Innes, Christopher. 'The (im)perfect Wagnerite: Bernard Shaw and Richard Wagner.' In *Text & presentation*, edited by Kiki Gounaridou (Jefferson, NC: McFarland, 2010) 22–31.

Irvine, W. "G. B. Shaw's Musical Criticism", *The Music Quarterly*, Vol. 32 (3), July, 1946, 319–332.

King, Carlyle. 'GBS and music, with a moral for Canadians.' *Queen's Quarterly* 63 (1956): 165–78.

Kramer, Ursula. 'Einsichten durch Aussensicht? oder, George Bernard Shaw und die Musikkritik.' In *Beiträge zur Geschichte der Theaterkritik*, edited by Gunther Nickel. (Tübingen: Francke, 2008) 313–34.

Laurence, Dan H. (ed.). *Shaw's Music: The Complete Musical Criticism of Bernard Shaw*. London: The Bodley Head, 1981. Vol I: 1876–1890; Vol II: 1890–1893; Vol III: 1893–1950.

Lee, Josephine. 'The skilled voluptuary: Shaw as music critic.' *SHAW* 12 (University Park, PA: Penn State University Press, 1992) 147–64.

Levinson, George. 'Some animadversions on Shaw as music critic.' *Independent Shavian* 22 (1984): 8–10.

Jacques Barzun. 'Another look at Shaw as music critic.' *Independent Shavian* 22 (1984): 29–30.

Loewenstein, F. E. 'Bernard Shaw, music critic.' *Hinrichsen's Musical Yearbook* 6 (1949): 147–52.

Lowenthal, Jerome. 'Beethoven, Shaw, and the literary sensibility.' *Piano Quarterly* no. 82 (1973): 14–15.

Mackerness, E. D. 'Corno Inglese: notes on the texture of George Bernard Shaw's musical criticism.' In *Renaissance and modern essays*, edited by G. R. Hibberd. (NY: Barnes & Noble, 1966) 147–57.

———. 'George Bernard Shaw and the English musical renaissance.' *Durham University Journal* 79 (1987): 303–10.

Mehus, Donald V. 'Shaw: a musical critic.' *Independent Shavian* 46 (2010/11): 18–30 (repr. from *Opera News*).

Nickson, Richard. 'The perfect Wagnerite? Wagner and his Shavian advocate.' *Independent Shavian* 28 (1990): 51–61.

Parakilas, J. P. 'Music for the people: George Bernard Shaw's musical socialism.' *Musical Newsletter* 7 i (1977): 21–28.

Pulido, E. 'Bernard Shaw (Corno di Bassetto), critico musical.' *Heterofonia* 44 1975 9–12; 47 1976 13–18; 48 1976 8–13.

Shenfield, Margaret. 'Shaw as a music critic.' *Music and Letters* 49 (1958): 378–84.

Stuckenschmidt, H. H. 'Shaw und Wagner.' *Stimmen: Monatsblätter für Musik* 1 (1947–48): 107–11.

Wandor, Michelene. 'Shaw and early music.' *Shavian* 11 iv (2010): 17–23.

Weimer, Michael. 'The well-tempered performance: Shaw as a critic of music.' *Yale / Theatre* 4 iv (1973): 15–19.

Wiedmann, Lutz. *Die Dramaturgie George Bernard Shaws und ihre Wurzeln in Musik, Philosophie, und in seiner Auseinandersetzung mit dem englischen Theater der Jahrhundertwende.* Bern: Lang, 1993.

Williams, Stephen. 'Bernard Shaw as music critic.' *Musical Times* no. 1295 (1951): 9–13.

Printed in Great Britain
by Amazon